How Do I Look?

How Do I Look?

Queer Film and Video

Edited by Bad Object-Choices

Bay Press   Seattle   1991

Published in 1991
Printed in Germany
Second printing 1992

Bay Press
115 West Denny Way
Seattle, Washington 98119
USA

Designed by Katy Homans
Cover design by Tom Kalin and Katy Homans
Set in Gill Sans and Walbaum by Trufont Typographers
Printed in Göttingen, Germany by Gerhard Steidl, Druckerel und Verlag.

"Lesbian Looks: Dorothy Arzner and Female Authorship," by Judith Mayne, is adapted from chapter 3 of *The Woman at the Keyhole: Feminism and Women's Cinema,* Indiana University Press, 1990.

Library of Congress Cataloging in Publication Data

How do I look? : queer film and video / edited by the Bad Object
  -Choices.
        p.   cm.
    Includes bibliographical references.
    ISBN 0-941920-20-8 : $16.95
      1. Homosexuality in motion pictures.   1. Bad Object-Choices
    (Organization)
    PN1995.9.H55H69   1991
    791.43'653—dc20   91-17052
                                                            CIP

Front and Back Cover:
Sheila McLaughlin, *She Must Be Seeing Things,* 1987. Production still by Christopher Boas.

We dedicate this book to Vito Russo and Ray Navarro. Vito was a pioneer of queer film history. Ray, twenty years younger, had begun to make significant contributions to the theory and practice of lesbian and gay media. Vito and Ray died during the same week in the fall of 1990 after long battles with AIDS.

Contents

Preface and acknowledgments

The papers and discussions published here comprise the proceedings of a conference entitled "How Do I Look? Queer Film and Video," held at Anthology Film Archives in New York City, October 21–22, 1989. The six papers have been revised for publication by the authors. The follow-up discussions have been edited to focus on the most productive exchanges; in many cases, the presenters, in editing the discussions, have extended and added pertinent points to their answers. The editors of this volume are less interested in fidelity to the moment than in furthering the debates raised at the conference.

The "How Do I Look?" conference was organized by Bad Object-Choices, a reading group formed in the spring of 1987 to address questions of gay and lesbian theory. The conference proceedings were edited by the following group members: Terri Cafaro, Jean Carlomusto, Douglas Crimp, Martha Gever, Tom Kalin, and Jeff Nunokawa. Other members who helped organize the conference were Amber Hollibaugh, Timothy Landers, Eileen O'Neill, and Lee Quinby.

The conference was held in conjunction with a film and video series organized by Bill Horrigan and Martha Gever and sponsored by the Collective for Living Cinema in New York City. Our thanks to Jack Walsh and Nancy Graham, respectively past and present directors of the collective, for their assistance. Bill Horrigan devised the title "How Do I Look?" for the entire series of events. Jason Simon was responsible for recording the conference and, with the help of Moyra Davey, transcribing the discussions. Siochain Hughes helped with many organizational details.

The "How Do I Look?" screenings and conference were supported by a grant from the New York State Council on the Arts; the conference was additionally funded by the New York Council on the Humanities, which allowed us to bring a number of film- and videomakers, critics, and theorists from Canada, England, and the West Coast to participate in discussions. Together with our six presenters, these informal discussants helped make the conference a success. Publication of the proceedings is supported by a separate grant from the New York State Council on the Arts. We wish to express our gratitude to the two state government granting agencies for so generously funding an avowedly queer event at a time when our federal government seeks to silence us.

Publisher's Note

The publication of this book was delayed two months as more than twenty printers refused to print—or in many cases—even bid on the project. At issue were images in the Patton, Mercer, and Fung essays.

I want to thank Cindy Peer at P. Chan & Edward for working so diligently to help us get this project on press. I also want to thank the editors and contributors for their patience and support. I am particularly grateful to Douglas Crimp for his good humor and outrage.

With the most generous support of Richard Serra and Clara Weyergraf we were able to have the book printed in Germany. We are indebted to their commitment to the project.

Introduction

Bad Object-Choices

When our reading group began planning the "How Do I Look?" conference in 1988, we didn't have a collective name, nor had we needed one. Two years earlier we had embarked on a project both simple and ambitious: to read and discuss texts related to the construction and representation of lesbian and gay subjects. We devised no program, but rather moved more or less at random from the writings of Michel Foucault to lesbian-feminist philosophy, from Freud to Freud's commentators and critics. We read recent work on identity, homophobia, AIDS, sex work, and lesbian sadomasochism. We also brought videotapes to meetings to view and discuss—videos by lesbian and gay media makers and tapes about AIDS.

The idea for a conference on queer film and video emerged from the casual, nonlinear development of our group's interest in theoretical and political questions raised by lesbian and gay media. Or, rather, it arose from our frustration at the scarcity of work on this topic, a scarcity we knew resulted from a lack of institutional support from the academy and the publishing industry. We also knew that our interests were shared by many who make, distribute, and program lesbian and gay films and videos and by their audiences.

We came upon the name for our group—Bad Object-Choices—in a similarly unprogrammatic way. In fact, we weren't looking for a name for ourselves at all, but rather one for the conference. We had charged one member of the group with the task of inventing a title; we realized how daunting the task was only when presented with a series of suggestions that relied on permutations of such well-worn terms as *desire, gaze, spectatorship,* and *representation.* Though these words have undeniable currency within contemporary theory, they are also endemic to discourses we wanted to question, as well as to an academic language that is off-putting to many of the people we wanted to attract to our conference. We were, however, tempted by one psychoanalytic concept that had not been the subject of recent theoretical analysis: object-choice. Ultimately, we appended the word *bad* to signal two things: the conventional presumption that a homosexual object-choice is wrong, and the popular reverse-discourse use of the word *bad* to mean precisely its opposite. We wanted to signal that for us the choice was not only right but right-on.

But as a conference title, "Bad Object-Choices" still indicated little about the event we planned, which became obvious when Bill Horrigan, who with Martha Gever organized a series of film and video screenings in conjunction with our conference, proposed "How Do I Look?" Desire, gaze, spectatorship, representation—it was all there, but with just the right camp inflection to suggest a queer event. Only then did we realize that *we* were Bad Object-Choices and that the question we wanted our conference to address was how we look—at/in film and video.

Although the structure for the conference—six presentations, each followed by an extensive discussion period—was intended to be rigorous, perhaps quite demanding for speakers and those in attendance, the event was not meant strictly for specialists in media studies. We were acutely aware of the traditional suspicion of academic theory among those actively engaged in lesbian and gay culture and politics but with no stake in scholarly institutions. Particularly at this moment, when the prospect of academic acceptance of lesbian and gay studies seems more auspicious than ever before, that suspicion needs to be respected. It is not simply, as many would prefer to think, anti-intellectualism. Rather this skepticism derives from the fact that lesbians and gay men have long been the *objects* of "knowledge," constructed *in* theory, not the agents of it. Our culture routinely demands an explanation of our desires, presumed in advance to be abnormal, deviant, aberrant, even pathological. Even in current theories of representation, where identity, subjectivity, and sexual difference figure prominently, *homo*sexual identities, subjectivities, and differences are frequently overlooked, disavowed, or otherwise declared irrelevant. This should not be news, not to any honest intellectual, straight or queer. Why then would we want to engage in a theoretical inquiry that seems so entangled in all-too-familiar homophobic dynamics? Will such an endeavor result in a dilution of our distinct, defiant cultures? Will what we regard as our cultures, our histories, be embraced merely as the latest intellectual trend? Will the mantle of respectability accorded lesbian and gay theory temper our political passions, those passions that historically have determined our claims to self-representation?

All of the essays in this collection describe intersections of theoretical study with collective political struggle—each with a different emphasis and implication. To take just one example, Judith Mayne's paper on Dorothy Arzner addresses an especially divisive but potentially productive conflict produced when these two domains clash. In her attempt, on the one hand, to claim Arzner as a specifically lesbian filmmaker and, on the other, to analyze the elision of Arzner's lesbianism by feminist film theory, Mayne sees "a tension between Arzner as a lesbian image and Arzner as a female signature to a text." Without rejecting the gains developed by feminist film theory, she proposes lesbian desire as crucial for understanding Arzner's films and suggests links between image and text that challenge heterosexist assumptions in feminist analyses of classical Hollywood cinema.

The repercussions of Mayne's arguments are manifold— hardly limited to academic debates. But that was the charge leveled at her, and at Teresa de Lauretis, during the conference's closing discussion, when both were told that their attention to feminist film theory was outmoded, hermetic, and therefore inconsequential for anyone producing lesbian media. Mayne's reply is instructive: "I realize these splits are very real, between activist and academic communities, between people who are film and video producers and people who work in the university, but I also think that these divisions need to be contested. And I still maintain that lesbian film history cannot be divorced from the concerns of media activists."

Rather than trying to ignore these conflicts or take sides in the debate, we deliberately structured the conference as a mix of presentations by people primarily known as writers (de Lauretis, Mayne, Mercer, and Patton—although Patton is equally well-known as a community activist) and as media producers (Fung and Marshall). To augment these voices, we sent abstracts of the conference papers to a number of film- and videomakers, critics, historians, and activists and invited them to the conference as informal discussants. Participants came from the West Coast, the Midwest, Canada, even England and Australia, as well as from the New York region. Exchanges were spirited, even heated, but however contentious the proceedings, we were left with a sense of accomplishment, of a community having come together to work on its own problems, problems within the community itself and problems that we face from an increasingly hostile political climate.

We have cooperated for a very long time in the maintenance of our own invisibility. And now the party is over.
—Vito Russo, *The Celluloid Closet*

The witty defiance with which Russo ended the introduction to his book on homosexuality in the movies takes on a special poignancy in 1990. For this is the year that Vito died of the disease syndrome that was first noticed among gay men at the very moment that his pioneering book was published. He never abandoned his high-spirited defiance of homophobia. But his optimism in 1981 that gay and lesbian visibility was about to do away with homophobic censorship turned out to be premature. No one in 1981 could have predicted the oncoming devastation of AIDS and the excuses it would provide for a renewal of virulent hatred against gay men and lesbians. Nor could any of us have foreseen the Supreme Court's denial of our constitutional rights in the 1986 *Bowers v. Hardwick* decision or the 1989 congressional attack on gay and lesbian culture.

It is in this renewed climate of oppression that *How Do I Look?* returns to and redefines questions first cogently raised in *The Celluloid Closet.* And our book, too, stands in defiance of a homophobic censorship that seeks to prevent us from producing queer representations and from presenting, discussing, and theorizing those representations in public forums. Just weeks before the "How Do I Look?" conference took place in New York City on October 21 and 22, 1989, and after a summer-long debate about "taxpayer-financed blasphemy and pornography," Congress passed a reappropriation bill for the National Endowment for the Arts; the new law contained the compromise version of Jesse Helms's notorious amendment proscribing "materials which . . . may be considered obscene, including, but not limited to, depictions of sadomasochism, homoeroticism, the sexual exploitation of children, or individuals engaged in sex acts. . . ."[1] Those words have been quoted again and again since the law was passed, nearly always to point out how slippery they are.[2] But queers have had reason to be especially alert to the list that follows what "may be considered obscene." Whatever the technical leeway in the law—those things might also be considered *not* obscene; the strictures of the Supreme Court's *Miller v. California* obscenity decision were meant to be the final arbiter—its language is clearly one of equation: of obscenity with what is on the list, of homoeroticism with, say, the sexual exploitation of children. The slipperiness is most pernicious when the language is most vague. Because of the inclusion of "individuals engaged in sex acts," it could be argued, for example, that no one, no sexual minority, is being singled out after all; but it is, on the contrary, that very phrase that alerts us

1
See *Congressional Record—House,* 2 October 1989, H6407.

2
For a particularly acute and thorough analysis of the amendment language and its implications, see Carole S. Vance, "Misunderstanding Obscenity," *Art in America* 78, no. 5 (May 1990), 49–55.

Production still from Isaac Julien's *Looking for Langston*, 1988.

Production still by Sunil Gupta.

3
Bowers v. Hard-wick, too, was often claimed to target heterosexual as well as homosexual sodomy, a cynical claim to anyone attentive to the specifics of the decision, the gay and lesbian movements' prolonged fight to erase all state antisodomy laws, and the ramifications of the decision for other legal challenges to antigay discrimination.

4
The writers were Chrystos, Audre Lorde, and Minnie Bruce Pratt. The law's reach was further indicated by the cancellation of performance grants to Karen Finley, John Fleck, Holly Hughes, and Tim Miller. The work of all four artists deals explicitly with sexuality, and three of the four—Fleck, Hughes, and Miller—are openly gay. John Frohnmayer, who withheld the grants, expressed fears that giving grants to these artists would bring down the wrath of Helms and other anti-NEA congressmen.

5
See Catherine Saalfield, "Overstepping the Bounds of Propriety: Film Offends Langston Hughes Estate," *The Independent* 13, no. 1 (January–February 1990), 5–8.

6
Caryn James, "A Trip to the Middle Ages, and a View of Langston Hughes," *The New York Times,* 1 October 1989, 61.

to the "difference" of *homoeroticism,* since homoeroticism is *not* a "sex act."[3] The breadth of what may be stigmatized with that term was made clear when Senator Helms declared that the NEA had in all probability violated the law because it awarded grants to three lesbian writers, the fact of their declared lesbianism sufficient in itself to indicate their law-breaking.[4]

Of course, *homoeroticism* is no more denotative of lesbian or gay identity than it is of an act; it merely indicates same-sex desire. Helms's suspicion nevertheless demonstrates exactly what the amendment is intended to do: it is meant to instill just enough fear in members of an NEA peer panel to make them withhold funding from any person, project, or event associated with homosexuality.

Around the time that Helms's amendment was signed into law, Isaac Julien's film *Looking for Langston* (1988) was screened at the New York Film Festival (it would be shown again a few weeks later in the "How Do I Look?" screening series and provide a central topic of discussion at the conference). Before the festival showing, the audience was informed that owing to a copyright dispute the film's sound would be blocked out in two archival sequences of Langston Hughes reciting his poetry. They were not informed, however, that the version they would see had already been altered in response to censorship: still more of Hughes's poetry had been replaced on the soundtrack by Julien in response to an injunction sought by the Hughes estate to prevent showing the film. Although the estate's legal claim was indeed one of copyright infringement, its wish to censor lay elsewhere: it objected to Julien's association of Hughes with homoeroticism.[5]

The New York Times contemptuously reported the censorship as "the most interesting aspect of 'Looking for Langston.'"[6] The reviewer apparently felt that the film would have been interesting *in itself* only if it had been more fully censored: "Mr. Julien's film would have been much more honest and effective if it had simply left Hughes out from the start." Hughes was, after all, "obsessively secretive about his sexuality," and that's how the *Times* reviewer would prefer to leave it, thus agreeing with the Hughes estate and not bothering to ask *why* an artist of the Harlem Renaissance might have felt compelled to be closeted about his homosexuality. The *Times* article fails to note that Julien's film, far from being a documentary, takes the form of a meditation, that it attempts to construct an imaginative Langston, a representation, by and for a new generation of black gay men. As Kobena Mercer writes of *Looking for Langston* in his essay published here:

Insofar as the aesthetic strategy of the film eschews the conventions of documentary realism in favor of a dialogic combination of poetry, music, and archival imagery, it does not claim to discover an authentic or essential homosexual identity (for Langston Hughes or anyone else). Rather, the issue of authorial identity is invested with fantasy, memory, and desire and serves as an imaginative point of departure for speculation and reflection on the social and historical relations in which black gay male identity is lived and experienced in diaspora societies such as Britain and the United States.

To understand this would require an act of imagination, perhaps even of identification, clearly impossible for a *New York Times* critic and the readers she presumes. A misconstrual of the film's documentary aspiration and a censorious dismissal is therefore expedient.

Censure is enjoined by the *Times* in its usual ignorance and arrogance, that of a privilege both heterosexist and racist. Because the *Times* is the most powerful newspaper in the United States, knowledge of the project to which Isaac Julien is a major contributor is not required. We therefore learn nothing about Sankofa, the black British film collective of which Julien is a member and which has, in a series of films including *The Passion of Remembrance* (1986) and *Territories* (1984), reshaped our very

idea of documentary, of historical memory, and of possible articulations of race, gender, and sexuality. Nor do we learn anything
of *Looking for Langston*'s relation to other gay and lesbian films
and videos that reorient documentary practice: John Greyson's
Urinal (1988) and Pratibha Parmar's *Memory Pictures* (1989) for
example. Thus, far more than Julien's film is censored: what is
effaced is an entire community of interest and an entire representational practice. The giveaway of the *Times* reviewer's
arrogance/ignorance is her reference to the poetry substituted
for Hughes's in *Looking for Langston* as that of "an obscure contemporary English poet named Essex Hemphill." To whom is
Essex Hemphill obscure? Would any queer fail to know that
Essex Hemphill is one of the foremost gay black *American* poets
writing today? It is, of course, the *Times* reviewer's pretense to
knowledge—that Hemphill is English—that renders him
"obscure."

Censorship was the background against which our conference on queer media representations took place in more than
these coincident senses. Vito Russo's *The Celluloid Closet* is
among other things a catalog of the ways that homosexuality
has been censored from movies—outright by the Hays code,
more subtly by industry homophobia—throughout the whole of
Hollywood's history. Gay and lesbian media theory thus takes
the effacement of queers from media representation as its point
of departure. But the effacement is greater still. Queer presences are censored not only from the screen, but from behind
the camera and from the audience as well. These latter censor-
ships are largely effected by film theory itself, which disavows or
disallows the sexual orientation of gay and lesbian filmmakers as
in any way meaningful, and which generally adheres to a heterosexual presumption in theories of spectatorship. A first answer
to the question "How do I look?" is, in theory, that I don't. I am
neither there to be looked at, nor am I the agent of the look.
But of course we know, we know *as* lesbians and gay men, that

we do, and Vito Russo's book was one way—one of the first ways—of telling us how we do.

If Russo's book, and much of the pioneering work of Richard Dyer as well, focused on exclusions and negative stereotypes of queers in mainstream cinema, feminist film theory, from the mid-1970s on, shifted attention from what is depicted on the screen—in its case the image of the woman—to how subjectivity is constructed through cinematic representation and how that construction might be changed by a different kind of cinema. But insofar as feminist film theory relies, for its conception of representation and subjectivity, on the psychoanalytic theory of sexual difference, several obstacles are posed for gay and lesbian study. First, gay men and lesbians have until now remained wary of psychoanalysis, whose *institutional practice* has a long and ignominious history of oppressing us—both directly and by lending its prestige to a widespread social opprobrium. Second, the psychoanalytic theory of sexual difference is a theory of *gender* difference; it therefore takes as normative a relation between the sexes, not between two members of the same sex. Indeed, this theory *presumes* heterosexuality to such a degree that it often appears to *demand* it. As Judith Mayne writes, "The preferred term *sexual difference* in feminist film theory slides from the tension between masculinity and femininity into a crude determinism whereby there is no representation without heterosexuality." And third, other differences, differences of race, ethnicity, class, and culture, are simply elided. These "other" differences have recently been placed on the agenda of feminist film theory, often by lesbians and women of color working within the ranks. In this one sense, then, lesbian theorists have had a distinct advantage over their gay male counterparts: they work directly out of the most developed body of film theory available, whereas gay men have only tentatively, if at all, taken up the questions advanced by feminist film theory.

There is, then, a gender divide at work within gay and lesbian media theory, a divide, that is, between gay theory and lesbian theory. The "How Do I Look?" conference can thus be seen to deal with distinctly uneven development, which is only exacerbated by the fact that there has until now been so little institutional support for the intellectual work that gay men and lesbians do on questions of our own sexualities. But if lesbians using the tools of feminist film theory might appear to have an advantage over their gay male counterparts, it was one of the major lessons of the conference to show that such an advantage could also serve to disadvantage lesbians. If "lesbian invisibility" has been a charge within the liberation movement whose *gay* rubric was most often taken as masculine, then that invisibility is doubly reinforced by feminist film theory: first, because of its heterosexual bias; second, because for this theory the image of the woman on the screen, and particularly the image of wo-men's sexuality on the screen, is a problem, even a taboo. Un-encumbered by qualms about their "objectification" for the pleasure of others, gay men have felt less reticent to represent their sexuality, to show it publicly, to talk about it directly. The moment when these differences came most to the fore at the conference was when Cindy Patton showed, at the end of a se-ries of safe sex pornography segments, one representation of lesbian sex. In the ensuing discussion, gay men apparently felt freer to discuss lesbian sexuality than did lesbians themselves, a fact that came sharply into focus when Patton told a story of self-censorship: when presenting the same video clips at Duke University, she had stopped the tape before the lesbian se-quence, so afraid was she of seeing an image of lesbian sex in mixed company.

That videotape, *Current Flow* (1989), made by Gregg Bor-dowitz and Jean Carlomusto for the Gay Men's Health Crisis Safer Sex Shorts series, demonstrated safe sex techniques for lesbians in a pornographic scenario enacted by a black "butch" and a white "femme." The explicit portrayal of lesbian sex, the butch-femme role-playing, the assumption of these roles by a mixed-race couple—all of these issues sparked discussion that would return throughout the conference as the most charged: discussion about the differences between the ways gay men and lesbians represent, talk about, and theorize our sexualities; about the meanings attached to sexual positions or roles—top-bottom, butch-femme; and about racial difference. But what is crucial is not only that these were the pervasive topics of debate, but that they constantly competed with and displaced each other.

The response to the conference's final paper provides a salient example. Teresa de Lauretis's subject was the representation of lesbian visibility in film. Using psychoanalytic theory to interrogate Sheila McLaughlin's *She Must Be Seeing Things* (1987), "Film and the Visible" is a complex argument about the construction of lesbian spectatorship through a butch-femme fantasy scenario doubled by a film-within-the-film. Through its portrayal of jealous hallucinations of heterosexuality, de Lauretis argues, the film implicates lesbian subjectivity in the inescapable heterosexual construction of sexuality:

In all the culturally dominant forms of representation that surround us, . . . desire is predicated on sexual difference as gender difference, the difference of woman from man or femininity from masculinity, with all that those terms entail—and not as a difference between heterosexual and homosexual, or straight and gay sexuality. This is the sense in which I read McLaughlin's statement that heterosexuality "defines and in a sense creates our sexuality." She means, of course, the *institution* of heterosexuality, and not heterosexual behavior, the event of sexual intercourse between a woman and a man, which may or may not occur. But even for those whose sexual behavior or whose desire has never been hetero-directed, even for them heterosexuality is "inescapable," though not determining. For, if sexuality is represented as gendered, as the direct result of the existence of two sexes in nature—on which basis culture has constructed gender, and onto which in turn civilization has attached meanings, affects, and values, such as love, social relations, and the continuation of the human species—then it follows that sexuality is finally inescapable for every single human being, as is gender; no one can be without them, because they are part and parcel of being human. Thus sexuality is not only *defined* but actually *enforced* as heterosexuality, even in its homosexual form.

But if this implication in She Must Be Seeing Things made it disturbing for some of its viewers, de Lauretis's analysis was perhaps even more disturbing: the follow-up discussion almost entirely avoided it. What occurred instead was a discussion of race, since the lesbian couple in She Must Be Seeing Things is not only butch-femme but also interracial, and in concentrating on *sexual* difference, de Lauretis ignored racial difference. What was criticized, though, and what increased the sense of displacement, was the conference itself—for not having a lesbian of color or a lesbian media maker among the presenters. The criticism of the conference was entirely valid; it was, however, borne by the speaker who took as her subject the difficult question of how the lesbian can be made visible in representation. Discussion of that question, posed implicitly and explicitly throughout the conference, was deferred at the very moment when it might have been most productive.

We mention this not to lament the loss, but to point to the urgency of all of these issues for our community and to suggest that their volatility is the result, on the one hand, of the shortage of occasions when we can address them fully and, on the other, of the underdevelopment of theoretical tools for their articulation. That such articulation is now squarely on the agenda was voiced by Kobena Mercer:

Today we are adept at the all too familiar concatenation of identity politics, as if by merely rehearsing the mantra of "race, class, gender" (and all the other intervening variables) we have somehow acknowledged the diversified and pluralized differences at work in contemporary culture, politics, and society. Yet the complexity of what actually happens "between" the contingent spaces where each variable intersects with the others is something only now coming into view theoretically, and this is partly the result of new antagonistic cultural practices by hitherto marginalized artists.

Several papers in this volume take up relations between gay and lesbian sexuality and ethnic or racial difference. The task of addressing them is by now fairly familiar: we have to imagine and produce a sense of solidarity sturdy enough to act collectively, but supple enough to interfere with ethnocentric pressures that feel at times like a cultural law of gravity, pressures that work everywhere to absorb ethnic and racial differences, casting others as mirrors or tools of a homogeneous (white) subject.

The papers address various questions: What are the patterns of reinforcement and resistance that define relations between scopic homoeroticism and racism? How can minority queer subjectivities imagine or produce a place for their own desires and their own desirabilities in a representational regime that appears to define itself through their exclusion or subordination? Can we characterize the relation between homophobia and racism as homologous, and what are the consequences of such a characterization?

Stuart Marshall addresses one particular hindrance to theorizing this difference within difference: the fact that "every political movement requires its points of imaginary identification, . . . a necessary fiction that is required not only for the construction of the subject as distinct from an external world of objects, but also in order for any political rallying and action to take place." In adopting the pink triangle as that point of identification, Marshall argues, both the lesbian and gay movements and the AIDS activist movement have relied on a problematic analogy between sexual identity and ethnic (Jewish) identity, especially insofar as the latter is constructed with a view to genocidal oppression. Marshall asks,

Why did this symbol representing only the extreme point of the Nazi regulation of homosexuality gain currency to represent gay people's commonality, our hopes, our struggles, and our belief in a better future? The answer to this question may be revealed in the very terms I have just used to ask this question. I think there is, and always has been, a fundamental problem about the status of the word *our* in this formulation. In what way are we a "we"? What is the common denominator of our putative community?

Kobena Mercer takes up the question of analogy from a different perspective, that of mapping sexual difference onto racial difference. In "Skin Head Sex Thing," Mercer revises his earlier critique of "racial fetishism" in Robert Mapplethorpe's photographs of black male nudes by introducing the notion of ambivalence, "something that is experienced across the relations between authors, texts, and readers, relations that are always contingent, context-bound, and historically specific."[7] Recognizing the altered context in the reception of Mapplethorpe's work in the wake of the Right's strategic deployment of it to charge the NEA with "financing obscenity," recognizing also his own shifting identifications within the representational structure—between desiring subject (as a gay man) and desired object (as a black man)—Mercer poses questions about his earlier transposition of feminist analyses of sexual difference to representations of racial difference:

Although analogies facilitate cognitive connections with important cultural and political implications, there is also the risk that they repress and flatten out the messy spaces in between. . . . Analogies between race and gender in representation reveal

7
The earlier essay is "Imaging the Black Man's Sex," in *Photography/ Politics: Two,* ed. Pat Holland, Jo Spence, and Simon Watney (London: Comedia/ Methuen, 1987), 61–69.

similar ideological patterns of objectification, exclusion, and "othering." In Mapplethorpe's nudes, however, there is a subversive homoerotic dimension in the substitution of the black male subject for the traditional female archetype.

But the introduction of homosexuality is not, of course, sufficient in itself to subvert racist codes. As Judith Mayne makes clear in her discussion of Arzner's *Dance, Girl, Dance* (1940), the troubling of heterosexual difference may in fact be *compensated* by reinforcing standard representations of racial difference: "The racial stereotype affirms the distinction between white subject and black object just when the distinction between male subject and female object is being put in question."

The most startling example of the compensatory use of racial stereotypes is revealed by Richard Fung in his discussion of Asian actors employed in gay male pornography. In one of the porn videos Fung examines, the "gendering" of roles in anal intercourse is accomplished through a racial substitution: in *Below the Belt,* the repressed desire of a white top man to be fucked is shown in a dream sequence in which, when dreaming of himself as a bottom, his character is assumed by the Vietnamese actor Sum Yung Mahn. Thus the Asian is not only represented as passive, but is the very representation of passivity as well. Fung comments:

Sex, especially anal sex, as punishment is a recurrent image. In this genre of gay pornography, the role-playing in the dream sequence is perfectly apt. What is significant, however, is how race figures into the equation. In a tape that appropriates emblems of Asian power (karate), the only place for a real Asian actor is as an exaggerated caricature of passivity. Sum Yung Mahn does not portray an Asian, but rather the literalization of a metaphor, so that by being passive, Robbie [the white character] actually becomes "Oriental." . . . As with the vast majority of North American tapes featuring Asians, the problem is not the representation of anal pleasure, per se, but rather that the narratives privilege the penis while always assigning the Asian the role of bottom: Asian and anus are conflated.

As has already been noted, a number of debates at the "How Do I Look?" conference took up questions of pornographic representation. Pornography's place in gay men's self-representation has a complex history. On the one hand, its centrality is in part determined by the fact that *any* image of homosexuality is thought by many to be inherently pornographic; on the other hand, pornographic images are the one type of representation that is made explicitly for, and often by, gay men, and therefore has offered a measure of self-determination. Such images as 1940s and 1950s physique photographs were, after all, *representations,* pictures that allowed some gay men to retaliate against prohibitions on overt, gay-identified erotica. Although Richard Fung's own work in video (notably *Chinese Characters* [1986]) has attempted to deconstruct mainstream gay pornography from an Asian perspective, he confessed at the conference, "Personally I am not very interested in producing porn, though I do want to continue working with sexually explicit material." Nevertheless, Fung noted that "whether we like it or not, mainstream gay porn is more available to most gay Asian men than any independent work you or I might produce. That is why pornography is a subject of such concern for me." One practical effect of the "How Do I Look?" conference was a commission to Fung from Gay Men's Health Crisis to produce a video for its Safer Sex Shorts series; the result is *Steam Clean/ Vapeurs sans peur* (1990), the first safe sex porn tape produced for a North American gay Asian audience.

As is suggested by Fung's decision to produce a porn tape for GMHC, debates about pornography occurring elsewhere in our culture (among feminists; in response to the Meese Commission or the NEA Mapplethorpe controversy) take on a very different cast among gay men facing the threat of AIDS. If pornography might be a possible means of teaching and encouraging safe sex practices, questions about its place within a subculture, its various uses and users, its representational codes, and its instrumentality are hardly academic. It was from this perspective that Cindy Patton began thinking about a "pornographic vernacular":

When AIDS emerged as an epidemic in which, as was often said, "prevention is the only weapon we have," new demands were placed on both the imagination and the languages of sex; theories of representation and of sexuality were ill-equipped to provide practical guidelines for representing safe sex in a culture in transition. The relationship between codes designed to negotiate sex, provide group identification for sexual subcultures, and resist the values of the dominant culture's repressive categories were largely untheorized. The apparent need to define unequivocal methods of conveying and reinforcing safe sex information collided with arguments about the limits of good taste, the meaning of sexual representation, and the role of fantasy in sexuality.

But the difficulty of inventing a safe sex pedagogy/ pornography for gay men (and eventually for lesbians) was not only theoretical; it was also material. In 1987, Jesse Helms was able with very little effort to persuade Congress to deny any federal funding to organizations providing gay-affirmative prevention education. Nevertheless, as has been the case since the beginning of the AIDS crisis, gay men and lesbians have proceeded without anything like sufficient help from government institutions.

Material constraints are central for any discussion of gay and lesbian representation, pornographic or otherwise. Access to power and resources and consequent visibility continue to be unequal across gender, maintaining a comparatively greater marginalization of lesbians than of gay men. The economic, social, and political ability to make sexual images by and about themselves represents a relatively new freedom for lesbians, one that has a history distinct from that of gay men and, which as a history in the making, cannot be typified.

Although the "How Do I Look?" conference was not conceived as a broad survey of queer film and video theory, the specific topics taken up in the six papers and the discussions they sparked do represent something of the range of current thinking in the field. In the hopes that this collection can serve both as an introduction to gay and lesbian media studies and as stimulation for new work, we have included a selected bibliography of writings on the subject. It does not pretend to be inclusive, but rather is a guide to some of the reading we ourselves did prior to "How Do I Look?" and what has been written in the year since the conference took place. Much of what has been written about queer film and video has appeared in the form of reviews published in local gay magazines; little of that is included here, largely because of its unavailability through library resources. The refusal to preserve these materials, except by a few struggling lesbian and gay archives, is only one among the myriad ways representations of us are effectively censored.

Safe Sex and the Pornographic Vernacular

Cindy Patton

Cindy Patton

Signifying
Safe Sex

The eight of us sat late into the night watching the same video-tape again and again. We ran the tape forward and backward, freeze-frame and slow motion. The cleaning man finished up and hurried past us, obviously disgusted that four men and four women were staying late at the office to watch homosexual pornography. But sexual desire was not the cause of our obsessive watching: we were searching for a condom. The actor had donned one early in the video, but once he began fucking, we couldn't see it. We freeze-framed the tape to scrutinize the base of the actor's dick. We considered whether he might be wearing one of the new ultrasheer condoms with no nubby end-ring.

"Well, I don't see it," said our videographer.

"There! There!" said the design assistant, jabbing his finger at the screen. "See that. It's shiny *here* and not shiny *here*."

This was not a censorship board, although our discussions sometimes had a moralistic tone. No, we represented, in varying combinations, professional sex educators, academics, seasoned community organizers, professional filmmakers, and "ordinary gay people" who wanted to make a contribution to slowing the HIV/AIDS epidemic. We had come together to design and produce an innovative, multiphase safe sex project for and by gay men in Boston. The women involved were also active members of the gay male subculture, and we hoped to develop a parallel safe sex organizing project for lesbians and bisexual women. Although we discussed gender differences in the construction and social organization of homosexualities, the first phases of the project focused largely on styles and strategies that might work among gay men. After months of reviewing other projects and discussing strategies, we decided that the adoption of safe sex practices depended on creating an environment in which gay men's sexuality (and at a later phase, lesbians' and bisexual women's sexualities) was once again celebrated and in which safe sex was assumed to be a *norm* rather than a *problem.*

To introduce the project, we wanted to include portions of a recent commercial porn film intercut with the project's logo. But we came up against a question in selecting segments for the trailer: how do you signify safe sex? Was it that magic edge of the condom, the line between shiny and not shiny? What might the effect on viewers be of the now-standard caution at the beginning of commercial porn films that all actors are practicing safe sex, even if the editing hides it? Or, if condoms are obviously donned early in a film, would viewers assume their presence later, even if they couldn't be seen? Was "condom continuity" necessary? Must the condom always be visible, along with technically proper application and removal? What about nonpenetrative (condomless) forms of safe sex? Could already-safe activities (licking, jerking off) be signified as safe? Should porn simply show (and therefore eroticize) safe sex? Must safe sex be constituted as a change in practice, requiring some signifier of sexual risk?

The concern to produce "responsible" sexual fantasy material was clear in most gay male video porn by 1989, but the approaches were contradictory and rested on widely divergent views of the role of fantasy and mediation in sexuality. As analysts of sexual representations, we, too, had dramatically different ways of interrogating the possibilities and requirements of teaching safe sex.

We eventually abandoned the porn component of our project, but the original reasons for wanting to use it and the debates that emerged are worth recounting, because they prompted me to begin theorizing a "pornographic vernacular" as a concept from which to produce better strategies for organizing communities or subcultures around safe sex.[1]

1 The term *community* has been nearly evacuated: the illusory unity of a "gay community" has been highlighted by the failure of mainstream AIDS groups to work effectively outside the white, middle-class gay-male core group. In addition, co-optation of the term by mainstream media—"heterosexual community" or "white community," for example— has robbed the term of its references to shared histories of oppression. *Subculture,* too, has its problematic connotations: sexual networks and the political groupings arising from resistance to policing are constituted through forms of "culture" different from those recognized in the dominant "culture." Specifically, the term *sexual subcultures* suggests exotic groups with values utterly divergent from the main culture. As I will suggest here, and develop in detail elsewhere, there are a variety of groupings of homosexual actors, and each needs to be theorized. I have made these tentative moves toward language theories in order to suggest, at least for the urgent project of communicating the *techne* and political significance of safe sex, how we might understand differences in these groupings. We seem stuck with the term for now, but rather than understand community as an essential, stable social institution, we might view it as a historically specific site of contestation that is in the process of reinvention. For all its undecidability, there is some notion of "community" to which urban gay men pay allegiance, and it is in this "ethno-methodologic," somewhat evacuated sense that I am using the term.

Safe Company: A Radical Experiment

2

In addition to reviewing specific gay male safe sex projects, we looked at theoretical work on sexuality (especially, Gayle Rubin, "Thinking Sex: Notes for a Radical Theory of the Politics of Sexuality," in *Pleasure and Danger: Exploring Female Sexuality,* ed. Carole S. Vance [Boston: Routledge and Kegan Paul, 1984], 267–319), on gay liberation (John D'Emilio, *Sexual Politics, Sexual Communities: The Making of a Homosexual Minority in the United States, 1940–1970* [Chicago: University of Chicago Press, 1983]; Michael Bronski, *Culture Clash: The Making of Gay Sensibility* [Boston: South End Press, 1984]; Dennis Altman, *The Homosexualization of America* [Boston: Beacon Press, 1983]), on AIDS politics (Dennis Altman, *AIDS in the Mind of America: The Social, Political, and Psychological Impact of a New Epidemic* [Garden City, N.Y.: Anchor Books, 1987]; Cindy Patton, *Sex and Germs: The Politics of AIDS* [Boston: South End Press, 1985]), and on pedagogy (Paulo Freire, *The Politics of Education* [South Hadley, Mass.: Bergin and Garvey, 1985]).

3

All of the major urban gay communities have gone through a "phase" of sexual austerity in the exhaustion from the epidemic. Boston has long been viewed as a more sexually conservative city, and if de-

Working from a complex and social constructionist community organizing model,[2] the members of our core group who designed the safe sex project, and who became peer educators, named themselves Safe Company. Subsequent recruitment and training produced an affinity-group-like team that engaged in innovative and militant safe sex work in the many places where gay men congregate—parks, bars, "tea rooms," porn cinemas—places familiar to the various members of Safe Company.

The name Safe Company was intentionally polysemous and suggested that anyone could be in safe company by openly celebrating the importance and eroticism of safe sex. Placing safe sex on the company/group/community level rather than the individual level resituated sex from a private, personal danger to a fundamentally social project. We wanted to affirm not only that safe sex can be hot sex, but also that working toward community-wide adherence to safe sex can be an act of resistance to the destructive political, social, and psychological effects of the HIV epidemic.

Promoting pleasure and energizing a cynical urban subculture a decade into a devastating epidemic was an ambitious project. Safe sex campaigns and slogans were considered gauche, even if fears of sexual danger had produced a marked decrease in sexual expression.[3] To make matters worse, the organization sponsoring Safe Company—the AIDS Action Committee of Massachusetts, an institution looked to for direction in the social and political issues surrounding the epidemic—was widely perceived to be prudish and even antisex, and there were few alternative institutional forces. In order to signal the difference between this project and earlier individualistic or psycho-therapeutically oriented programs, porn producer and star Al Parker—a Boston boy made good—was invited to join Safe Company at Boston's gay pride celebrations.

Safe Company asked Parker to participate for a variety of reasons: first, of course, because he was a nationally known porn star and, second, because his style and age were easily identified with by the "clone generation" of gay men, the thirty-five to forty-five-year-old mustachioed and LaCoste shirt—clad cohorts who had been hard hit by AIDS. Parker was also raunchy enough to appeal to the leather/denim crowd, who, although long active in AIDS volunteer work, had been publicly disenfranchised by the major AIDS groups and the wider gay and lesbian community. In addition, Parker had already appeared in several safe sex campaigns on the West Coast and had been a vocal advocate for safe sex in the gay media and in a controversial appearance on the "Phil Donahue Show." Parker required absolute adherence to ultrasafe sex on his sets and had produced a commercial porn video that was a primer on the use of condoms, surgical gloves (for finger fucking), and plastic wrap (to cover the anus for rimming).

Finally, there was a historical reason to work with Parker: his film career as actor, writer, director, and producer (Parker is the co-owner of Surge Studios, the only fully gay-owned commercial gay porn producer) spanned and mirrored the gay liberation era. Parker's films, like those of his competitors, were self-consciously stereotyped fantasies of male-male sex, but they also included scenes from or alluded to urban gay life. In the 1970s, gay porn makers generally tried to give their films a particular style or content to mark them as gay and thus different from films that showed men having sex with each other for the erotic pleasure of ostensibly heterosexual male consumers. In Parker's films—especially those from the 1970s—emotional issues and problems of gay life made up the erotic narrative into which sex scenes were slotted. Even Parker's films from the highly competitive 1980s were less "hunk"-dominated than other commercial gay porn: they played on the heat of sexual scenarios instead of conforming to narrow, if changing, notions of masculine beauty. The men in Parker's films were more diverse, and their activities seemed more perverse. Like gay films made before the explosion of gay and straight home video porn in the early 1980s standardized the genre, Parker's films were less insistently focused on intercourse as narrative closure, proposing instead a range of sexual activities to be pursued as objectives in themselves.

Safe Company felt this broadening of what constitutes sex was critical. Whereas gay male sexual practices before AIDS and safe sex discourse had included a wide variety of activities, the equation of condoms with safe sex had "heterosexualized" gay male sex, reconstituting many activities as "foreplay" to an ultimate "intercourse." This shift in perception of "already always safe" activities like jerking off, licking, tit play, verbal scenes, and so forth, which once constituted ends in themselves, was evident in high-production-value commercial pornography, in which virtually every sexual narrative ended with intercourse. Parker's films, however, had always included a wide range of already-safe erotic activities, and his work also met our requirements for a diversity of male types, a gay liberation ethos, and a message that safe sex was perverse and fun, not a limitation. We hoped Parker and his films would help us promote the idea that sex was integral to the strength of the gay male community and that aggressively promoting safe sex, rather than fear, was essential to individual and community survival. But, the videographers returned from their initial edit of Parker's film *Better Than Ever* (1989) with the charge that the film was not safe.

Containing Safe Sex

Better Than Ever began with the usual notice to the viewer that all actors were practicing safe sex, even though, for artistic reasons, barrier devices might not always be visible. Condoms were indeed donned on camera, but could not always be seen thereafter. Although a wide range of safe activities occurred—use of dildos and "stubbies" (short condoms that cover the head of the penis, useful for fellatio)—safe sex was not signaled or problematized within the narrative of the film. Was that safe?

The representational issues raised were not unlike those debated at art schools. But we were working on an immediate, practical problem: using cultural artifacts to revitalize a besieged community in order to change sexual norms and behaviors and reduce the risks of a new disease syndrome. Theory and practice could not be separated: each argument about the nature of representation, the meaning of safe sex, and the modes through which community change might occur was conducted against a background of death witnessed and community destruction survived. While the arguments outlined below and the preliminary theorizing about sexual languages seem abstract, they represent the heart of a struggle for group self-determination.

The group could not decide what constituted the representation of safe sex, in part because although safe sex appears to have a real reference in medical data, it is, in fact, a cultural construction that joins science, fantasy, group histories and identities, and health logics. The relation (or distinction) between fantasy sex and "actual sex" and the capacity for sexual agents to rework the symbolic meaning of particular acts were far from clear. Moreover, the nature of porn watching was in dispute: is watching porn a sexual activity in itself (a *parasocial* relationship, in clinical terms)? Or are porn videos an aid to the imagination, doing the work of fantasy production for the viewer? The underlying issues concerned whether videos are taken to be real by viewers and what people *do* with the videos. Do they imitate what they see? Does watching unsafe sex provide a viable substitute for practices now out of bounds? Do unsafe videos image and stabilize activities that ought to be erased from any moment of desire? The dozen or more people involved at some stage of the discussion had their own stories to tell about their relationship to pornography, their experiences of both sexual pleasure and sexual danger, their own vision of what a "safe company" might look and feel like.

Three basic, partially overlapping positions emerged:

1. Gay male porn videos must show proper application, use, and removal of a condom in logical order and with a kind of episodic structure that leaves no doubt in the viewer's mind about the pragmatics of condom use. The viewer should be able to clearly see the condom on the dick when the actors are fucking. This argument assumes that some measure of imitation of the process will occur, and, thus, "learning" requires real-time, accurate presentation of condom use. The primary goal of safe sex advocacy in a video is information, not eroticization. Although pornography might be able to provide information, the specific requirements of safe sex representation are probably at artistic odds with pornographic conventions.

2. The now-standard disclaimers in commercial gay pornography—insisting that actors are practicing safe sex and explaining the cinematic technique of editing—are effective and enable the viewer to imagine that condoms are in place. Porn is understood as fantasy, and viewers supply or ignore any number of details or elements. This argument assumes that safe sex is already accepted in gay male sexual practice and that explicit visual description is not required. Overemphasis on condom use, especially by signaling its "difference," comes at the expense of celebrating the many other already-safe activities. Safe sex is a symbolic concept for a range of practices, only one of which is condom use.

3. Individuals have a wide range of reactions to pornography and are strongly influenced by intratextual characteristics, such as stereotyping or narrative structure, and by viewing context. What porn tapes say about gay male sexuality and how porn relates to the social context of gay male culture are larger issues than the specifics of condom use. Interpretations and enactment of safe sex depend on cultural attitudes, not on the presence or absence of specific representations. Porn videos are useful if they suggest positive attitudes about gay male sexuality, since they help create and sustain a social environment in which safe

The cum shot is the "climax," in which the actor "pulls out" or disengages from mutual sexual activity and masturbates to orgasm. In fact, I have found several younger men whose porn viewing experience has occurred only in the context of a world in which safe sex was already thematized and who believed that the cum shot was in fact a specific technique of safe sex within the films. Lacking any other explanation for this convention, they interpreted the cum shot as a form of safe sex representation.

The only weapon we have . . .

5
Unequivocal, but not univocal: the "education" for gay men was initially offered as a mode of breaking the silence about AIDS promoted by the mainstream culture. It was recognized that information could and should be offered in a variety of forms. As control over this enterprise of "spreading the word" shifted away from a small number of well-informed and politically engaged groups to mainstream news media and as divisions in strategy arose between AIDS groups, educators began seeking something like "teacher/learner-proof" ways of communicating about safe sex. The media and government—and many gay groups—were initially criticized for their silence.

sex is practiced *because* it is viewed as a positive aspect of gay male sexuality. Thus, nuances in pornography narratives about sexuality and about interrelationships between men will promote the confidence men need in order to practice safe sex and not feel limited by condom use. Making no reference to the issue of safe sex is not acceptable, but a range of textual strategies—narrative, overt visual representations, specific dialogue, the instruction before the tape—can cue the viewer to interpret the video in the context of safe sex. This argument posits viewers as already actively interpreting porn texts in the larger context of their lives and sexual practices and suggests that the traditional cum shot might be reinterpreted as an enactment of the safe sex slogan "On me, not in me."[4]

When AIDS emerged as an epidemic in which, as was often said, "prevention is the only weapon we have," new demands were placed on both the imagination and the languages of sex; theories of representation and of sexuality were ill-equipped to provide practical guidelines for representing safe sex in a culture in transition. The relationship between codes designed to negotiate sex, provide group identification for sexual subcultures, and resist the values of the dominant culture's repressive categories were largely untheorized. The apparent need to define unequivocal methods of conveying and reinforcing safe sex information collided with arguments about the limits of good taste, the meaning of sexual representation, and the role of fantasy in sexuality.[5] But picturing change and tapping the fantastic interior of erotic possibilities put pornography in conflict with pedagogy. "Your brain is the biggest sex organ" became a cry of the 1980s, but the thought police were ready to set limits on imagination.

Safe sex education evolved rapidly as various strategies met with mixed success. At first (1981–82), information was categorical and sexological, declaring promiscuity, penile-anal penetration, and oral-genital contact suspect. Very soon, the

After about 1985, safe sex
informational materials
were criticized for overlay-
ing "neutral information"
with coded moral
judgments—for example,
use of the term *promiscuity*,
with its long-standing cultural meanings, was said to
misdirect risk reduction efforts toward reducing partners and producing an
unefficacious "trust." The
problematics of safe sex information have shifted over
time in relation to the investments of the producers
of the information. But, as I
have argued elsewhere,
nearly all positions were
based on a belief in the potential neutrality of information as well as the belief
that antibody testing produced a relatively uniform
experience.

6
In 1983, *How to
Have Sex in an Epidemic*, a
forty-two-page pamphlet,
was published by longtime
gay activists involved in
health organizing in the
newly described epidemic.
Beginning in 1984–85,
workshops and events with
titles like "Hot, Horny, and
Healthy" attempted to
counter the growing per-
ceptions of limitation and
de-eroticizing associated
with safe sex. These workshops continue and are
probably useful in initially
proposing interpersonal
and conceptual categories
that facilitate change in
sexual behavior and nor-
mative shifts in the com-
municative requirements
of sexual relationships.
In my view, how-
ever, they overemphasize
verbal negotiation and re-
constitute the late 1970s as
a mythical time when "anything went," implying that
gay male culture was re-

how-to style took over as men were encouraged to "eroticize safe sex."[6] But cultural and subcultural variations in gay sexual and learning styles threw up obstacles to the largely middle-class, psychobabble-oriented "Hot, Horny, and Healthy" and "Meeting Men" style of workshops, however successful these were/are at introducing a new set of relational styles, values, and terminologies to a select group within the visible gay male community.

The terms *culturally sensitive* and *sexually explicit* were bandied about as if the former were a category of narrative preference and the latter a marker of realist representation. But both terms were already overdetermined, and they began to cut both ways. *Culturally sensitive* suggested a hands-off, community self-determination ethos. Sexuality is not, however, a culture in itself, but rather, an artifact *of* cultures. By the time "cultural differences" were a common concern in gay community-based AIDS groups (around 1985 or 1986 in the dozen hardest hit cities), the "clone" core of the gay community was well into a new sexual austerity, the complex roots of which related not only to the multiple problems of the epidemic—caring for friends and lovers, fear, and despair—but also to the aging of, and career demands on, this upwardly mobile baby-boom group. This austerity was visible in the closing of many bars, a declining attendance in other gay clubs and entertainment businesses, an apparent increase in monogamous relationships (or at least reversal of stated values about monogamy and "leisure sex"), and the increase in concern about so-called sexual compulsion and substance abuse.[7]

Outside of the gay communities' grappling (however badly) with their own diversity, "cultural sensitivity" became a new form of voyeurism for public health officials and clinicians, who mastered the quaint vernaculars of their charges. Both in the discourse of the gay community and that of public health practices, those who "need" cultural sensitivity are measured

strictionless and normless. There is an uncomfortable assumption that sexuality must be tamed by "mature" and rational limit-setting. While components of these programs foreground non-penetrative sexual options, the overall context situates intercourse as a telos now problematized, rather than viewing the range of sexual possibilities as a menu. I now believe that differences in perception about what constitutes "real gay sex" are a key underlying problem in accomplishing normative changes. Too much safe sex education is constructed against the "old style" of gay sex, idealized (or idolized) as the abandon of the 1970s. Thus, safe sex practice is overdetermined by its role in demarking transgressive sex from "mature" or natural (safe) sex. For men who viewed gay sex as intrinsically transgressive (of cultural or particular psychic norms), the loss of transgressiveness that safe sex ("Bambi sex") now implies means that a critical component of erotic performance (desire) has been eliminated.

7
Whatever the numerical realities of the latter, the rise in concern about excesses of pleasure marched in lockstep with the mainstream, Reaganite views on drugs and sex. Some effort was made to articulate drug/alcohol abuse as an effect of homophobic oppression rather than individual pathology ("addiction is a disease"), but this view was difficult to assert relative to sex (no doubt because of its centrality to gay identity) without appearing to claim that

against a middle-class, white norm and found lacking in both the decoding skills and the behavioral and social values of the mainstream society. Their perceived deficiencies are gauged by their distance from the mainstream and by whether or not they "change" once they receive a "culturally sensitive message." The distinction between those who "want" information and those who "need" a culturally sensitive message creates two target audiences: those who have a right to (and could be counted on to respond to) education and those who could be held legally and medically liable (through arrest or denial of health care) for the ignorance their infection or "risk behavior" was presumed to represent.[8]

Cultural sensitivity came to mean addressing the way *those* people who can't understand straightforward medical terms talk about sex. In some arenas this meant softening medical terms that might seem offensive for some groups, notably those not perceived to be "truly at risk." Thus, when speaking to mainstream heterosexuals, we were to talk of "making love" rather than penile-vaginal intercourse. For other groups, such as gay men, it meant not blinking an eye when speaking of rimming or fisting as opposed to oral-anal contact or manual-anal insertion. In all cases, cultural sensitivity entailed scientists begrudgingly giving up their stuffy clinical terms in order to water down the "real" and "specific" language *for* sex into derivative popular terms considered less accurate and thus at the opposite pole from "documentary" on a realist representational continuum.

Despite the nod toward pluralism, the notion of cultural sensitivity posits a reality of acts existing prior to the meanings created around them and constructs a double-entry system that equates specific acts with corresponding, technically correct words. Scientific language for acts is presumed to be more correct than vernacular terms, which are slightly confused translations. The task of the culturally sensitive educator is to match

gay men are in some essential way self-destructive. Within the gay community, sex was perceived to be more importantly linked with HIV/AIDS, both as the precondition for the epidemic and as the mechanism—as "safe sex"—for stemming the epidemic. Thus, "sexual compulsiveness" had a different valence and was less accepted as an "issue" than gay substance abuse, although the latter appeared as a separate issue. Indeed, the ad for a major gay-operated detox and therapy unit (Pride Institute) claims that more gay people die each year from chemical dependency than from AIDS, an obviously problematic set of rhetorical equivalences. This stands in marked contrast to the claim of the Black Power movement in the 1960s, and to a lesser extent of the African-American political infrastructure, that drug control patterns have resulted in a disproportionate degree of drug use and trade within the urban African-American neighborhoods.

8
I take up this complex issue of the cultural-political economy of safe sex education in *Inventing AIDS* (New York and London: Routledge, 1990), Chapter 2.

up existing vernacular terms with corresponding scientific terms in order to ensure that the message conveyed is true to its ideal form. The process involves treating vernacular concepts as "found" and static artifacts of a pre- or protoscientific thought system: the educator is "sensitive" when he or she leaves such language as is and covertly determines its match to the ideal terms.

What are ignored are the ways in which the vernacular terms are altered or are reinvested once they are linked to the dominant discourse through an enforced equivalency determined and policed by the culturally sensitive educator. Like the subtle imperialism of late twentieth-century anthropology, uncritical educators and clinicians unconsciously accept their own scientific language as the standard for reality effects even as they celebrate the "richness" of the speech of the *indigene*. This pseudo-aesthetic appreciation masks the educators' inability to understand the meaning potentials of vernacular terms, which constitute a surplus in their system of equivalencies. Although the education occurs in the vernacular, some amount of cultural violence occurs in ripping loose the sexual vernaculars from the objects of scientific/educational intervention. Using vernacular terms in the charts and graphs of scientific conferences or educational materials designed by outsiders may appear to mark the scientist or educator as culturally sensitive, but appropriation robs the vernacular of its linguistic polysemy and temporal specificity. *Rimming* and *knocking boots* sound like a foreign language when pronounced back into subcultures, however proficient the accent.

An interesting study in England, for example, showed that people preferred being addressed by interviewers in medical-sounding language, even though they often did not fully understand or recognize the terms. Likewise, injecting drug users and street teens feel offended when outsiders use their vernacular, sensing that the professional is using the street terms in quotes.

9

Kay Welling, "Preliminary Report on a Pilot Study," Social Aspects of AIDS Conference, South Bank Polytechnic Institute, London, February 1989.

10

It is common for "sensitive" educators to buy the line "we don't talk about sex" offered by many subaltern groups when confronted with outsiders who try to get them to talk about sex in colonialist terms. Rather than incite subalterns to (Western) discourse, truly sensitive educators discover how sex is understood locally, how sexual concepts and practices are learned and communicated. It often turns out that what counts as "sex" is radically different across microcultures.

11

It is important to the history of the political economy of both AIDS education and access to clinical trials and prophylaxis that we recognize the ideological significance, in 1985 and through the present, of linking antibody testing with "risk behavior change." It was assumed with this first funding requirement that knowledge of antibody status would change behavior; no data supported this view, and health education wisdom was divided on this "confrontation with reality" style of education. The original testing mandates were an experiment in social engineering, one that most current data suggest failed. Studies by the Centers for Disease Control and more recently by the National Cancer Institute find no re-

Vernacular cloaks group identification; boundary defenses are diminished when a vernacular is colonized.[9]

Like cultural sensitivity, the idea of sexual explicitness bears a realist mark. It is as if there were a bare, mirror representation or language of sex. But instead of filtering "correct terms" through a posited "culture," the notion of sexual explicitness views the downest, dirtiest words as most accurate to the user: anything less than unvarnished prose is marred by repression. Bawdy terms place sex in a bodily rather than a clinical context. When used in clinical discourse, bawdy terms are treated rather like foreign words that become standard usage but are italicized to indicate their otherness and their magic power to defy translation. But because bawdy terms are perceived by educators as having privileged access to a bodily or sexual reality, there is no mechanism for deciding which bawdy terms to use, no assessment of the context or mode of address in which the terms are conveyed, no appreciation for the ways in which sexual rhetorics reinscribe systems of power.

In this framework, linguistic transgression is equated with realism: rather than evaluating specific, local bawdy terms as they operate doubly and performatively in their contexts, the most naive educators use their own discomfort or amusement with "dirty words" as the criterion for closeness to sexual reality. This constitutes an inverted, romantic imperialism: dominant culture's rejection of the validity of "talking sex" in bawdy terms is taken as a *validation* of those terms. But when a subaltern population, unconsciously idealized as "naturally" less "uptight" about sexuality, rejects those very same terms, the educator searching for explicitness deems the subaltern *culture* lacking in the verbal tools to express their sexuality.[10] The fact that the dirty words of a culture function to constitute, resist, and protect sexual identities is missed when these words are stripped of context and inserted into another culture's linguistic system of sexual constructions.

liable correlation between knowledge of antibody status and behavior change. Certainly, such knowledge affects individuals in a wide variety of ways, related to health beliefs, social and psychological support, community attitudes, to suggest only a few. With new calls for early testing in order to take advantage of regimens that boost the immune system and prophylaxes for pneumocystis carinii pneumonia and other opportunistic infections, it is critical to understand how behaviorist ideas are embedded within the testing system and in public attitudes toward HIV policy development. It will be a difficult task politically and educationally to transform the testing system, designed as a sexual behavior change experiment, into a system for early diagnosis of HIV disease. The relationship between the testing system and AIDS/HIV policy is pursued at greater length in my *Inventing AIDS*.

Community educators worked from one of these two frameworks (or from both) in the shadow of U.S. government silence about AIDS. The downside of no government response was no government funding. On the other hand, no government response meant no government interference: education by and for gay men and injecting drug users could stay within the borders of these fragile communities. The first federal funding for education became available in late 1985, more than four years after the identification of the first cases of what came to be called AIDS. And the $400,000 came with restrictions, including potential censorship by a "community standards" board and a requirement that the then-new antibody testing had to be a part of the package.[11] In 1987, Senator Jesse Helms of North Carolina displayed on the floor of the Senate some sexually explicit, culturally sensitive brochures from Gay Men's Health Crisis (GMHC) in New York City. The pamphlet that drew the most ire was a cartoon book, by a well-known gay artist, about s&m sexuality. It was sensitive to this minority sexual culture and explicit in visuals and language. Although scrupulous bookkeeping records at GMHC demonstrated that no federal monies had been used for the project, Helms was able to leverage personal revulsion into political terrorism by alleging that American taxpayers had paid for the pamphlets.

Pornography of Life

Helms's attack had a chilling effect on gay male health education. In sorting out how far to go in producing material "direct" enough to be useful without bringing wrath down on the gay community, two questions emerged: first, are realist portrayals of gay male sexuality pornographic by definition to a mainstream culture that wants to hear nothing about it? And, second, the question I've already raised: is conventional pornography used as stimulus for solo-sex "safe" regardless of whether or not its content conveys a message about nontransmitting sexual behaviors?

Porn producers, educators, and community activists were divided over the above questions, and discussions ran through another range of questions: Is sex a drive? Is it a compulsion in some men? Can men make choices about safe sex? Do certain environments lessen one's ability to stick to safe sex? Can someone consent to unsafe sex? Whose responsibility is an individual occasion of safe sex? Who is responsible for establishing new norms?

Debate over the relative balance between sexual pleasure and sexual danger brought accusations, on one hand, of denying the reality of an epidemic and, on the other, of denying the demands of desire; of promoting unsafe sex or of promoting paranoia about sex. The value of specific safe sex educational interventions was difficult to assess because of a failure to clarify assumptions about sexuality and representation. How sex is accomplished and how sexual vernaculars evolve needed to be more rigorously theorized. Simply stated, I want to argue, first, that groups (audiences, target populations, subcultures, mainstream culture) bring a range of readings to a particular representation of sex and, second, that safe sex educators must work within the logics of interpretation established and/or evolving within subgroups. This preliminary move toward a theory of sexual vernacular makes no sharp distinction between "sex" and "text," but views sexual performance, sexual identities, and sexual networks as constructed in and *as* language.

In this framework, sexual expression is learned through communication and observation in both public and private social venues as well as through mediated observation and communication, including medical texts, the popular press, how-to books, and pornography. The particular matrix of public/private, communication/observation, texts, identification with social categories, and subsequent punishments and pleasures experienced "from" a range of subject-positions in a range of social fields creates for each person a set of registers, or decoding strategies, or a hermeneutic, which in turn positions him or her in a network of policing, advice, sexual possibilities, style, erotic "preferences," and closets.

Sexual vernaculars are learned contextually: members of various language communities experience cultural recognition not through visual identification, but when performances—*what is said*—are meaningfully decoded by another person. Sexual vernaculars are the identifying characteristics of liminal sexualities—being "in the life" historically precedes more visual markers of subcultural affinity. Only when a vernacular achieves hegemony does it appear to be a "natural," coherent language (instead of "dirty words") with a legitimate parentage. Thus, by its claim to naturalness, the dominant language of heterosexuality (for example, "making love") intimidates those who operate within the liminal space of a minority sexual vernacular.[12]

Every culture—and subgroups within every culture—has public and private sexual languages, with strong rules concerning the appropriateness of speaking such languages "out of bounds." Dirty jokes, double entendre, and sexual leers are probably the classic and nearly universal modes of public sexual discourse, but medicalized discourses about the sexual (like the charts of Ronald Reagan's colon in an era obsessed with anality) as well as graffiti, euphemisms, and pointed polite silence are also forms of public sexual signification.

In addition, gendered and class-based differences in access to "the public" intersect with public/private languages, so that, for example, men engage in a public language (for example, porn film viewing in X-rated cinemas) in the absence of women, and it is precisely this absence of women that constructs as "public" those particular words/texts/performances on that particular occasion.

Sexual languages vary dramatically and are important in some cultures—gay culture, for example—and unimportant in others. Sexual languages vary by class, gender, ethnic group, age,

12
I want to be clear that heterosexualities also have local vernaculars, but users' relations to state and psychiatric policing are different, since all heterosexuals, at least in the contemporary era, are viewed as enacting variations on a sexual category viewed as normal. With the exception of extreme forms of sex-linked violence and overt child-oriented sexualities, liminal heterosexuals are largely considered "kinky" rather than pathological.

Safe Sex and the Pornographic Vernacular

location, and even time of day: sexual language employed in the marketplace is not the same as that used late in the evening in the bar, even between the same interlocutors. Thus, determining what is an "appropriate" use of sexual language, or how a set of sexual ideas will be interpreted, requires understanding the register of usage and the people likely to recognize that register.

Sexually explicit materials are not a form of representation on the opposite end of the spectrum from euphemism; that is, there is not a spectrum with liberated sexuality on one end and repressed sexuality on the other, each with its own "natural" language. A better term might be *sexually consistent material,* that is, material consistent in *form*—oral, written, pictorial, gestural—in *style,* and in *mode of cultural circulation.* This latter is probably the least examined area and the one most often violated in the quest for cultural sensitivity. Safe sex is a cultural intervention that may work entirely within existing cultural economies or may stretch the edges of those economies, but it cannot be imposed from outside without making participants feel ridiculed or even attacked. Sexually consistent material is not more "real" or "accurate" material thrust upon a repressed or ignorant group. That is sexual imperialism. Sexually consistent material must work within the conceptual logics of a group and must circulate within the borders of the microculture.

Some would argue "if you don't like it, don't look at it." Unfortunately, "public" and "private" collide in contended areas of social power: the live-and-let-live politics of pluralism is impossible in a society in which a mobile media threatens previous linguistic cordons (*Playboy* at the 7-Eleven; gay newspapers offered as "evidence" in right-wing publications). The curious ideology of taxation, which constructs the public will within the collectivity of purchasers, made the Gay Men's Health Crisis pamphlet fair game for public debate. Direct-mail letters informed right-wing constituents of the details of the pamphlets, which the *The New York Times* did not find "fit to print." Although the language in the GMHC pamphlet was "targeted" and considered "private" by participants in s&m culture, the right wing considers it not a language to be left in its venue, but a language to be scrutinized in order to reveal the hidden truth about homosexuality and AIDS.

Unfortunately, most sexual vernacular is very offensive to those for whom it is not a native tongue. Sexual vernaculars may be more open to misreading than other vernaculars because they rely on "found" symbols and syntax, but sexuality is also chiefly regulated through the policing of speech and gesture—from psychiatry's attempts to elicit the hidden psychic language of deviant sexuality to the queer-bashing that results from a "reading" of a victim as "homosexual." Queer-bashers may perceive their victims through dominant-culture stereotypes, such as effeminacy; or through presumed subcultural codes, such as having a particular haircut; or through the perception that the "gay man" was attempting to deploy a subcultural code, that is, to "cruise" the queer-basher, or that the lesbian was refusing to participate in a verbal/gestural performance of heterosexuality/femininity.

Thus, people from certain subgroups become afraid to speak their native tongue when their "texts"—a red hanky, a turn of phrase or cut of suit, a pamphlet, a book—thought private, suddenly come under scrutiny and become public, rendering the private language and symbols of the subculture vulnerable to unanticipated readings by someone with greater social power. And, on the other side, members of dominant language communities feel their territory has been invaded with languages they do not wish to acquire (perhaps because these languages highlight, perhaps for the first time, the experience of the irregularity of the borders of their arbitrary and unjustifiable concentration of power).

**Finding the
Limits:
Our Sex,
Our Cinema**

The borders of microcultures are precarious, changing, co-opted by commercialism, and facilitated by the interpenetration of commercial culture that serves as camouflage for encoded desires. At the risk of ripping particular artifacts out of their natural habitat, I'd like to explore several approaches to representing safe sex in porn films, including both commercial and independent productions.

Play Safely, 1986, directed by David McCabe, Fantasy Productions. Commercially available, but produced with the consultation of educators, *Play Safely* uses a before-and-after narrative structure to display gay men's concerns about their changing sexual culture. The film's premise is that a "brush with reality" (in the encounter of a "promiscuous" man who is rumored to have AIDS with a character who tests antibody negative) enables the men to make positive and hot changes. Like most porn films, the narrative weaves together the stories of several characters, allowing producers to show more icons having more types of sex. In this film, one member of each couple is "anxious" and articulates specific concerns common in urban gay male culture. The partner responds with words of comfort and wisdom. Various strategies—monogamy, testing, avoiding people who "don't look well"—are proposed, but proper use of condoms is always the chosen solution. The film makes unusual use of dialogue to voice and elaborate logics concerning decision-making in the context of safe sex.

We are shown the practical aspects of safe sex in exhaustive, almost didactic detail from the middle of the film on. Sexual danger is produced by representing characters as having unsafe sex in equally hot flashback scenes. The film is thus anxiously poised on the edge of realism, asking the viewer to believe in the recounted dangers in order to appreciate the importance of taking up safe sex practices.

This film contains one of the few coming-in-the-condom shots I have found (Al Parker's *Turbo Charge* trailer also has such a shot). In terms of safe sex practice, there is no good reason not to remove the condom upon pulling out (as many men do in "real life"). The film does not appear to be suggesting that men actually duplicate this activity; rather, it assumes that the traditional "cum shot" of porn (where the man pulls out and masturbates to copious orgasm) is a metonym for what is happening "inside," out of camera view. Thus, the coming-in-the-condom shot helps the viewer visualize condom efficacy: the condom actually will contain coming, even if we can't observe this happening "inside."

Top Man, 1988, written, produced, and directed by Scott Masters, Catalina Video and Newport Video. One of the top grossing films of 1988, this coproduction has extremely high production values and humor and incorporates condom use

Al Parker and Justin Cade,
Turbo Charge Trailer,
Surge Studios, 1987.

without foregrounding safe sex. The use of condoms is not problematized: all scenes of fucking include both condom application and clear "meat" shots (penis-in-anus) in which the line of the condom is visible. Two scenes include dialogue about condom use incorporated into stereotyped scenarios of "teaching" another man how to have homosexual sex. Thus, the film inculcates a sense of collective responsibility for ensuring condom use. In a final orgy scene, there are plenty of condoms for everyone, and everyone uses them. Again, condoms are completely normalized, both something you can give to someone who is not initiated into gay sex and something you can freely use and ask for in front of men within gay male culture.

Turbo Charge Trailer, 1987, written and produced by Al Parker and Justin Cade, Surge Studios. Presented as a public service announcement, this how-to trailer to the then soon-to-be-released *Turbo Charge* shows Al Parker and Justin Cade using condoms, surgical gloves for fingering, and plastic wrap for ass licking. No reference is made to safe sex, per se, until the end title of the clip. The smooth acting and ease with which the men employ safe sex techniques suggest that this is simply what

Safe Sex and the Pornographic Vernacular

men do. The men snap the condoms in mock dick-torture, suggesting not only that condoms are *ordinary*, but also that they are an improvement in the game. Split-second repeat editing provides viewers with a clue to the problem points in safe sex technique: getting the plastic wrap out and smoothly covering the ass and getting the condom rolled down past the foreskin are foregrounded without interrupting the flow of the sexual narrative. The five-plus-minute clip is didactic insofar as time and care are taken to present safe sex techniques, but the techniques are "taught" in the course of a scenario that shows the men having fun and sexual ecstasy.

The Gay Men's Health Crisis Safer Sex Shorts, 1989, directed by Gregg Bordowitz and Jean Carlomusto. These videos, ranging in length from three to four minutes, are part of an ongoing project by activist videomakers working with members of target groups to create vernacular safe sex representations. The first two were screened at the Fifth International AIDS Conference in Montreal in June 1989: *Something Fierce* is a rock-video-style guide to fantasizing, touching, and fucking using a condom, including a didactic interlude in which the dancer applies and removes a condom. *Midnight Snack* shows two men meeting at the refrigerator and using whipped cream and honey to sweeten fellatio (with a condom). Neither shows the traditional cum shot, but both signify sexual pleasure through the men's facial expressions.

Car Service was designed by a black gay men's focus group and shows a more typical porn story progression: a yuppy black man discovers he has lost his wallet and pays his macho black cab driver with three condoms. The cab driver pulls into a quiet place, and the men have sex. Although we see the condoms, a penis, and a greedy, winking anus, we do not actually see the condom applied or the penis inserted, even though the men appear to have anal sex. The focus group preferred an erotic, soft core representation in which the condom signifies

Gregg Bordowitz and
Jean Carlomusto,
Current Flow,
Gay Men's Health Crisis
Safer Sex Shorts, 1989.

both anal sex and safe sex. The video is an implicit critique of the more hard core, fuck-focused eroticism of mainstream, largely white-oriented gay male porn.

Current Flow, one of the first projects aimed at safe sex for lesbians, acknowledges that the concepts, techniques, and tools of safe sex are new for most lesbians. One woman interrupts another, who is masturbating, and unrolls a towel containing the full complement of safe sex devices. The camera pans slowly over dental dams, surgical gloves, lubricant, and a dildo. The camera pan, which was commonly used in early gay male and heterosexual safe sex films, is a critical didactic moment for lesbians, many of whom are only beginning to be introduced to safe sex ideas and have little idea of what a dental dam looks like. The women engage in a variety of activities using all of the latex accouterments. *Current Flow* is remarkable both as a safe sex video for lesbians and as an early and cine-realist contribution to the emerging field of lesbian-produced lesbian porn. The video does not suffer from a lack of generic reference and sets an interesting aesthetic standard in using longer takes and women's music in the background.

Discussion

Audience member

I was struck by the extreme butch-femme role-playing in the lesbian porn video you showed. I thought the radicalism of the gay movement was in the equality and reciprocity of our relationships, unlike those of heterosexuals.

Cindy Patton

I want to say something briefly and then turn your question over to Gregg Bordowitz and Jean Carlomusto. Both their work and mine attempt to consider political and representational strategies developed largely in academic environments while simultaneously working with people who have had little access to that discussion. One thing I discovered in the Safe Company project was that the men I was working with had very stereotyped notions about representation, particularly about the representation of their own sexuality. This indicated to me that there might be a larger project involved in producing safe sex material: once we've named our sexuality, what do we want it to look like?

Jean Carlomusto I don't want to let the issue of butch-femme drop, because these are roles that have been greatly contested over the years. Historically lesbians who were particularly butch or femme have been subject to a great deal of discrimination, and these roles went out of vogue in the 1970s. They have since returned, but with a new sense of how the roles are enacted. Still, I think that any woman who might be seriously into this kind of role-playing would find my tape's representation of these sexual-psychic positions to be quite unreal. We were playing with these roles. There was an intentional sense of fun about them, and I have no qualms about having evoked them.

Gregg Bordowitz This project was conceived at Gay Men's Health Crisis as one in which Jean and I would organize task groups to develop a safe sex tape for a specific community. There was a black men's task group, a Latino group, a women's group, and people interested in making an s&m tape. That's what's unique about our project: it's trying to be very focused in its address and its distribution strategies.

I also have a comment about the role-playing in the work. It became clear to me in making these tapes that we cannot just cast off these roles. When working in the realm of fantasy, it's not merely a matter of saying "we're all equal." For example, in our most recent tape, the s&m one, we had to confront all the different hierarchical—top-bottom—positions at play in the cop-and-construction-worker scenario we were filming. It was not a matter of just dismissing them. Therefore, we tried to explore, on the one hand, what were the affirming aspects in this kind of sexual imagery, and on the other, what were the implicitly ideological messages structuring them. So we tried to play with the roles, reverse them, take pleasure in them, to show that they can be within our control.

Carlomusto The "problems" of the s&m tape are even greater because the scenario is also interracial. When you have an s&m scene played with a white cop and a black construction worker, the potency of the images of different kinds of power in this culture is undeniable. I'm sorry that this tape wasn't ready to be shown here, since it, more clearly than the others, raises the issue of self-determining groups producing what will most likely provoke enormous conflicts for viewers outside the target communities.

Bordowitz One of the good things about producing these tapes is that it has occasioned this kind of discussion. Without this project, for example, such a dialogue wouldn't have occurred in the education department at GMHC. Against all the odds of limited resources and the kinds of forces arrayed against us, this project has served as an opportunity for us to work through some very difficult issues.

Patton I began developing the idea of a sexual vernacular in part because this kind of conversation occurs informally all the time. Sexual languages are very much tied to particular communities, and each community has its own very rich and special way of speaking: a sexual artifact that makes sense in one community often looks very strange or offensive or stereotypical when taken outside that context. In this presentation, I did exactly what I just argued one shouldn't do: I ripped seven artifacts out of the communities in which they are symbolically meaningful. Still, to think of them as vernacular is useful when addressing criticisms made against them. When someone has problems with one of these tapes, it's useful to ask whether they understand the way in which the language operates for the community that designed it and how it is meaningful for that community. This is not to say that you can't criticize the work, but I think you have to understand yourself as outside of the symbolic language of the community it's meant for.

Safe Sex and the Pornographic Vernacular

John Greyson	Can you comment on the difficulty of producing safe sex materials when criteria for safe sex actually change very radically and can be very different from community to community.
Patton	This idea that safe sex information changes rapidly is, I think, misleading. What people know now is not really different from what people knew when *How to Have Sex in an Epidemic* came out in 1983. So I think it's a mistake to launch campaigns to change the safe sex guidelines every time a new study shows some 3 percent difference in something or other. What really needs to be dealt with is what the symbolic structures and the actual practices are at a given point in time for a given community.

In Boston we interviewed people to find out what they thought about safe sex. By and large, gay men were very aware of what safe sex is and why it is practiced. It wasn't a question of knowledge, but if and when they applied that knowledge.

Eventually we had focus groups draw up lists of problems with safe sex. Some of the problems mentioned were that younger men are often afraid they don't know how to have sex at all, so how can they negotiate safe sex? Or men in committed relationships often associate safe sex only with sex outside the relationship, even though they know they should always practice safe sex. After we compiled information about the real problems men were having with safe sex, we developed a pornographic pamphlet with stories in which only ultrasafe sex occurs. In these scenarios men always use condoms and pull out before coming. But the words *safe sex* never appear. The stories just progress, and safe practices are described. This worked incredibly well in the Boston community, because by 1989 there was already a fairly standard set of concepts about what constituted safe sex.

Bordowitz	I want to return to John's question, because I agree that there are competing criteria for what constitute safe sex practices. One tendency focuses on blocking the transmission of HIV specifically, and another tries to develop a broader understanding of

sexual health. These two tendencies sometimes seem to be in competition. For example, as illustrated in the "Safer Blow-Job" segment of John's video *The Pink Pimpernel* (1989), the Toronto view of a safe blow job is just a blow job—based on the assumption that HIV transmission is not very viable orally—while the New York view is that there are other viruses and organisms that can compromise your immune system that can be transmitted in oral sex. Therefore you have to make sexual decisions in relation to your health status.

Dennis Altman   I want to make a couple of comments as someone who comes from outside the U.S. It's worth remembering that there are some people doing safe sex education—I'm thinking particularly of the Dutch—who are still committed to trying to persuade gay men not to fuck at all. I thought that was really the complicated part of John's question; that is, from that position, most of the videos we saw would not be promoting safe sex at all. I don't agree with that position, but it is worth remembering that for some people the definition of safe sex is not to have sex at all.

The other comment I wanted to make was that you speak about "communities" as if the whole world consisted of self-defined communities. In Australia, over the last three years, a major concern has been to reach people who do not belong to a sexual community, individuals who have sex in very isolated ways that may put them at risk. I don't want to stereotype these people. They are not only married bisexual men, but also lonely people, immigrants, kids, people who for all sorts of reasons do not have a sense of affiliation with a community. From the context in which I work, it doesn't make sense to say, "Let's have a focus group for these people." No one would come to such a focus group.

So I'm curious, how you would take account of such people, people who are the least likely to receive safe sex information while needing it the most?

Patton	The problem you're raising is the very reason I started thinking in terms of vernaculars rather than something like "language communities," which would be another possible sort of organizing concept. I think that there are large numbers of men having sex with other men, or women having sex with other women, who don't self-identify as part of a gay community, a bisexual community, an s&m community, or whatever. But this is, I think, different from saying that people don't communicate about having sex. Bodies somehow manage to connect, people manage to have sex, and I think there are regular or, perhaps, irregular rules for finding people who will engage in those activities with you. And this is what I mean by sexual vernacular.

For people who are not part of a self-identified sexual community, you have to find out how they negotiate sex, how, for example, men who have sex at a truck stop find out that the truck stop exists as a place for sex. In Boston we have a number of men who work for Safe Company in the porno cinema—and I use the singular advisedly—and others who work in the parks. Part of the time they just hang out there, but they also have sex with the men who go there. Part of what they're doing is producing sort of folk ethnographies of how sex occurs in those places; and then they bring their observations to the group, and we discuss them in order to figure out what we can do. What we learned, first, was that there is not a lot you can do in the porno cinema or the bushes with traditional educational strategies. So, what the men in Safe Company do is this: they engage in sexual encounters in these places and steer their partners away from unsafe activities. And when they are done having sex, they say something like: "That was really hot. I'm really glad we had safe sex. It's really important."

Richard Fung	Could you talk a bit about distribution strategies and to what extent the tapes you discussed have managed to penetrate the commercial market?
Patton	I can speak only about the first three, which are widely available

commercial videos. *Top Man* was an incredibly successful video in 1986 and continues to be rented and sold; in fact, it promises to become a porn classic. If you rent porn videos much, you know that the unpopular ones disappear from the shelves after five or six months. *Play Safely* is no longer available in stores, but is available in most gay-oriented porn catalogs. And the Al Parker films are widely available.

Fung

Have there been attempts to use the shorter ones—those by Gregg and Jean—as shorts in longer pieces?

Bordowitz

That's our intention. They're also made to function like music videos in bars and bathhouses and will be distributed to those places as soon as we've finished the project. We're going to premier them at Mars, a club in New York, and we're going to put them in as many other clubs as possible. Also, some of the prevention and outreach workers at GMHC have taken some of the tapes to the baths. We designed them so that they would have a wide range of distribution possibilities.

Ray Navarro

I'm working with Gregg and Jean on the safe sex porn shorts, and I wanted to say something that relates to what you said about men doing safe sex education in porno theaters. We all have a personal stake, as sexual beings, in investigating the kinds of production practices and distribution strategies for these safe sex images. I'm doing outreach to people in the porn industry, trying to convince people who run porn theaters to run our safe sex tapes as trailers before and after feature films that may or may not have safe sex in them.

I initially got involved with the sex industry when trying to cast one of these videos. The people I've spoken to have all been really nice queers who are completely sympathetic to our project. It's not that these people are unwilling to help; it's just that they're not well informed about what the industry could be doing to promote safe sex. These people's stakes are not necessarily different from ours. And I always approach them that way. I tell them I'm a porn producer, too.

Ruby Rich   I wanted to ask something, Cindy, that I'm sure you've thought about but didn't talk about today. I guess if there were a headline for the tapes we saw today it would read: "See Dick Come, Did Jane Come?" There was an enormous difference between the male and female vernacular in the pornography you presented. I agree with Linda Williams that pornography is a genre that can be situated next to the musical and the western [Linda Williams, *Hard Core: Power, Pleasure, and the "Frenzy of the Visible,"* University of California Press, 1989]. However, given this notion of porn as a genre, and given that Williams doesn't deal with gay porn at all, what do you see as a lesbian vernacular within this? For example, if a central icon in straight and gay male porn is a cum shot, what would constitute a lesbian vernacular? In short, where is the lesbian situated in this discourse?

Patton   I wrote an essay for the fall 1988 issue of *Screen* addressing the appearance of lesbians in heterosexual porn ["Hegemony and Orgasm, or the Instability of Heterosexual Pornography," *Screen* 30, no. 3 (Fall 1988), 72–77]. However, I would like to comment on Linda's work and the idea of porn as a genre. In the 1980s, with the new market in home video, the older forms of porn broke down. Porn now participates in many different genres utilizing all kinds of textual and narrative strategies. I've identified at least five or six types of pornography available in the average video store that cannot be viewed as belonging to the same genre. This means, I think, that Linda's thesis has to be revised. I'm uncomfortable with seeing porn as a single genre based on a set of codes of sexual representation, or the centrality of, say, the cum shot.

The question of how to represent lesbian sexuality or what a lesbian genre would look like complicates the problem even further. This is the case because women will require various structures for looking. There will be those who want a narrative, with a beginning, a problematic, a denouement, and an ending. There will be others who want something that's much more antinarrative, in which there is little textual justification for the sexual activity being shown. And then there are those lesbians who will want something altogether different.

One problem for lesbian porn is that we have inherited the feminist discourse about objectification. There's a desire to produce lesbian pornography that's not objectifying. For example, Andrea Dworkin would argue that mediated sexuality, or a sexuality based on objectification, is a bad thing—wrong, immoral, and unfeminist. But if we take the big political step beyond that and accept that there could be such a thing as lesbian video porn, then we must grapple with the question of what it will look like.

Martha Gever   I'm interested to know if you have any thoughts about—if we are going to create pornography for lesbians—how to get lesbians to watch it, or how to reach its intended viewers. Distribution circuits for lesbian porn are almost nonexistent. I would think the GMHC video aimed at a lesbian audience, for example, would require a completely different distribution strategy than the tapes for men.

Carlomusto   I agree. We have to develop distribution markets. For example, I sent *Current Flow* to Susie Bright to see what *On Our Backs* could do with it. She liked the video, and she's trying to put together a feature about it in the magazine. I think we need to explore these kinds of venues, as well as show the videos in more social, public spaces like lesbian bars. In the outer boroughs, or places where lesbian culture is not as easily accessible, we'll have to be more creative about distribution—maybe Tupperware parties!

Gever   *On Our Backs* has done some of the best safe sex education for lesbians there is, and if you are a reader of it, then you already know about safe sex. I think my question has much in common with Dennis Altman's comment about belonging to "communities"—that is, what about those lesbians who can't find or don't read *On Our Backs?*

Patton	I think it first has to be established how lesbians find out about having lesbian sex in the first place, and then work through those networks. I also feel it's a mistake on two levels to think that because gay men seem to have it so good—they can see great porn, ostensibly anywhere—that you can imitate that with other groups of people. This is a mistake, first, because the market doesn't exist. Second, it's probably quite comfortable for gay men to watch themselves being represented as having sex. For most lesbians such an experience is probably incredibly uncomfortable.
	I gave this same lecture at Duke University about three weeks ago, and I ended the talk before getting to the lesbian sex tape because I decided I couldn't cope with showing it to that audience. I simply pretended it didn't exist. I performed this act of self-censorship because I wasn't sure what it meant for members of this audience (mostly straight white men) to see lesbians "doing it." It's important to take such a factor into account, because what you hear women say most frequently, lesbian or straight, is "pornography is assaultive to me." Although we may be critics of this position, the context has to be taken quite seriously, especially since this kind of representational sexual language is very underdeveloped. What happens when I present it for public scrutiny?
Alexandra Juhasz	I believe there are many people, particularly women, although I don't know if it divides along gender lines, whose sexual vernacular is not pornography. And I was, therefore, wondering if you would be willing to talk about what might be a more complicated issue; that is, what might a representation of safe sex and sexuality be that doesn't use the conventions of pornography?
Patton	The booklet I coauthored with Janis Kelly, *Making It: A Woman's Guide to Sex in the Age of AIDS* [Ithaca, N.Y., Firebrand Books, 1987], was an example of something done in another vernacular. We realized that women in general, whether they were bisex-

ual, lesbian, or straight, did not exist in anything like a sexual community. And it was therefore unworkable to try to approach women in the way that we had approached a sector of the gay male community. So we said, okay, where do women talk about sex? We decided it was in places like the kitchen, the living room, the office, and usually only to close friends or associates. So we tried to convey the necessary information in a writing style akin to talking with a friend. The book, which is in English and Spanish, uses the second person much of the time, and it's illustrated with casual cartoons. It's been extremely well received in a number of different cultures and countries. High school curriculums have been developed from it. We seem to have succeeded in reproducing something like a women's way of talking in the book, a vernacular that seems to work with straight, lesbian, and bisexual women.

Jim Fouratt

I have a number of questions about the lesbian porn safe sex video, and one of them is: are all lesbians at risk? The tape seems to presume that all lesbians are at risk and should be having safe sex.

Patton

I am going to return to something Gregg said earlier, which is that there have been a number of different strategies regarding safe sex practices. We use the term *safe sex* as if it were a scientific term, but it is not. It's an evolving concept for a whole range of practices. One thing discussed in *How to Have Sex in an Epidemic* was that, because we have experienced a great deal of medical oppression for our sexuality, we have never received proper sex education. Because we have never been given the tools to have both psychologically and physically healthy sex, we are generally unable to get the information necessary for keeping germs away.

Now, if this is the approach, then the question of whether lesbians are at risk for HIV is in some ways secondary, since lesbians first need to respond to our past history of never having been properly educated about sexually transmitted diseases. That's what we're doing—changing the whole range of modalities around lesbian sexuality.

Another strategy is, of course, to ask if *people* are at risk for HIV, and if so, let's educate them. As Gregg was mentioning earlier, those two things are constantly in conflict, both in the educator's mind and in that of the individual who's receiving the information.

Carlomusto Yes, it's not just a question of HIV, but of a whole spectrum of illnesses that can result from the sexual exchange: yeast infections, chlamydia, and so on. The motivation for making *Current Flow* was to make women aware of the option of using a dental dam.

I am also in agreement with Alex. I don't think that porn is the only way to address women. For example, if a woman doesn't feel good about her sexuality, then a dental dam is not going to be relevant anyway. You have to create avenues for discussions about negotiating the sexual act, about feeling good about yourself—good enough so that you would get into a sexual situation in the first place. Then, our tape would just be something that would give a technical demonstration of how you actually use a dental dam when having sex.

Isaac Julien I want to open the debate to questions of racial difference in relationship to the lesbian porn tape. In trying to visualize safe sex or sexual desire, the creation of porn tapes is a minefield in terms of trying to grapple with the different dichotomies constructed around racial difference. I felt, regarding your tape, that the butch-femme role-playing was really based on racial difference.

Since there is already a stereotypical discourse in representations of the black subject, how can we, as image makers, make these identities more complex, or more dialectical?

Carlomusto I think there's an unfair burden placed on a work when it is one of the only ones out there or when you only have the opportunity to make one tape. If this tape existed within a series of tapes about lesbian sexuality, there wouldn't be as much tension around this particular frame or that particular image.

I'll talk just a bit about the making of this tape, since very real contingencies affected the final product. I wanted to have a butch role and a femme one, and from the outset the well-known porn star Annie Sprinkle was cast as the femme. Annie loves using vibrators, or whatever kind of toy, and really wanted to be the femme. But finding someone to play the butch was not so easy. The black woman in the video is somebody I went to high school with, whom I happened to run into one day on the street. She told me she would be really interested in being in the video, and much of the staging of the sexual scenario grew out of her input. In fact, both women designed their own costumes and invented their characters.

What we ended up with is perhaps problematic. It's difficult when you think of what the five-minute video was trying to accomplish, especially when you have an interracial scene. Still, we tried to play with the roles by putting the femme on top and the butch on the bottom.

Julien Unfortunately there is a world of difference between the anecdotal knowledge of how someone came to be in a work and played with a role and how spectators—unaware of this history—relate as voyeurs to the images. These pressures apply to my work as well. I have received similar criticism about the two black men in *Looking for Langston* [1988], both of whom are light skinned. People have kind of whispered in my ear, "Make sure there's a darker brother next time." And though this can lead to essentialism, where there is thought to be some kind of authentic representation of race, I do think there's a responsibility to do something more dialectical. We work within the realm of fantasy, and in that realm there are a number of things we can do against the grain of stereotypical representations and discourses.

The Contemporary Political Use of Gay History
The Third Reich

Stuart Marshall

In 1983 I made a proposal to Channel Four Television in England for a program about media representations of AIDS. At that time, only two television documentaries about AIDS had been broadcast on British television. Although these demonstrated an emerging televisual agenda, I decided to confine myself to the horrific printed journalism about AIDS that had begun to dominate British tabloids. The upshot of this proposal and the subsequent research was the videotape *Bright Eyes* (1984), in which I sought to deconstruct the journalistic representations to reveal their historical determinations. Stated concisely, the point I wanted to make was that the historical construction of homosexual identity as an inherently pathological subjectivity formed the powerful subtext of contemporary journalistic representations of AIDS as "the gay plague." According to this subtext, if homosexuality was a diseased form of subjectivity, then it was inevitable that this condition would eventually reveal itself in a medically identifiable form of morbidity.

Bright Eyes took the form of a collage of different historical discourses, images, and meanings about homosexuality and disease. As part of this collage, I included a sequence about the history of the gay rights movement in Germany in the early part of this century, as represented by the work of Dr. Magnus Hirschfeld and his Scientific-Humanitarian Committee. *Bright Eyes* tells this story in the form of a recollection, as Hirschfeld sits in a cinema in Paris watching newsreel documentation of the destruction of his Institute of Sexual Science in Berlin by members of the Nazi youth movement. The videotape then goes on to depict a young homosexual man's interrogation by the Nazis and his eventual internment in a concentration camp.

As I have said, *Bright Eyes* is a kind of collage, a series of

Sacking of Magnus Hirschfeld's Institute of Sexual Science in Berlin, 1933.

Marshall

temporal juxtapositions of textual units. I chose this form because it allowed me to collide different historical episodes in such a way that the viewer would be presented with the problem of assembling their mutual relationships. The viewer would participate in the construction of meaning by juxtaposing large, seemingly self-contained units of discourse. What, then, are the possible relationships between a presentation of the worst kind of tabloid AIDS journalism and a partial history of the demise of the German homosexual rights movement? My intention in 1984 was to draw out the historical continuity of antihomosexual persecution. There is a strong clue to this when the Hirschfeld character describes an antihomosexual media smear campaign that was conducted by the French and Italian press in the 1910s in an attempt to discredit Kaiser Wilhelm II. Hirschfeld explains that this campaign created enormous public hostility toward the homosexual rights movement and permanently set back its political agenda to achieve equal rights for homosexual people. The sequence registered my fears that the international lesbian and gay rights movements might suffer a fate in the 1980s similar to the eventual demise of the German movement in the 1930s, when it was totally destroyed by the Nazis.

There were other relationships as well. At that time in Britain, the Right was demanding that people with AIDS (PWAs) be quarantined, a demand that evoked the specter of condemning social undesirables to the concentration camps. My intention at that time, however, was not to draw a parallel between the AIDS epidemic and the Holocaust—a point to which I will return in greater detail.

Several years after completing *Bright Eyes,* I submitted a proposal to Channel Four television for *Desire* (1988), a film about the experiences of lesbians and gay men under National Socialism. My reasons for proposing this project were complex. On a personal level, I felt I was not done with this subject, or rather it was not done with me. On a political and intellectual level, I thought it was necessary to examine the particular period of history that has provided the gay rights movement with potent symbols—the pink and, more recently, the black triangles—symbols with which, in Europe and North America at least, we have often represented our common movement for liberation.[1] The symbols of the Nazi persecution of homosexuals have been given a privileged status in contemporary gay politics since the late 1970s. I wanted to discover some of the historical facts—if you will excuse me such a positivist endeavor—that lay behind the use of these symbols in contemporary political discourse. It seemed necessary to confront the fact that, although these pink and black triangles had become such a common form of self-identification within the gay and lesbian communities, they had been extracted from a specific historical and political conjuncture that lay outside the life span and therefore beyond the memory of the contemporary generation of gay activists. Furthermore, this history, precisely because it was gay history, had not been documented in a form accessible to the kind of analysis that could usefully inform contemporary political practice. My goal, therefore, was to lay out this history in such a way that it could resonate with our contemporary experience.

I was also curious as to why the pink triangle had been taken up by the gay movement at a time of its greatest optimism for the future of lesbian and gay civil rights. Other symbols, such as the butterfly and the lambda, had been considered as well, but had never found widespread popularity. I had never felt comfortable about the use of the pink triangle in contemporary gay politics. After all, this symbol represented the limit point, the inconceivable and unspeakable possibility of annihilation. I wanted to know why such a horrific symbol had gained currency for representing our commonality, our hopes, our struggles, our belief in a better future. I wanted to tease out the political meanings and effects of using for affirmative group

[1] Because lesbianism was not illegal under German law, lesbian women could not be imprisoned on account of their sexuality. However, they were frequently classed as asocials and imprisoned under the black triangle along with prostitute women, the "work-shy," and other "enemies of the German people."

identification an image that was once so cruelly used to stigmatize gay men in the Nazi death mills.

During the filming of *Desire,* I began to acknowledge a repressed agenda, which became painfully clear to me in the
course of conducting one particular interview. While making the
film, I met some extraordinary elderly lesbians and gay men
who thrilled me with their dignity and courage. One man, Gert
Weymann, who survived this period as an active gay man, ended
his harrowing account of persecution by saying, "It was very
hard then, but it was easier to survive Nazism than it is to survive AIDS." Suddenly part of my investment in this project was
made clear to me. It was the pressing need to discover for myself, in the context of the AIDS crisis, what it was like to survive that limit point, that inconceivable experience of terrifying
persecution. What price was paid? What were the strategies of
survival? How deep were the scars? Who lived and who died,
and why?

During the later stages of the making of *Desire,* I became
aware that the American AIDS activist movement had begun to
use the pink triangle and to employ genocide and Holocaust
analogies. Some participants in this movement were drawing a
rhetorical parallel between the Nazi state's persecution and extermination of its homosexual population and the United States
government's treatment of PWAs. Although I absolutely support the use of historical analysis to assess the successes and
failures of earlier political struggles and to implement that
knowledge in the form of considered contemporary political
practice, I believe, as I have stated earlier, that for reasons of
historical suppression this harrowing period of lesbian and gay
history has not been sufficiently researched and understood in
all its intricacies and complexities to be available for comparison.

A simple example of the problem relates to the AIDS activist group ACT UP's use of the pink triangle (albeit ironically
inverted) in conjunction with the legend SILENCE = DEATH.

Herr Weymann told a very different story. According to him, the only way to avoid the concentration camps and death was precisely to remain silent. Those lesbians and gay men who lived to tell their tales survived by subterfuge, self-concealment, and secrecy. Both his testimony and the testimony of another gay man, who was tortured by the Gestapo in its attempt to gain a confession of homosexual activities and the names of homosexual partners, demonstrated that at that time the equation would have been SILENCE = SURVIVAL.

It might be argued that my objection is nothing more than an academic one to the powerful rhetorical deployment of a potent symbol to galvanize a community and express its fears of annihilation. Such an argument is encapsulated in the slogan Never Again. It is my contention, however, that we must examine this period of gay history to determine whether the analogy holds, and if so, what possible lessons and survival strategies can be learned. The analogy proceeds from a commonly held belief that the Nazi treatment of homosexuals was a form of *genocide*—the annihilation of a *race*—and thus comparable to the Nazi treatment of Jews and Gypsies. Furthermore, the analogy equates the Nazi state's extermination of homosexuals and the contemporary liberal democratic state's treatment of PWAs. It can, of course, be argued that the juxtaposition of the legend SILENCE = DEATH and the pink triangle can produce meaning on a number of different levels, and it is clear that the inversion of the pink triangle is intended to skew its meaning. But even though the meaning of the pink triangle has been changed by its use in the context of the gay liberation movement, it is apparent that among AIDS activists a contemporary perception of its earlier historical meaning is being called upon to produce a specific ideological effect. This intended effect is the evocation of a "memory" of mass extermination.

I hope that the following remarks will not be construed as an attack upon the dynamism, the energy, the political importance, and the successes of the AIDS activist movement in general, or of ACT UP in particular. I offer them simply as a series of reflections.

Constructing the Homosexual Identity, Racial Analogies, and Reverse Discourse

Returning briefly to my earlier comments on *Bright Eyes,* I would like to restate a commonplace observation of social constructionist theory. The contemporary homosexual identity was first formulated in the late 1860s by European medics intent on extending their purview, their domain of professionalism, and their arena of social power by increasingly medicalizing aspects of human behavior that had previously been supervised by the church. This medicalization of homosexuality—a transition from notions of sin within ecclesiastical law to notions of sickness and deviancy within criminal law—is part of a general process of the medicalization of deviancy that was to result in a proliferation of new social identities, a whole set of new species of human beings. The new characters to be added to the social drama were, among others, the prostitute, the criminal, the mentally enfeebled, and the drunkard. Within the realm of sexual deviancy, the process of categorization was to become so refined that by the end of the nineteenth century, sexologists such as Havelock Ellis and Krafft-Ebing were to describe literally dozens of sexual types, all of which were absolutely characterized by sexual proclivities. It is important to note that this process constructs and categorizes not only the deviant but also the norm itself. The notion of the norm, particularly when coupled with the concept of the "natural," was to become one of the most important reference points for describing the relationship between the individual and society from the mid-nineteenth century up to the present day. As Michel Foucault wrote:

The nineteenth-century homosexual became a personage, a past, a case history, and a childhood, in addition to being a type of life, a life form, and a morphology, with an indiscreet anatomy and possibly a mysterious physiology. Nothing that went into his total composition was unaffected by his sexuality. It was everywhere present in him: at the root of all his actions because it was their insidious and indefinitely active principle; written immodestly on his face and body because it was a secret which always gave itself away. We must not forget that the psychological, psychiatric, medical category of homosexuality was constituted from the moment it was characterised—Westphal's famous article of 1870 on "contrary sexual sensations" can stand as its date of birth. . . .[2]

2
Michel Foucault, *The History of Sexuality, Volume One: An Introduction* (New York: Vintage Books, 1980), 43.

Nineteenth-century criminal anthropologists, sexologists, and medics attempted to categorize and classify social deviancy by using models that vacillate between notions of personal identity, physiological specificity, racial characteristics, psychological complexes, subclasses of the population, genetic predispositions, and patterns of criminal behavior.

Most of the scientific work that proceeded from physiognomy, or the study of the relationship between internal predispositions toward deviancy and their external physiological characteristics revealed in human anatomy, concentrated on "the distinguishing feature." The distinguishing feature was that anatomical characteristic that absolutely characterized all individual subjects of a particular deviant social type. The work of the English physiognomist Francis Galton is exemplary of this endeavor. Using recently developed photographic technology, Galton superimposed a number of individual photographs of a particular deviant type in the belief that all the variable physiognomic features would blur through the superimposing process, while the distinguishing feature or features that were common to all examples of a particular deviant social type would be amplified through successive superimpositions.[3]

3
For a detailed account of Galton's theories and techniques, see Allan Sekula, "The Body and the Archive," *October* 43 (Winter 1987), 3–64; and David Green, "Veins of Resemblance: Photography and Eugenics," *The Oxford Art Journal* 7, no. 2 (1985), 3–16.

Running through the discourses of physiognomy and social categorization is a notion of racial similarity. In the case of Galton, there are a number of photographic studies of "the Jewish type," for example. It is important to note that the broader social backdrop to this scientific endeavor was the expansion of European imperialism. There is a complex and self-validating interrelationship between attempts to categorize, control, and regulate the colonized subjects of imperialism "abroad" and the potentially rebellious, politically seditious subjects of the social underclass "at home." In fact, the residuum—the "primitive" un-socializable lumpen proletariat thrown into existence by the massive social reorganization of the Industrial Revolution—was frequently characterized as another race—always potentially politically disruptive and subversive—living parasitically within the healthy social body. The process of civilizing the primitive world outside the seat of empire was part and parcel of the at-tempt to regulate and control the primitive society of the social underclasses within the seat of empire. The two were mutually interdependent. Attempts to describe social differences by the use of racial analogies do not absolutely characterize all work of this kind, but they do form a dominant discourse that was even-tually to be rationalized as the discourse of eugenics. Hence the physiology of social deviancy was profoundly inflected by a racial understanding of social groupings, behaviors, and demographic patterns.

Foucault has noted that attempts to control and categor-ize deviant social behavior through the construction of a deviant identity also open up the possibility of a reverse discourse, a political struggle, based upon and made possible by the con-struction of the deviant identity. Thus the nineteenth-century German homosexual rights movement proceeded from the new notion of a homogeneous homosexual identity, but contested the social persecution of individuals characterized by this iden-tity. Magnus Hirschfeld, the leader of the liberal-left wing of the German homosexual rights movement was very much a man of his time. As a physician and sexologist, his struggle for equal rights for homosexuals was based on an absolute acceptance of the medical science of his day. But Hirschfeld made use of a contradiction internal to the discourse of deviancy in order to construct a reverse discourse of resistance to the process of social stigmatization. The contradiction that lay at the heart of criminal anthropology and the new psychiatry was the problematic status of nature itself. The concept of nature was highly unstable: on the one hand, it represented the truth of human society uncorrupted by the artificiality of developed industrial capitalism; on the other hand, it represented the dark forces of uncivilized primitive man, which had to be transcended in order to perfect human society.

Hirschfeld employed the notion of the "naturalness" of nature in order to argue that if the homosexual was constitutionally homosexual then he was only doing what came "naturally," and therefore he should not be discriminated against for being true to "his nature." So strong was Hirschfeld's belief in the scientific premises about homosexual identity and the rational nature of his own argument that, in the early 1920s, he mounted the motto Justice Through Science above the doorway to his Institute of Sexual Science in Berlin.

Though it is clear that small subgroupings of homosexual men could be found long before the 1860s—in English society for instance—it seems probable that these groupings were motivated by the need to meet others who participated in the same sexual behaviors rather than the need to identify as a society of individuals who were absolutely and inherently different from other social subjects. The English molly houses of the eighteenth century were places where sodomitical behavior could be enjoyed, but it is doubtful whether the participants recognized each other in their discrete sexual identities in the same way that contemporary gay men recognize each other.[4] At this time, the sodomite was understood not so much as a homosexual identity but as the person who indulged in the act of sodomy, irrespective of whether the partner was man, woman, or beast. By Hirschfeld's time, it is evident that a separate homo-

4
For a study of the molly houses, see Alan Bray, *Homosexuality in Renaissance England* (London: Gay Men's Press, 1982), 81–114.

sexual identity had been constructed and that this was an essential aspect of homosexual subculture and self-acknowledgment. This is clearly obvious in the right-wing German homosexual rights movement, which saw itself as a movement of a particular and special people and which adopted the name *Gemeinschaft der Eigenen* (Community of the Special).

Though this reverse discourse of struggle has provided gay men and lesbians with a variety of political possibilities, ranging from Hirschfeld's liberal movement of the beginning of the century to the 1970s gay liberation movement (whose name also reflects the influence of Third-World Marxist liberation struggles of the same period), we are still employing a problematic agenda of sexual identity and community, an inherited agenda that determines the very terms of our self-recognition and our discourse of contestation. Perhaps the most problematic aspect of this agenda is the nature of our community, how we define ourselves *as* a community. Precisely because the nineteenth-century discourse slid between concepts of race, community, subculture, underclass, and criminal conspiracy, we have inherited imprecise and sometimes mutually contradictory options to conceptualize our society.

The Nazi Regulation of Homosexuality

It is precisely this problem that Nazism set out to address in its attempts to eradicate homosexuality. In order to produce a range of regulatory strategies toward homosexuality, Nazism made use of a variety of *understandings* of our society and our individual appearances, understandings that reflect the numerous conceptualizations of homosexual identity and homosexual society available within scientific discourse at the time. To understand the complexity and sophistication of the Nazi position, it is essential to comprehend the particular form of racial eugenics developed by Nazi scientists and the Nazi state.

It is clear that eugenics had many different faces, including, for example, the arguments put forward by the British birth control movement's struggle for women's reproductive rights. In this case, the eugenic argument for the need to control and develop racial purity and strength was deployed in a form that gave individual women the right to choose motherhood. The fascist development of eugenics, however, denied women control of reproduction and lodged all power in the state, supported by legal and penal power structures. In this case the purification of the race not only depended upon the absolute extermination of those other "races" to be found "like a disease within the social body"—the Jews and the Gypsies—but also required the imposition upon all "true Aryans" of a duty to reproduce prolifically.

It is often stated that abortion and contraception were outlawed by the Nazi state, but this is only partly true. In 1943, after three years of preparation, a law was indeed introduced for the "Protection of Marriage, Family, and Motherhood," calling for the death penalty, "in extreme cases," for carrying out or aiding abortions. However, this legislation covered only the abortion of an "Ayran" fetus. In fact, in June 1935, aborting "defective pregnancies" on grounds of race hygiene, which was already in practice, had been legalized. For Jewish women, or Aryan women who were pregnant by a Polish worker, for example, abortion was then required by law. In July 1933, the cabinet, led by Hitler, had passed the "Law for the Prevention of Hereditarily Diseased Offspring," which was used to limit the propagation of "lives unworthy of life." Paragraph 12 of this law allowed the use of force against those who did not consent to being sterilized. This law was used to deny reproductive rights to "Aryans" who were criminal, disabled, or mentally disturbed (and eventually the long-term unemployed and the work-shy). Also in 1935, a law against "habitual delinquents legalized castration of men in specific cases. This was extended to women in the form of ovariectomy and sterilization by X ray in 1936. Only after having experienced three cesarean births was a woman entitled to an abortion and then only on condition that she accepted sterilization. Between 1934 and 1937, about eighty men and four hundred women died in the course of sterilization. Furthermore, hundreds of thousands of Jewish women who entered the extermination camps but were not sent immediately to the gas chambers were forcibly sterilized by X ray. Many of them were unaware of the meaning of the "treatment" they were being given.

The eugenic control of the population was therefore twofold. On the one hand, it required genocide—the mass extermination of the Jews and the Gypsies and forced sterilization for those who would be used as labor but not allowed to reproduce. On the other hand, for Aryan women there was an enormous social pressure to have as many children as possible, and this demand frequently contradicted the official Nazi position on the sanctity of the family. Pregnancy outside marriage was to some extent sanctioned, and the notorious *Lebensborn* institutions were set up to provide illegitimate mothers with social support when they were rejected by their families. It is well known that Lebensborn were to come into their own when privileged young SS officers fulfilled the demands of the chief of the SS, Heinrich Himmler, that every good SS officer should father at least three children. "If both parents are pure Aryans," Himmler stated, "illegitimate children should be accepted with as much joy as legitimate offspring."[5]

It is true that Himmler, when speaking about homosexuals, frequently employed racial eugenic analogies: for example, "We must exterminate these people root and branch."[6] He also described homosexuals as "symptoms of dying races" and conjured up an image of an early pure Teutonic race that drowned homosexuals in bogs.[7] But this is nothing more than political rhetoric appealing to the discourse of racial purity already in place. No real parallel can be drawn between the extermination of Jews in the Final Solution and the extermination of homosexuals. The

5
Quoted in Hans Peter Bleuel, *Strength Through Joy: Sex and Society in Nazi Germany*, trans. J. Maxwell Brownjohn (London: Secker and Warburg, 1973), 221.

6
Quoted in Felix Kersten, *The Kersten Memoirs 1940–1945* (New York: Macmillan, 1957), 57.

7
Ibid.

The Contemporary Political Use of Gay History

extermination of Jews was conceived by the Nazis precisely as the extermination of a "race," which unless sterilized and gassed would continue to propagate its putative racial characteristics. The problem with homosexuals, as far as the Third Reich was concerned, was the fact that they supposedly did *not* reproduce. In this sense, they did not propagate themselves or their "race." Hence this remark, from the speech of Himmler's just quoted: "Just think how many children will never be born because of this." According to Rudolf Diels, the founder of the Gestapo, Hitler "lectured me on the role of homosexuality in history and politics. It eliminated from the reproductive process those very men on whose offspring a nation depended."[8] First and most im-

8
Quoted in Bleuel,
Strength Through Joy, 218.

portant, then, homosexual men were not available for the propagation of the Aryan race. From this perspective, we can see that the regulation of homosexuality was understood as a part of eugenic politics only by way of reproductive politics. On October 26, 1936, Himmler established the Central Agency for Jointly Combatting Abortion and Homosexuality. It was headed by SS Captain Joseph Meisinger, whose previous job had been administrating the redistribution of property confiscated from Jews.

But, this is not the full story. Whereas it is clear that the Nazis saw homosexuals as constitutionally deviant, they also simultaneously made use of a much more modern theory of homosexuality, a theory not of racial or even sexual identity, but rather a theory of sexual desire. Homosexuality as a non-identity-specific desire was frequently represented by disease analogies. For example, again from the same speech by Himmler: "Just think how a people can be broken in nerve and spirit when such a plague gets hold of it." Or Hitler: "Once rife, it extended its contagious effects like an ineluctable law of nature to the best and most manly of characters."[9] As I said, there is a long Western European sociological tradition that describes the effects of homosexuality as a moral contagion. This is not spe-

9
Ibid.

cific to Germany, but its manifestation there was more complex.
For Hitler, paradoxically it would seem, it is the best and most
manly of characters who are vulnerable to the disease of homosexual desire. Homosexuality is therefore made to bear a historical anxiety in German culture about masculinity, femininity,
and the nature of friendship. The anxiety may be couched in the
language of disease and contagion, but this language simply covers over a contradiction fundamental to Nazi attitudes toward
masculinity.

The Nazis appropriated a history of male friendship popu-
larized in eighteenth-century literary society that included the
open display of affection as well as the writing of what can best
be described as love letters. From the Napoleonic wars to the
First World War, romantic friendship was politicized into
comradeship—the mutual bonding of men in the service of the
state. This is the origin of the *Männerbund,* or male bonding
which was to form such a powerful ideology in German culture.
The Nazis aestheticized and eroticized the *Männerbund* as part
and parcel of their overvaluation of the masculine fighting man.

They produced endless representations of male beauty for the populace to identify with or to idealize, most notably through their official art, which made frequent references to Hellenic Greek art and culture (a fascination of right-wing German cultural commentators).

The overvaluation of masculinity carried within it, however, the possibility not just of identification but also of object-choice. It is absolutely clear that the German language of male comradeship was shot through with homoeroticism. In German philosophy and culture, eroticism connoted a desexualized relationship; it was about a cosmological love relation and not about sexual desire. But homoeroticism can easily become transmuted into homosexual desire, and this was the root of the Nazis' problem. Homosexual desire radically challenged the fixed relationships between the sexes fantasized by the Nazi state as an absolute difference between the maternal reproductive desire of the woman and the domineering active desire of the man. As Himmler stated, "It would be a catastrophe if we foolish males wanted to make women into logically thinking instruments. . . . If we try to masculinize them, well, there we conjure up the danger of homosexuality."[10] "If a man just looks at a girl in America, he can be forced to marry her or pay damages . . . therefore men protect themselves in the USA by turning to homosexuals. . . . Women in the USA are like battle axes—they hack away at the males."[11]

The recognition that the finest fighting men of the German nation might be open to the influences of homosexual desire produced a violent paranoia about homosexuality in the Third Reich. The Nazis promoted all-male organizations, which were constantly open to accusations of homosexual perversion. From very early on, the Hitler Youth was commonly referred to as the "Homo Youth." In a speech in 1934 Hitler said:

I expect all SA leaders to preserve and strengthen the SA in its capacity as a pure and cleanly institution. In particular, I should

10
Bradley F. Smith and Agnes F. Peterson, eds., *Heinrich Himmler Geheimreden 1933–1945* (Frankfurt: Propylaen, 1974), 97.

11
Ibid.

12
Quoted in Bleuel,
Strength Through Joy, 219.

13
Karl Werner
Gauhl, *Gleichgeschlechtliche
Handlungen Jugendlicher:
Statistische Untersuchungen
über Gruppenbildung bei
Jugendlichen . . .* (Ph.D.
thesis, Marburg 1940), Uni-
versity Library, Marburg/
Lahn.

like every mother to be able to allow her son to join the SA, the Party, and Hitler Youth without fear that he may become morally corrupted in their ranks. I therefore require all SA commanders to take the utmost pains to ensure that offenses under Paragraph 175 are met by immediate expulsion of the culprit from the SA and the Party.[12]

In 1940 Karl Werner Gauhl produced a dissertation at the University of Marburg entitled *Gleichgeschlechtliche Handlungen Jugendlicher*—an extraordinary work of pseudoscience that claimed to trace the networks of homosexual contagion infecting the Nazi youth movement.[13] This fear had existed among

The Contemporary Political Use of Gay History

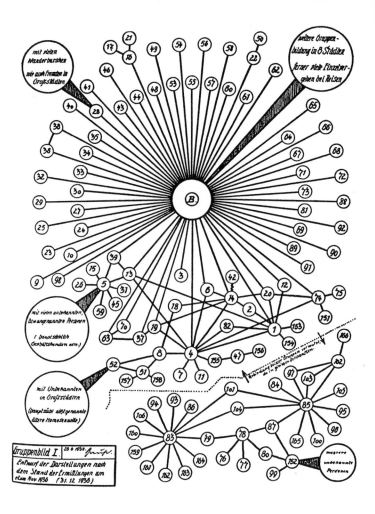

the Nazis for some time. In 1928 Adolf Brand of the *Gemeinschaft der Eigenen* canvassed all German political parties for their views on the reform of Paragraph 175, the law that made homosexuality a criminal offense. The Nazi Party replied as follows:

It is not necessary that you and I live, but it is necessary that the German people live. And it can only live if it can fight, for life means fighting. And it can only fight if it retains its masculinity.

Marshall

And it can only retain its masculinity if it exercises discipline, especially in matters of love. Free love and deviance are undisciplined. Therefore we reject you, as we reject anything which hurts our people. Anyone who even thinks of homosexual love is our enemy.[14]

14
Rudolf Klare, *Homosexualität und Strafrecht* (Hamburg: Hanseatische Verlagsanstalt, 1937), 114.

It is this focus of paranoia about the possible promotion of homosexuality among the members of the leading male Nazi organizations that explains the lack of uniformity in the Nazi persecution of homosexual men. In the SS—the most prestigious Nazi organization—homosexual offenses were punishable by death. There was no trial; the individuals involved were immediately executed. In the army, homosexuality was dealt with slightly more leniently. In civil society, the due processes of law were meticulously used, followed by imprisonment. In the early days of the regime, only habitual offenders were sent to the concentration camps. Second offenders were sometimes punished by castration. As Himmler gained power, however, he used the so-called *schutzhaft,* or "protective custody," to enable the police to rearrest homosexuals after their release from prison and specified that they should be sent to Level Three camps—the death mills: "After serving the sentence imposed by the court, they will, upon my instructions, be taken to a concentration camp and there shot while trying to escape."[15]

15
Quoted in Bleuel, *Strength Through Joy,* 223.

This focus of fear on homosexual desire itself is best illustrated by the 1935 amendment to Paragraph 175 that criminalized homosexual kisses, embraces, glances, and even fantasies. A person could even be charged on suspicion that these offenses were about to be committed. Nevertheless, many homosexual artists and performers were not subject to these penalties. Some famous homosexual stage and film stars were protected by Hermann Goering's wife, and in 1937 Himmler advised that no actors or performers could be arrested for Paragraph 175 offenses without his personal consent unless they were caught by the police engaging in homosexual activities. It has also been documented that some Aryan homosexual first-time offenders were offered the possibility of psychotherapy in an attempt to reclaim their desire for the propagation of the race.

Professor Rüdiger Lautmann of Bremen University has established from official records that between five and fifteen thousand homosexual men were sent to concentration camps.[16] In the period of the Third Reich, fifty thousand men were sentenced for homosexual offenses by the courts. It is therefore clear that only a minority of convicted homosexuals, all of whom must have been known to the Gestapo, were sent to concentration camps. This information has been available since the late 1970s. In 1985 the German gay historian Manfred Herzer stated that a description of the life of homosexual men in the Nazi state was not exhausted with their unspeakable suffering in concentration camps. In fact, some homosexual men who survived the period reminisced about the brown dictatorship as the "happiest time of their lives." This is incompatible with the usual clichés "according to which the unimaginably demonic Nazis launched an entirely unique and unparalleled holocaust against gays in which the pink triangle was to have even more horrible connotations than the yellow star."[17]

The Contemporary Use of the Pink Triangle

Herzer's observation takes me back to my original question about the use of the pink triangle in contemporary gay politics. Why did this symbol representing only the extreme point of the Nazi regulation of homosexuality gain currency to represent gay people's commonality, our hopes, our struggles, and our belief in a better future? The answer to this question may be revealed in the very terms I have just used to ask this question. I think there is, and always has been, a fundamental problem about the status of the word *our* in this formulation. In what way are we a "we"? What is the common denominator of our putative community? In 1927 Magnus Hirschfeld uncharacteristically decried

16
Rüdiger Lautmann, *Seminar: Gesellschaft und Homosexualität* (Frankfurt: Suhrkamp, 1977), 333.

17
Manfred Herzer, "Nazis, Psychiatrists, and Gays: Homophobia in the Sexual Science of the National Socialist Period," The Cabirion and Gay Books Bulletin, New York, no. 12 (Spring/Summer 1985), 1–5.

the lack of solidarity between homosexuals, probably during a moment of extreme frustration at the lack of activist support for his campaign.

It is untrue that homosexuals form a sort of "secret society" among themselves with all sorts of code signals and mutual defence arrangements. Aside from a few minor cliques, homosexuals are in reality almost totally lacking in feelings of solidarity; in fact, it would be difficult to find another class of mankind which has proved so incapable of organizing to secure its basic legal and human rights.[18]

18
Magnus Hirschfeld, "Die Homosexualität," *Sittengeschichte des Lasters,* ed. Leo Schidrowitz (Vienna: Verlag für Kulturforschung, 1927), 309.

From the very beginning of the homosexual rights movement, there has been a very real problem, not only from a theoretical but also from an organizational point of view, about the roots of our commonality. Nothing anchors our bonding other than our sexual desires. We come from different classes, different ethnic backgrounds, different genders, and different positions of social privilege. The sexual liberationists and libertines of the 1970s saw sexual desire as the great leveler of these differences. Many gay male theorists argued that, at the level of organs connecting with organs, social, racial, and class differences were erased. The bathhouse was seen as the privileged site of this collapse of difference, the place where democracy of desire reigned supreme. In the world outside, however, these differences returned. These problems are not, of course, specific to the lesbian and gay movements. After the heady heyday of "sisterhood," second-wave feminism was riven with questions of class and racial difference.

For gay people in the 1970s, then, the mistaken belief that homosexuals had been massively exterminated as a group by the Third Reich filled an enormous gap. This mythical genocide of homosexuals provided us with a group identity similar to that of the Jews. The pink triangle expressed our commonality as victims; we could recognize our community through the eyes of our Nazi persecutors. How potent, then, the use of the pink triangle in the midst of a health crisis that represents, in our worst fears, the annihilation of our community. Hasn't history repeated itself? Have we not found ourselves again faced by the genocidal actions of a fascist state?

Every political movement requires its points of imaginary identification. Using the term in the sense given it by Jacques Lacan, the *imaginary* is a necessary fiction that is required not only for the construction of the subject as distinct from an external world of objects, but also in order for any political rallying and action to take place. It would be naive to suggest that an effective political movement could be based entirely upon the recognition of difference. A passionate identification of similarity is an absolute necessity. This political identification does not and cannot exhaust our subjectivities. Although our reverse discourse of political struggle necessarily proceeds from the need to contest the dominant social construction of our identity as pathologically diseased, we cannot and do not fall for the lie that this historically constructed identity exhausts our subjectivities as gay people. The very use of the word *gay* has been an effective means of insisting upon the complexity of subjectivities over and above the reductive notion of identity implicit in the term *homosexual*. AIDS education campaigns that target gay men have had to address these issues on a day-to-day basis. They recognize that there is no singular gay community and that many of the men who most urgently need to be reached are those who do not identify as gay and who do not participate in gay subcultures.

I believe that problems arise when we reactivate the horrifically stigmatizing pink triangle in order to reunite our political struggles against AIDS around the central figure of the victim of the fascist state. Clearly the fact that this symbol is being used in the context of an angry and powerful political movement shows that certain paradoxes are consciously being used. But this grounding symbol, which has already been used historically to unite gay people around the idea of a group experience of persecution, is now being reinvested with an intensified experience of victimization horribly linked to questions of survival, of life and death. It seems entirely inappropriate to me to compare the complex and sometimes murderous actions of a fascist state toward homosexuals to the contemporary response of a supposedly liberal democracy to a health crisis in a number of populations it actively discriminates against. But more important, lost in the analogy are all those aspects of difference and subjectivity that identity politics subordinates and suppresses precisely to ensure political solidarity and action. This has, on a subtle level, far-reaching and possibly reactionary consequences.

What PWAs have in common with homosexuals at the time of the Third Reich is not the status of the concentration camp victim. Rather it is being a recruit within a complex and contradictory regime concerning the state's regulation of desire by means of moral, legal, and ideological manipulation of a society's anxieties about sex and deviancy. The parallel is to be found in the positive and negative pressures to conform to a politically defined imaginary moral norm and the construction of the hierarchy of susceptibilities, vulnerabilities, predilections, and fears of reprisal used by Nazism to construct different levels of disposability within a population. It should not be forgotten that the system of colored triangles was used by the Nazis to construct a hierarchy of differences within the enclosed society of the concentration camp. This system not only allowed the Nazis instantly to determine the disposability of a prisoner, but also produced a consciousness of divisions among the prisoners themselves, which, by working on preexisting social, religious, and racial differences, set the inmates against each other in a world of dog-eat-dog.

AIDS has resulted in the regulation of desire throughout the entire population. We cannot understand this if we focus on genocide metaphors. People with AIDS are not of a piece. The simplest division of this population into guilty and innocent victims within dominant regimes of representation shows how contemporary society itself constructs and capitalizes upon differences. It is for this reason that I have difficulties with the notion of a singular AIDS community. Although this notion may be an important imaginary point of identification for political struggle, it cannot account for the different experiences of AIDS even within New York City. There can be no global or all-encompassing representation of AIDS. The experiential and political reality of AIDS for a migrant worker in South Africa is mostly dissimilar to that of a white middle-class gay man living in New York. There are many AIDS communities, which both intersect and differ in their needs, their priorities, their agendas, and their strategies. Rather than assume a political cohesion, AIDS offers us the possibility of building alliances that do not yet exist. Our differences are to be welcomed, and our similarities are to be built upon. Furthermore, these differences should be raised to the level of representation. The dominance of identity politics united around a specific symbol of Nazi terror tends to obfuscate not only the issues of how a community struggling against a health crisis imagines itself in its commonality and its differences, but also the relationship between this community and the many others affected by other health crises.

I am utterly convinced of the appropriateness of the legend SILENCE = DEATH, but I am unconvinced about anchoring this equation to the pink triangle. The powerful message contained in the slogan is the necessity of representation, but the use of the pink triangle immobilizes representation by locking it into an agenda of victimization and annihilation. One of the most problematic consequences of this agenda is how it affects the consciousness of people living with AIDS. Throughout this epidemic it has been very difficult to construct a discourse of survival. AIDS discourse divides into three dominant types. First, there is the moralistic discourse of the Right, which has lost no opportunity to drive home its racist, antifeminist, and antigay agenda with complete disregard for the suffering of massive portions of the population. Second, there is the discourse of AIDS activism, which has tended to stress death, annihilation, and holocaust and genocide analogies in its attempts to stir the state into a caring response to the crisis. Third, there is an often unheard discourse of people living with AIDS that stresses hope, survival, healing, and personal triumph. To some extent this third discourse finds itself pitted against not only the punitive right-wing discourse, but the discourse of political activism as well.

There is a pressing need for a range of representations of AIDS. We need to find languages and images that begin to approach the complex and contradictory realities of AIDS. I don't believe this language can be homogeneous and consistent. By necessity it must be polysemic, multiple, and perhaps, when it speaks about difference, contradictory. I would like to suggest that the most useful, confirming, and productive forms of representation for us to develop will be those that help us understand and respect our differences while at the same time suggesting a multiplicity of mutually supportive political and cultural strategies. Although the political issues of AIDS are of enormous immediate concern to the gay communities, they can also fruitfully be linked to far wider political struggles around the politics of health care as they affect many other sectors of the population.

I am indebted to the historians Manfred Herzer, Burkhard Jellonnek, Ilse Kokula, Harry Oosterhuis, Richard Plant, and James Steakley, and to Nicola Field, who researched *Desire*, for providing information for this essay.

Discussion

Ray Navarro

Could you speak about the parallels and differences between the use of the pink triangle in gay politics and the historical rearticulation of such words as *black* within the black community or *Chicano* by Mexican Americans? As you probably know, both of these words were originally used pejoratively by the white ruling classes in this country, but they have since been appropriated and turned around by the very people they were meant to oppress and are now empowering terms within those communities.

Stuart Marshall

In order to create a political movement, oppressed people must construct their commonality precisely as an oppressed group. As you say, one of the ways this can be achieved is by taking the pejorative language used by the oppressors and throwing it back at them, demonstrating that you do not recognize the power represented by their language and that you are reusing this oppressed status as the basis for an identity forged for political action. This is an example of what Foucault calls reverse discourse. But in the black and Mexican-American communities, for example, there are other commonalities, such as the family, that underpin the political identity of the community; the community does not construct itself only in the political recognition of oppression. The pink triangle has by contrast been used to construct a commonality solely around an ideological history of persecution.

The notion of community is always problematic, but this is doubly so in the case of lesbians and gay men, because we do not have this other, "positive" means of experiencing community. This is the problem of the notion of gay people as a minority community. While we may build social networks, these do not provide the same experience of family, for example, as one finds in Chicano or black communities. It is this analogy between the gay community and the ethnic minority that I have tried to contest in this paper. The Nazis recognized that we could not be disposed of in the same way as the Jews and the Gypsies—that we were not, in Hirschfeld's terminology, "the third sex," not, that is, a distinct people or race that could be prevented through genocide from reproducing itself. The Nazis understood that we were potentially everywhere and that we were best regulated through the control of the population as a whole.

Another difference between the examples you've given and the adoption of the pink triangle by the gay community is that terms like *Chicano* were in common use at the time they were politically appropriated by Mexican Americans. But the pink triangle was not being used by the oppressor at the time it was adopted by the gay community; it was hidden in history to such an extent that some gay people do not understand its meaning even today. Ironically, it has only been used against us by our contemporary oppressors since we excavated it—I'm thinking of a homophobic English councilor who recently stated that gay people should be sent to the gas chambers.

I've spoken with people who were forced to wear the pink triangle in concentration camps, and they were horrified by its contemporary use by the gay movement. The memories they associate with the image are unspeakable. Ironically, it is the very lack of a sense of a protective, nurturing community that has made them so reluctant to speak about their experiences in the camps.

My question is, what are the effects of constructing a community identity solely around an imaginary representation of a gay holocaust, and, more particularly, what are the effects of this on people with AIDS?

As for the continuing use of reverse discourse by other political movements, it seems to me that they have started to move on from the need for an imaginary identity to a greater appreciation of difference.

Marusia Bociurkiw   I was interested in what you were saying about Nazi ideology concerning childbirth and abortion. I'm from Canada, where the rhetoric of the reproductive rights movement has been reduced to one of individual choice, whereas those opposing abortion have formed coalitions with, for example, white supremacists. I'm sure much the same thing is happening here. So perhaps this knowledge about fascist regimes can help us develop strategies to form our own more broadly based coalitions. And perhaps analogies can be made to lesbian politics as well. My father is a concentration camp survivor, and his experiences of victimization and survival have helped shape my own politics, although his homophobia has not. There are contradictions, but there are also powerful historical continuities that I'm unwilling to ignore.

Marshall   Yes, I agree with you, and I'm sure that other analogies can be made. What I am arguing against is drawing analogies based on supposed genocidal attitudes toward a particular race, because Nazi attitudes toward homosexuality were much more complicated and concerned the regulation of desire throughout the whole population; the Nazis were very modern in that sense. This is where the contemporary gay movement and the AIDS activist movement can find their analogies between contemporary and Nazi society. I could find no historical English political discourse on the regulation of sexuality that paralleled the sophistication of Nazi discourse. The Nazis even made it an area of "respectable" scientific study—respectable in their terms, that is. The doctoral thesis I mentioned, which was written by Karl Werner Gauhl at the end of the 1930s, investigated the spread of homosexuality throughout Nazi organizations, particularly in the Hitler Youth. This study was worked out in great detail and was given an aura of scientificity, with diagrams and flow charts that visualized a theory of homosexual desire rather like the transmission of disease. When people see these diagrams today, they immediately notice their similarity to the early "contact tracing" diagrams purporting to describe the transmission of HIV among gay men in Los Angeles.

The Nazis also developed the psychotherapeutic treatment of homosexuality, and "Aryan" gay men could, albeit infrequently, avoid concentration camps by agreeing to such treatment. One learns of this happening most often in Berlin. In fact, I met someone who had been given that option. These two examples show that analogies made to this era must be more complex. Even if we focus solely on the concentration camps, it is inaccurate to describe the Nazi regulation of homosexuality as a holocaust. The accurate figures of gay men put into "protective custody" were published by Rüdiger Lautmann in the late 1970s, but whenever the specter of the gay holocaust is evoked, the numbers are given in the tens of thousands. Fifteen thousand does not have the emotional impact of seventy-five thousand.

It is crucial that we rethink our imaginary relationship to that historical episode, for it was not so free of contradiction and cannot be grasped through the simplistic concepts of victimization and annihilation.

Tom Kalin

I would like to respond to one aspect of the appropriation of the pink triangle, and that is in relation to the AIDS activist movement. I agree with you that the AIDS activist movement is turning into anything but a univocal movement—a reality that is evidenced in the fact that the activism of primarily white gay men has now extended beyond that community. White gay men have been forced in this health crisis to deal with issues that lie outside our own domain, issues that cut across a whole range of historical dilemmas. For example, reproductive rights or pediatric AIDS cases have now become compelling issues within a general concern for how health care is structured in this country. I think your project of examining specific historical references is crucial as the AIDS movement and the AIDS pandemic, globally, are seen to affect other communities in greater numbers. The discussion about health care and other policies in this country is becoming increasingly complex. That's why I think your project is a really important one—it coincides with a change in the AIDS activist movement.

Marshall May I ask you a question? How has this complex discussion of the epidemic by the AIDS activist movement impacted official policy in this country?

Kalin Governmentally, there's little happening. There's still no "targeted" or "culturally sensitive" education campaign. And, of course, this reflects how issues have or have not been handled in our health care system generally. For instance, the value placed on the baby in our health care system—at the expense of the health needs of the mother—finds its corollary in the AIDS crisis. A child of color who is born HIV-positive or with AIDS is often more likely to be enrolled in an experimental drug trial than its mother, who may be HIV-positive or living with AIDS as well. Or if the mother is accepted into a drug trial, she's often unable to participate—due to economic or other circumstances—because she's trying to get health care for her child. People are becoming aware that there are countless factors that disenfranchise people, factors that are amplified in regard to health care in this country.

Douglas Crimp I'd like to extend that answer a bit. I do think that the AIDS activist movement has been able to apply some degree of pressure on government agencies as we have grown more sophisticated about the nature of the problems of affected communities. For example, the inclusion of women and people of color in drug trials has been an insistent demand of the movement at least since the demonstration against the Food and Drug Administration in the fall of 1988, and the bureaucrats at the National Institutes of Health and the FDA have been forced to pay some attention to these demands.

I would also like to add a comment. You made a division at the end of your talk that I feel is somewhat reductive. You suggested that we in the AIDS activist movement insist upon an identity structured around victimization, in contrast to people living with AIDS, who employ a rhetoric of survival. I don't think that such a clear opposition should be made. First, there are many people living with AIDS in the AIDS activist movement—a movement that has, by now, a very strong rhetoric of survival. At the same time, I would say that a problem for AIDS activists is the sense that there is always an identifiable externalized enemy. This does seem to obscure all kinds of other psychological, spiritual, or personal ways in which we must negotiate this crisis. Still, I'm nervous with a reading of the AIDS activist movement that claims that we privilege victimhood, because I think we insist very strongly on survival.

Marshall   You recognize that the discourse of AIDS activism problematically effaces the spiritual dimension and also what you describe as our own personal problems. Shouldn't these be an important part of the community's agenda? One might, of course, argue that the political dimension cannot be all-encompassing, but does this obviate the need for the AIDS activist movement to consider the effects of its political discourse upon the spiritual well-being of the community's individual members?

Thousands of us are now confronted with our own mortality and are forced into considering this precisely as our own personal problem. When the political domain is filled with messages of holocausts, one must withdraw into an individual, private space in order to sustain the hope of one's own survival. The AIDS activist movement has rejected the notion that we are "AIDS victims," and it argues that we are the victims of state negligence. In order to do this, it stresses the devastation of our community. But a problem appears when, for example, the health status of an individual gets confused with the survival of the community in the rhetoric of AIDS activism. I've heard the slogan "We're all living with AIDS" used here. Of course, in some sense we are all living with AIDS, but we are all living *differently* with AIDS. A slogan like this negates the specific lived experience, the subjectivity if you will, of a person who actually has AIDS and replaces it with an imaginary political identity, a "we" who all live in an undifferentiated relationship to AIDS. And it's that kind of collapse that worries me and that I'm trying to address. ACT UP San Francisco has distributed a poster that states, "Women are not living with AIDS, they are dying from AIDS." Obviously one can see the point that is being made about women's limited access to health care, but I would not like to be a woman with AIDS reading that poster, particularly if it were accompanied by a pink triangle. We now know from innumerable psychological studies that people with potentially fatal diseases who have a strong belief in their own survival live much longer than people who have accepted their disease as a death sentence. Shouldn't AIDS activists consider this when formulating slogans?

The lesbian and gay movements have been profoundly suspicious of spirituality, probably because the Church, as the traditional repository of spirituality in the West, has been the source of so much homophobia. Nevertheless, there is a pressing need to develop a discourse of hope, of spirituality, and of caring, which are not adequately represented in the political anger of AIDS activists. Anger may be an important requirement for activist politics, but it is only one form of individual empowerment.

I think that different strategies are needed for different situations. When one is trying to provoke a government into a paternalistic response toward a minority, or minorities, against which it actively discriminates, one uses a particular kind of language, one which stresses suffering, death, and devastation. But this language can be very disempowering to people with AIDS. I don't think the AIDS activist movement fully appreciates the need to develop a discourse of hope and survival as well.

Gregg Bordowitz   I thought of an example that might illuminate this discussion. Early on, in the formation of ACT UP, Larry Kramer, who has used holocaust and genocide analogies in his analysis of AIDS, was a primary motivating force. Kramer used to stand up and say we should be more like the Irgun, which represented the most violent tendency within the Zionist movement. I think this illustrates the danger of facile historical analogies. It also says something about the inadequacy of this particular analogy, since people found the idea of our being like the Irgun ridiculous and the rhetoric was dropped. To some extent the development of the movement in the direction of diversity has shown that certain analogies have currency but they don't necessarily have valence, and that they are, in fact, inadequate.

José Arroyo

I would also like to comment on the use of the pink triangle, because for the gay groups at the University of Montreal, it is not only a symbol, but a powerful tool as well. Instead of looking at it as reductive, perhaps we should employ the concept of condensation. When we learn what the pink triangle means—which most of us do before wearing it—we are put in touch with the history of the gay movement. And the risk of wearing it, the terror of wearing it in a non-gay place, also has a powerful effect. It also puts one in touch with the present situation of AIDS as another kind of risk. The pink triangle condenses all of these meanings and acquires its power from this ability to stand in for all of these issues.

Marshall

As I said at the beginning, I am not suggesting that the pink triangle is not an extremely powerful rhetorical device or that it cannot function as an important point of identification for a community. What I was trying to say is that there is a cost, and then go on to describe that cost.

Victoria Starr

I'm not sure that I recognize the cost of using this symbol by its painting us as victims. In the United States, many people are passive for the very simple reason that they don't recognize their victimization. Organizing or activating people often begins with helping people to understand that, in fact, they are victims. And then you go from there to the next phase of the process, which is to determine what can be done to give ourselves hope

Photograph and "diagnosis" of Jenny Shermann, selected for "euthanasia" in Ravensbruck concentration camp, Nuremberg State archive (photographs used in *Desire*, 1988). Diagnosis reads: "Jenny Sara Shermann, compulsive lesbian, frequenting only such bars. Avoids the name 'Sara' [a name imposed on all Jewish women]. Stateless Jew."

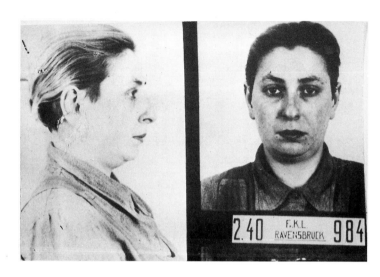

Marshall

or to empower ourselves to change the situation. If this is the case, what is problematic in using this symbol?

To put it in a nutshell, if I can, it seems to me that to dwell on this notion that now, as then, the state is intent upon eliminating, through genocide, a particular group of beings does not help us understand the complex manner in which AIDS is being used to regulate the behavior of the population as a whole. Another interesting example of a different kind of agenda being mapped onto an available symbol is the fact that in Britain, for about two or three years now, some lesbians have been wearing black triangles. The belief is that the black triangle was the symbol used to stigmatize lesbians in concentration camps. There is documentation of lesbian women in concentration camps wearing the black triangle. But that triangle by no means denoted their lesbianism. It was used to identify "asocials," people of both sexes whose actions ranged across a whole set of so-called antisocial behaviors. Now, being a lesbian in the Nazi period would probably lead one to certain kinds of "asocial" behavior, such as being unmarried, not having children, shunning traditional notions of femininity. The historian Ilse Kokula has described the celebration of lesbian culture during the Weimar period. These women drank a lot, smoked in the street—behaviors considered antipathetic to the spirit of the German people and punishable by confinement in a concentration camp.

But what does the black triangle represent in contemporary lesbian politics? I think it attempts to confer the same level of stigmatized identity on lesbians as the pink triangle does for gay men. But it establishes a fictional relationship to the lesbian in Nazi Germany. In the Nazi state, lesbianism was not illegal. Furthermore, the question of lesbianism never needed to be directly addressed because lesbians could be controlled as women. Lesbians were invisible. Because of this, it is very difficult to research the history of lesbians in the concentration camps.

It seems to me that it is precisely this invisibility of lesbian desire that is the interesting parallel between then and now and that this is what should be discussed, rather than this historically inaccurate notion of a specifically stigmatized lesbian identity represented by the black triangle. This symbol represented a wider variety of independent and deviant women than its current use seems to suggest.

Kobena Mercer I think one of the most important things about your paper, Stuart, was that it drew attention to the ways that certain political identities not only dehistoricize, but also lend themselves to reductionism; they flatten out and homogenize the complex differences that exist between them. What's been missing in some of the responses, particularly regarding the political issues of AIDS activism, is a relational sense of those ambiguities that exist between identities. To return to Ray Navarro's point about the appropriation of *black* and *Chicano* by those communities, and in relation to what you said about the necessarily fictional nature of identity in the Lacanian account of the imaginary: before the 1960s, black people didn't exist as such, they were Negroes or colored people. The rearticulation or reversal of that stigmatized racial metaphor was based on a nationalist, "back to Africa" discourse. In fact, diasporic black people in the Caribbean, Latin America, and North America have only an imaginary relationship to Africa. What I'm trying to ask through this analogy is, whom does it empower and whom does it disempower? Which is what I think lies behind your objection to the rearticulation of the pink triangle.

If one grasps the relational character by which political identities are constructed, what's important is not the particular symbol. The symbol itself is meaningless—not meaningless, polyvalent—it can also be articulated into a reactionary discourse. As Gregg said, genocide can be rearticulated into a Zionist discourse or it can be articulated into a discourse of the left, a discourse of, in this particular case, the state's responsibility for the provision of health care. So I think the question of context is really crucial, because political positions can't be decided either by the symbol itself or by the identity of the group that's articulating it at the time.

There's a word that was missing from the responses to your paper, and that word is *alliances*. Alliances are based on an imaginary identification, whether it's Mary Wollstonecraft in the eighteenth century, talking about the position of women in relation to the abolition of slavery, or any of a number of other historical examples. What determines political identity is not where it comes from, not its "essence"; rather it's the relationship to other struggles, the alliances that are made possible by certain forms of imaginary identification. And I think it might be helpful to bring those other historical analogies to bear on the current situation, not so much to ask whether the pink triangle is a problem in the abstract, but what alliances it makes possible and what alliances it forecloses.

Lesbian Looks
Dorothy Arzner and Female Authorship

Judith Mayne

Some cinematic images have proven to be irresistibly seductive as far as lesbian readings are concerned: Greta Garbo kissing her lady-in-waiting in *Queen Christina* (1933), Marlene Dietrich in drag kissing a female member of her audience in *Morocco* (1930), Katharine Hepburn in male attire being seduced by a woman in *Sylvia Scarlett* (1935)—all these images have been cited and reproduced so frequently in the context of gay and lesbian culture that they have almost acquired lives of their own. By lives of their own, I am referring not only to their visibility, but also to how lesbian readings of them require a convenient forgetfulness or bracketing of what happens to these images, plot and narrative-wise, in the films in which they appear, where heterosexual symmetry is usually restored with a vengeance. Depending upon your point of view, lesbian readings of isolated scenes are successful appropriations and subversions of Hollywood plots, or naive fetishizations of the image. Put another way, there is a striking division between the spectacular lesbian uses to which single, isolated images may be applied and the narratives of classical Hollywood films, which seem to deaden any such possibilities.

Feminist film theory, as it has developed in the last fifteen years, has scorned the subversive potential of such appropriations. Although the narrative of feminist film theory does not exactly follow the plot of a classical Hollywood film, the writings of feminist film theorists have affirmed, in a rather amazingly mimetic fashion, that the Hollywood apparatus is absolute, the codes and conventions of Hollywood narrative only flexible enough to make the conquest of the woman and the affirmation of the heterosexual contract that much more inevitable. In countering "spectacular" lesbian uses with "narratives"—those

of Hollywood or of feminist film theory—I am, of course, evoking what has become the standard feminist account of the classical Hollywood cinema, where the spectacle of the male gaze and its female object and the narrative of agency and resolution make for a perfect symmetrical fit, with heterosexual authority affirmed.

Although much may be said about the relation between feminism, Hollywood plots, and lesbian images, my purpose here is to explore another cinematic image with unmistakable lesbian

contours, one which has attained—at least in feminist film theory and criticism—the kind of visibility more commonly and
typically associated with the female star. Dorothy Arzner was
one of the few women to have been a successful director in
Hollywood, with a career that extended from the late 1920s to
the early 1940s. Arzner was one of the early "rediscoveries" of
feminist film theory in the 1970s, and that rediscovery remains
the most significant and influential attempt to theorize female
authorship in the cinema. As one of the very few women direc-

tors who were successful in Hollywood, particularly during the studio years, Arzner has served as an important example of a woman director working within the Hollywood system who managed, in however limited ways, to make films that disturb the conventions of Hollywood narrative.

A division characterizes the way Arzner has been represented in feminist film studies, a division analogous to the tension between the lesbian reading of Dietrich, Garbo, and Hepburn and the textual workings of the films that, if they do not deny the validity of such a reading, at least problematize it. For there is, on the one hand, a textual Arzner, one whose films—as the by-now classic feminist account developed by Claire Johnston would have it—focus on female desire as an ironic inflection of the patriarchal norms of the cinema. On the other hand, there is a very visible Arzner, an image that speaks a kind of desire and suggests a kind of reading that is quite notably absent in discussions of Arzner's films.

Noting that structural coherence in Arzner's films comes from the discourse of the woman, Claire Johnston—whose reading of Arzner has defined the terms of subsequent discussions of her work—relies on the notion of defamiliarization, derived from the Russian formalists' *priem ostrananie,* the device of making strange, to assess the effects of the woman's discourse on patriarchal meaning: "the work of the woman's discourse renders the narrative strange, subverting and dislocating it at the level of meaning."[1] In this context Johnston discusses what has become the single most famous scene from Arzner's films, the scene in which Judy (Maureen O'Hara), who has played ballet stooge to the vaudeville performer Bubbles (Lucille Ball) in *Dance, Girl, Dance* (1940), confronts her audience and tells them how *she* sees *them.* This is, Johnston argues, the only real break between dominant discourse and the discourse of the woman in Arzner's work. The moment in *Dance, Girl, Dance* when Judy faces her audience is a privileged moment in feminist film theory

1

Claire Johnston, "Dorothy Arzner: Critical Strategies," in *The Work of Dorothy Arzner: Towards a Feminist Cinema,* ed. Claire Johnston (London: British Film Institute, 1975), 6.

and criticism, foregrounding as it does the sexual hierarchy of the gaze, with female agency defined as the return of the male look, problematizing the objectification of woman.[2] The celebrity accorded this particular scene in Arzner's film needs to be seen in the context of feminist film theory in the mid-1970s. Confronted with the persuasive psychoanalytically-based theoretical model according to which women either did not or could not exist on screen, the discovery of Arzner, and especially of Judy's "return of the gaze," offered some glimmer of historical hope as to the possibility of a female intervention in the cinema. To be sure, the scope of the intervention is limited, for as Johnston herself stresses, Judy's radical act is quickly recuperated within the film when the audience gets up to cheer her on and she and Bubbles begin to fight on stage to the delight of the audience.

Other readings of Arzner's films develop, in different ways, the ambivalence of the female intervention evoked in Johnston's analysis. In responses to Arzner's work, one can read reflections of larger assumptions concerning the Hollywood cinema as an apparatus. At one extreme is Andrew Britton's assessment of Arzner (in his study of Katharine Hepburn) as the unproblematized *auteur* of *Christopher Strong* (1933), the film in which Hepburn appears as an aviatrix who falls in love with an older, married man. That *Christopher Strong* functions as a "critique of the effect of patriarchal heterosexual relations on relations between women" suggests that the classical cinema lends itself quite readily to a critique of patriarchy, whether as the effect of the woman director or the female star.[3] At the opposite extreme, Jacquelyn Suter's analysis of *Christopher Strong* proceeds from the assumption that whatever "female discourse" there is in the film is subsumed and neutralized by the patriarchal discourse on monogamy.[4] If the classical cinema described by Britton seems remarkably open to effects of subversion and criticism, the classical cinema described by Suter is just as re-

2
Lucy Fischer reads *Dance, Girl, Dance* in terms of this "resistance to fetishism." See *Shot/Countershot* (Princeton: Princeton University Press, 1989), 148–54.

3
Andrew Britton, *Katharine Hepburn: The Thirties and After* (Newcastle upon Tyne: Tyneside Cinema, 1984), 74.

4
Jacquelyn Suter, "Feminine Discourse in *Christopher Strong*," *Camera Obscura*, no. 3–4 (Summer 1979), 135–50.

markably closed to any meanings but patriarchal ones; one is left to assume that female authorship, as far as Hollywood cinema is concerned, is either an unproblematic affirmation of agency or virtually an impossibility. That Britton is the only openly gay critic among those I've mentioned thus far suggests, of course, a familiar desire to assert the possibility of lesbian authorship, to identify the conventions of Hollywood cinema as less absolutely consonant with heterosexual and patriarchal desire than other critics have suggested.

Interestingly, however, the appearance of Arzner within the context of lesbian and gay studies is quite literally that—a persona, an image quite obviously readable in lesbian terms. In Vito Russo's *The Celluloid Closet,* a striking photograph of Arzner and her good friend Joan Crawford appears in the text, along with a brief mention by another director concerning Arzner's lesbianism and her closeted status, but none of her films are cited: even by the measure of implicit gay content, Arzner's films seem to offer little.[5] This photograph is adapted in the images included in Tee Corinne's *Women Who Loved Women,* and Corinne's description of Arzner emphasizes again an isolated image that is readable in lesbian terms only when placed within Corinne's narrative sequence: "Quiet closeted women," she writes, "like film director Dorothy Arzner worked in Hollywood near flamboyant and equally closeted bisexuals like Garbo and Dietrich."[6]

The textual practice that has been central to a feminist theory of female authorship disappears when Arzner is discussed in the context of lesbian and gay culture, suggesting a tension between Arzner as a lesbian image and Arzner as a female signature to a text. This tension is addressed explicitly in the introduction to the *Jump Cut* special section on lesbians and film that appeared in 1981. The editors of the special section note that Arzner's "style of dress and attention to independent women characters in her films has prompted the search for a

5
Vito Russo, *The Celluloid Closet: Homosexuality in the Movies* (New York: Harper and Row, 1981), 50.

6
Tee Corinne, *Women Who Loved Women* (Pearlchild, 1984), 7.

Dorothy Arzner.
Museum of Modern Art Film Stills Archive.

7
Edith Becker, Michelle Citron, Julia Lesage, and B. Ruby Rich, "Special Section: Lesbians and Film: Introduction," *Jump Cut*, no. 24–25 (March 1981), 18.

lesbian subtext in her work—despite the careful absence of any statements by Arzner herself that could encourage such an undertaking."[7] It is curious that Arzner's dress is not readable as such a "statement"; and the term *subtext* seems curiously anachronistic at a time in film criticism when so much attention was being paid to the apparently insignificant detail through which an entire film could be read deconstructively or at least against the grain. Yet the awkwardness of the term suggests the difficulty of not only reconciling but also accounting for any connection between Arzner's image and her films. Despite the supposed absence of lesbian "subtexts" in Arzner's films, Arzner looms large as an object of visual fascination in the *Jump Cut* text.

It is not only in gay and lesbian studies, however, that Arzner's persona acquires a signifying function seemingly at odds with her film practice. Even though what I've said thus far suggests a gap between feminist readings of Arzner's films and lesbian and gay readings of her image, Arzner has proven to be a compelling image for feminist film theory and criticism. Although Arzner favored a look and a style that quite clearly connotes lesbian identity, discussions of her work always seem to stop short of any concrete recognition that sexual preference might have something to do with how her films function, particularly concerning the "discourse of the woman" and female communities, or that the contours of female authorship in her films might be defined in lesbian terms. This marginalization is all the more striking, given how remarkably *visible* Arzner has been as an image in feminist film theory. That Arzner's image and appearance would find a responsive audience in gay and lesbian culture makes obvious sense. But in a field like feminist film theory, which has resolutely bracketed any discussion of lesbianism or of the female homoerotic, such visibility seems curious indeed, and in need of a reading. With the possible exception of Maya Deren, Arzner is more frequently represented visually than any other woman director central to contemporary feminist discussions of film. And unlike Deren, who appeared extensively in her own films, Arzner does not have the reputation of being a particularly self-promoting, visible, or *out* (in several senses of the term) woman director.

Not only has Arzner been consistently present as an image in feminist film studies, but two tropes are obsessively present in images of her as well—tropes that have been equally

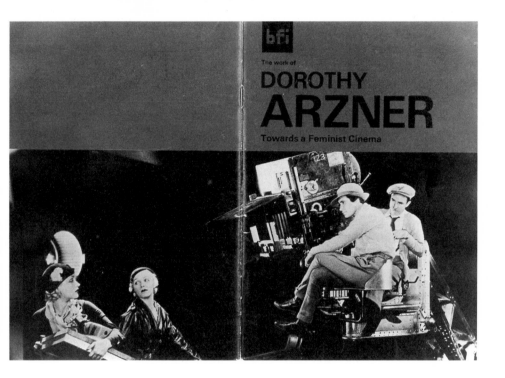

obsessive points of departure and return in feminist film theory. She is portrayed against the backdrop of the large-scale apparatus of the Hollywood cinema, or she is shown with other women, usually actresses, most of whom are emphatically "feminine," creating a striking contrast indeed. Both of these tropes appear in the photograph on the cover of the British Film Institute (BFI) collection edited by Claire Johnston, *The Work of Dorothy Arzner: Towards a Feminist Cinema*. On the front, we see Arzner in profile, slouching directorially in a perch next to a very large camera; seated next to her is a man. They both look toward what initially appears to be the unidentified field of vision. When the cover is laid out flat, however, we see that the photograph "continues" on the back: two young women, one holding packages, look at each other, their positions reflecting symmetrically those of Arzner and her male companion.

It is difficult to read precisely the tenor of the scene (from *Working Girls* [1930]) between the two women: some hostility perhaps, or desperation. The camera occupies the center of the photograph, as a large, looming—and predictably phallic— presence. The look on the man's face strongly suggests the cli- chés of the male gaze that have been central to feminist film theory: from his perspective the two women exist as objects of voyeuristic pleasure. Arzner's look has quite another function, however, one that has received very little critical attention, and that is to decenter the man's look and eroticize the exchange of looks between the two women.[8] Although virtually none of the feminist critics who analyze Arzner's work have discussed her lesbianism or her lesbian persona, a curious syndrome is sug- gested by this use of "accompanying illustrations." The photo- graph on the cover of the pamphlet edited by Claire Johnston teases out another scene of cinematic desire, complete with the devices of delay, framing, and even a version of shot/countershot more properly associated with the articulation of heterosexual desire in the classical narrative cinema.

Conversely, the representation of Arzner with the camera and with more "feminine" women can be read in relation to one of the most striking preoccupations of feminist film theory, that of the preferred notion of sexual difference, which has consis- tently displaced marginal desires from the center stage of het- erosexual symmetry. Whether blending into a background of the cumbersome and quite literal cinematic apparatus or gazing longingly at another woman, whether assuming the phallic ma- chinery of the classical cinema or the position of spectatorial de- sire, Arzner's image oscillates between a heterosexual contract assumed by feminist theorists to be absolute, on the one hand, and another scene, another configuration of desire, on the other. Arzner's persona has acquired a rather amazing flexibility as well, if not always with the same teasing play of front and

8
Jackie Stacey dis- cusses female sexual at- traction as a principle of identification in *All About Eve* (1950) and *Desperately Seeking Susan;* see "Des- perately Seeking Differ- ence," *Screen* 28, no. 1 (Winter 1987), 48–61.

Mayne

back cover evident in the BFI pamphlet. One of the early, "classic" anthologies of feminist film theory and criticism (Karyn Kay and Gerald Peary's *Women and the Cinema: A Critical Anthology*, New York: E. P. Dutton, 1977), for instance, features Arzner on its cover along with three other women, all of them well-known actresses, in a rectangle of shifting opposing poles: the good girl (Bardot in wedding dress)/bad girl (Jane Fonda as prostitute in *Klute*) dichotomy characteristic of an "images of women" approach to film analysis and a classically feminine (Bardot and Fonda) demeanor as opposed to a more androgynous one (Arzner and Dietrich). In a recent collection of essays on feminist film theory, not one of the several reprinted essays on Arzner discusses erotic connections between women. Yet on the cover of the book is a photograph of Arzner and Rosalind Russell exchanging a meaningful look with more than a hint of lesbian desire—enough, certainly, to provide images for the flyer advertising the "How Do I Look?" conference.

9
For an excellent discussion of the very possibility of a feminist fetishism, see Jane Marcus, "The asylums of Antaeus. Women, war and madness: Is there a feminist fetishism?" in *The Difference Within: Feminism and Critical Theory,* ed. Elizabeth Meese and Alice Parker (Amsterdam and Philadelphia: John Benjamins Publishing Co., 1989), 49–83. Marcus examines how feminists in the suffrage movement oscillated "between denial and recognition of rape as the common denominator of female experience" (76). Naomi Schor has examined the possibility of female fetishism in the writings of George Sand; see "Female Fetishism: The Case of George Sand," in *The Female Body in Western Culture,* ed. Susan Suleiman (Cambridge, Mass.: Harvard University Press, 1986), 363–72.

10
See Christian Metz, *The Imaginary Signifier,* trans. Ben Brewster (Bloomington: Indiana University Press, 1982), 69-80. A chapter in Octave Mannoni's *Clefs pour l'imaginaire ou l'autre scène* (Paris: Editions du Seuil, 1969) is entitled "Je sais bien, mais quand même . . ." ("I know very well, but all the same . . .").

One begins to suspect that the simultaneous evocation and dispelling of an erotic bond between women in Arzner's work is a structuring absence in feminist film theory. Arzner's lesbianism may not be theorized in relation to her films, but her remarkable visibility in feminist film criticism suggests that feminists replicate the very fetishism they have identified as being "criticized" in Arzner's films. To be sure, any parallel between a classical, male-centered trajectory like fetishism and the dynamics of feminist theory can only be made tentatively.[9] But there is nonetheless a striking fit between Octave Mannoni's formula for disavowal ("I know very well, but all the same . . ."), adapted by Christian Metz to analyze cinematic fetishism, and the consistent and simultaneous evocation and disavowal of Arzner's lesbian persona.[10] The evidence of lesbianism notwithstanding, feminist critics would speak, rather, through a heterosexual master code, where any and all combinations of "masculinity," from the male gaze to Arzner's clothing, and "femininity," from conventional objectification of the female body to the female objects of Arzner's gaze, result in a narrative and visual structure indistinguishable from the dominant Hollywood model. To be sure, Arzner's work is praised for its "critique" of the Hollywood system, but the critique is so limited that it only affirms the dominance of the object in question.

Some feminist work on Arzner does acknowledge her supposed "mannish" appearance, and one of the preferred phrases for avoiding any mention of lesbianism—"female bonding"—is fairly common in writing on Arzner. However, the two separate but interconnected questions I am raising here—whether there is any fit to be made between the persona and the films, and why feminist film theorists are so drawn to the dykey image yet so reluctant to utter the word *lesbian*—have not been widely addressed. To my knowledge, the only feminist critic to suggest that Arzner's films cite the persona, and are therefore informed by lesbian desire, is Sarah Halprin. Halprin suggests, fairly generously, that the reason for the omission of any discussion of Arzner's obvious lesbian looks in relation to her films is, in part, the suspicion of any kind of biographical information in analysis of female authorship; and she suggests that a reading of marginal characters in Arzner's films, who resemble Arzner herself, might offer, as she puts it, a "whole new way of relating" to Arzner's work.[11] As with the term *subtext* mentioned earlier, in relation to the *Jump Cut* essay, there is an acknowledgment here that the wish to read Arzner's films through Arzner's appearance may resurrect a traditional form of auteurism, a form of biographical criticism that would seem to be hopelessly naive in an era of poststructuralist suspicion of any equations between the maker and the text. But the Arzner persona as it circulates in feminist film studies does not seem to me to be a simple case of the "real woman" versus the "text," since those illustrations of Arzner have themselves become so thoroughly a part of the web of both feminist film theory and Arzner's work. More strikingly, the "illustrations" of Arzner in the company of a female star echo uncannily in the stills from her films that illustrate the discussions of textual practice—like Billie Burke and Rosalind Russell in *Craig's Wife* (1936) (with Russell now assuming the more Arzneresque position), or Madame Basilova and Judy in *Dance, Girl, Dance*.

Take Madame Basilova, for example. What has been read, in *Dance, Girl, Dance*, as the woman's return of a male gaze she does not possess might be read differently as one part of a process of the exchange of looks between women that begins within the female dance troupe managed by Basilova. Judy's famous scolding of the audience is identified primarily as a communication, not between a female performer and a male audience (the audience is not, in any case, exclusively male) but between the performer and the female member of the audience (secretary to Steven Adams, the man who will eventually become Judy's love interest) who stands up to applaud her.[12] And

11
Sarah Halprin, "Writing in the Margins (review of E. Ann Kaplan, *Women and Film: Both Sides of the Camera*)," *Jump Cut*, no. 29 (February 1984), 32.

12
Barbara Koenig Quart stresses the relationship between Judy and the secretary in her reading of the scene. See *Women Directors: The Emergence of a New Cinema* (New York and Westport, Conn.: Praeger, 1988), 25.

the catfight that erupts between Judy and Bubbles on stage
seems to me less a recuperative move—transforming the potential threat of Judy's confrontation into an even more tantaliz-
ing spectacle—than the claiming by the two women of the
stage as an extension of their conflicted friendship, not an alienated site of performance. The stage is, in other words, *both* the
site of the objectification of the female body *and* the site for the
theatricalizing of female friendship.

This "both/and"—the stage (and by metaphoric implication, the cinema itself) simultaneously serving as an arena of patriarchal exploitation and of female self-representation—contrasts with the more limited view of Arzner's films in Johnston's work, where more of a "neither/nor" logic is operative—neither patriarchal discourse nor the "discourse of the woman" allows women a vantage point from which to speak, represent, or imagine themselves. Reading Arzner's films in terms of the "both/and" suggests an irony more far-reaching than that described by Johnston. Johnston's reading of Arzner is suggestive of Shoshana Felman's definition of irony as "dragging authority as such into a scene which it cannot master, of which it is not aware and which, for that very reason, is the scene of its own self-destruction. . . ."[13] But the irony in *Dance, Girl, Dance* does not just demonstrate how the patriarchal discourse of the cinema excludes women, but rather how the cinema functions in two radically different ways, both of which are "true," as it were, and totally incompatible. I am borrowing here from Donna Haraway's definition of irony: "Irony is about contradictions that do not resolve into larger wholes, even dialectically, about the tension of holding incompatible things together because both or all are necessary and true."[14] This insistence on two equally compelling and incompatible truths constitutes a form of irony far more complex than Johnston's analysis of defamiliarization.

Johnston's notion of Arzner's irony assumes a patriarchal form of representation that may have its gaps and its weak links, but which remains dominant in every sense of the word. For Johnston, Arzner's irony can only be the irony of negativity puncturing holes in patriarchal assumptions. Such a view of irony has less to do, I would argue, with the limitations of Arzner's career (for example, as a woman director working within the inevitable limitations of the Hollywood system) than with the limitations of the film theory from which it grows. If the cinema

13
Shoshana Felman, "To Open the Question," *Yale French Studies*, no. 55–56 (1980), 8.

14
Donna Haraway, "A Manifesto for Cyborgs: Science, Technology, and Socialist Feminism in the 1980s," *Socialist Review*, no. 80 (1985), 65.

is understood as a one-dimensional system of male subjects and female objects, then it is not difficult to understand how the irony in Arzner's films is limited, or at least would be *read* as limited. Although rigid hierarchies of sexual difference are indeed characteristic of dominant cinema, they are not absolute, and Arzner's films represent other kinds of cinematic pleasure and desire.

An assessment of Arzner's importance within the framework of female authorship needs to account not only for how Arzner problematizes the pleasures of the cinematic institution as we understand it—for example, in terms of voyeurism and fetishism reenacted through the power of the male gaze and the objectification of the female body—but also for how, in her films, those pleasures are identified in ways that are not reducible to the theoretical clichés of the omnipotence of the male gaze. The irony of *Dance, Girl, Dance* emerges from the conflicting demands of performance and self-expression, which are linked, in turn, to heterosexual romance and female friendship. Female friendship acquires a resistant function in the way that it exerts a pressure against the supposed "natural" laws of heterosexual romance. Relations between women and communities of women have a privileged status in Arzner's films. To be sure, Arzner's films offer plots—particularly insofar as resolutions are concerned—compatible with the romantic expectations of the classical Hollywood cinema: communities of women may be important, but boy-still-meets-girl. Yet there is also an erotic charge identified within those communities. If heterosexual initiation is central to Arzner's films, it is precisely in its function as rite of passage (rather than natural destiny) that a marginal presence is felt.

Consider, for instance, *Christopher Strong*. Katharine Hepburn first appears in the film as a prize-winning object in a scavenger hunt, for she can claim that she is over twenty-one and has never had a love affair. Christopher Strong, the man

Katharine Hepburn in Dorothy Arzner's _Christopher Strong_, 1933.
Museum of Modern Art Film Stills Archive.

with whom she will eventually become involved, is the male version of this prize-winning object, for he has been married for more than five years and has always been faithful to his wife. As Cynthia Darrington, Hepburn dresses in decidedly unfeminine clothing and walks with a swagger that is masculine, or athletic, depending upon your point of view. Hepburn's jodhpurs and boots may well be, as Beverle Houston puts it, "that upper-class costume for a woman performing men's activities,"[15] but this is

15
Beverle Houston, "Missing in Action: Notes on Dorothy Arzner," _Wide Angle_ 6, no. 3 (1984), 27.

also clothing that strongly denotes lesbian identity and (to stress again Sarah Halprin's point) that is evocative of the way Arzner herself, and other lesbians of the time, dressed. Cynthia's "virginity" becomes a euphemistic catch-all for a variety of margins in which she is situated, both as a woman devoted to her career and as a woman without a sexual identity. The process the film traces is, precisely, that of the acquisition of heterosexual identity.

I am not arguing that *Christopher Strong*, like the dream that says one thing but ostensibly "really" means its mirror opposite, can be decoded as a coherent "lesbian film" or that the real subject of the film is the tension between gay and straight identities. The critical attitude toward heterosexuality takes the form of inflections—bits and pieces of tone and gesture and emphasis—that result in the conventions of heterosexual behavior becoming loosened up, shaken free of some of their identifications with the patriarchal status quo. Most important perhaps, the acquisition of heterosexuality becomes the downfall of Cynthia Darrington.

Jacquelyn Suter has described *Christopher Strong* in terms of how the feminine discourse, represented by various female characters in the film, is submerged by patriarchal discourse, the central term of which is monogamy. The proof offered for such a claim is, as is often the case in textual analysis, convincing on one level but quite tentative on another, for it is a proof that begins from and ends with the assumption of a patriarchal master code. Even the "feminine discourse" described by Suter is nothing but a pale reflection of that master code, with nonmonogamy its most radical expression. The possibility that "feminine discourse" in *Christopher Strong* might exceed or problematize heterosexual boundaries is not taken into account in Suter's analysis.[16] As should be obvious by now, I am arguing that it is precisely in its ironic inflection of heterosexual norms, whether by the mirroring gesture that suggests a reflection of

16
See Jacquelyn Suter, "Feminine Discourse in *Christopher Strong*."

Arzner herself or by the definition of the female community as resistant to, rather than complicitous with, heterosexual relations, that Arzner's signature is written on her films.

These two components central to female authorship in Arzner's work—female communities and the mirroring of Arzner herself—are not identical. One, stressing the importance of female communities and friendship among women, may function as a pressure exerted against the rituals of heterosexual initiation but is not necessarily opposed to them. This foregrounding of relationships among women problematizes the fit between female friendship and heterosexual romance, but the fit is still there; that is, the compatibility with the conventions of the classical Hollywood cinema is still possible. The representation of lesbian codes, mirrored in Arzner's and other lesbians' dress, constitutes the second strategy, which is more marginal and not integrated into narrative flow. These are the images that lend themselves to lesbian appropriation. Moreover, these two authorial inscriptions—the emphasis on female communities, the citations of marginal lesbian gestures—are not situated on a "continuum," that model of continuity from female friendship to explicit lesbianism so favored in much contemporary lesbian-feminist writing.[17] Rather, these two strategies exist in tension with each other, constituting yet another level of irony in Arzner's work. Female communities are compatible with the classical Hollywood narrative while they problematize it. The lesbian gesture occupies no such position of compatibility; it does not mesh easily with narrative continuity in Arzner's films.

Thus, in *Dance, Girl, Dance,* Arzner accentuates not only the woman's desire as embodied in Judy and her relationships with other women, but also secondary female figures, who never really become central but who do not evaporate into the margins, either—such as the secretary (who leads the applause during Judy's "return of the gaze" number) and Basilova. That

17
The phrase *lesbian continuum* comes from Adrienne Rich, "Compulsory Heterosexuality and Lesbian Existence," *Signs* 5, no. 4 (Summer 1980), 631–60.

these figures do not simply "disappear" suggests even more strongly their impossible relationship to the Hollywood plot, a relationship that *is* possible insofar as Judy is concerned. Now, Basilova *does* disappear in *Dance, Girl, Dance*, but in one of the most absurdly staged death scenes imaginable. In *Craig's Wife*, however, there is a more immediate relationship between marginality and female communities, although significantly the marginality has less of a lesbian inflection, both in dress and gesture. Julia Lesage has noted that in *Craig's Wife* Arzner rereads George Kelly's play, the source of the film, so that the secondary women characters are treated much more fully than in the play.[18] *Craig's Wife*—preoccupied with heterosexual demise rather than initiation—shows us Harriet (Rosalind Russell), a woman so obsessively concerned with her house that nothing else is of interest to her. At the conclusion of the film, virtually everyone has cleared out of Harriet's house, and Harriet seems pathetically neurotic and alone. The widow next door (Billie Burke) brings Harriet some roses. In Kelly's play, Harriet has become a mirror image of her neighbor, for both are portrayed as women alone, to be pitied. But in Arzner's film, the neighbor represents Harriet's last chance for connection with another human being. Thus the figure who, in Kelly's play, is a pale reflection of Harriet becomes in the film the suggestion of another identity and of the possibility of a female community. The resolution of Arzner's version of *Craig's Wife* has little to do with the loss of a husband and more to do with situating Harriet Craig's fantasy come horribly true alongside the possibility of connection with another woman. And, although Billie Burke is hardly evocative of lesbianism (like Basilova is in *Dance, Girl, Dance*), she and Rosalind Russell offer a play of contrasts visually similar to those visible in photographs of Arzner with more "feminine" women. The other woman portrayed by Billie Burke is, quite literally, a marginal figure in the original play who,

18
Julia Lesage, "The Hegemonic Female Fantasy in *An Unmarried Woman* and *Craig's Wife*," *Film Reader*, no. 5 (1982), 91.

through Arzner's reading, becomes a reflection on marginality itself.[19]

The female signature in Arzner's work is marked by that irony of equally compelling and incompatible discourses to which I have referred, and the lesbian inflection articulates the division between female communities that can function, although problematically, within a heterosexual universe, and the eruptions of lesbian marginality that do not. This lesbian irony taps differing and competing views of lesbianism within contemporary feminist and lesbian theory—as the most intense form of female and feminist bonding and as distinctly opposed to and

19
Melissa Sue Kort also discusses Arzner's reading of the Kelly play, noting that the "shift from play to film changes Harriet from villain to victim." See her discussion of the film in " 'Spectacular Spinelessness,' " in *Men by Women*, ed. Janet Todd (1982), vol. 2 of *Women and Literature* (New York and London: Holmes and Meier), 196–200.

Lesbian Looks

20
See Esther New-
ton, "The Mythic Mannish
Lesbian: Radclyffe Hall and
the New Woman," *Signs* 9,
no. 4 (Summer 1984), 557–
75. See also Lillian Fader-
man, *Surpassing the Love
of Men: Romantic Friend-
ship and Love between Wo-
men from the Renaissance
to the Present* (New York:
William Morrow and Co.,
1981), esp. parts II and III.

21
Nancy K. Miller
makes this observation
about irony: "To the extent
that the ethos (character,
disposition) of feminism
historically has refused the
doubleness of 'saying one
thing while it tries to do
another' (the mark of classical femininity, one might
argue), it may be that an
ironic feminist discourse
finds itself at odds both
with itself (its identity to itself) and with the expectations its audience has of its
position. If that is true, then
irony, in the final analysis,
may be a figure of limited
effectiveness. On the other
hand, since nonironic, single, sincere, hortatory feminism is becoming
ineffectual, it may be worth
the risk of trying out this
kind of duplicity on the
road." See "Changing the
Subject: Authorship, Writing, and the Reader," in
*Feminist Studies/Critical
Studies*, ed. Teresa de Lauretis (Bloomington: Indiana
University Press, 1986), 119
n. 18.

22
See the Camera
Obscura Collective, "An Interrogation of the Cine-
matic Sign: Woman as
Sexual Signifier in Jackie
Raynal's *Deux fois*," *Camera Obscura*, no. 1 (Fall
1976), 11–26.

other than heterosexuality (whether practiced by women or men). In Arzner's own time, these competing definitions would be read as the conflict between a desexualized nineteenth-century ideal of romantic friendship among women and the "mannish lesbian" (exemplified by Radclyffe Hall), defined by herself and her critics as a sexual being.[20] Arzner's continued "visibility" suggests not only that the tension is far from being resolved, but also that debates about lesbian identity inform, even (and especially!) in unconscious ways, the thinking of femi-nists who do not identify as lesbians.

I am suggesting, of course, that lesbian irony constitutes one of the pleasures in Arzner's films and that irony is a desir-able aim in women's cinema. Irony can, however, misfire.[21] It has been argued that in Jackie Raynal's film *Deux fois* (1970), for in-stance, the ironic elaboration of woman-as-object-of-spectacle is rendered decidedly problematic by the fact that it is only in of-fering herself as an object of spectacle that the category of woman-as-object-of-spectacle can be criticized; that is, it is only by affirming the validity of patriarchal representation that any critique is possible.[22] I have in mind here another kind of misfir-ing, when the ironic reading of patriarchal conventions collides with other coded forms of representation that may serve, quite disturbingly, as a support for that irony. In *Dance, Girl, Dance*, for instance, racial stereotypes emerge at three key moments in the narrative of the film. In the opening scenes of the film, at a nightclub in Akron, Ohio, the camera moves over the heads of the members of the audience as it approaches the stage, where the female dance troupe is performing. Intercut is an image of the black members of the band, who are smiling as the prover-bially happy musicians. Although an equivalence seems to be es-tablished between women and blacks as objects of spectacle, I see little basis for reading this as a critical use of the racial stereotype.

Later in the film, when Judy longingly watches the rehearsal of the ballet company, another racial stereotype emerges. The performance number portrays the encounter between ballet and other forms of dance and body language within the context of the city. At one point in the performance, the music switches suddenly to imitate a jazzy tune, and a white couple in blackface strut across the stage. During one of the concluding scenes of the film, when Judy and Bubbles resolve their friendship in a court of law, the ostensibly amusing conclusion to the scene is provided when the clerk announces the arrival of a black couple whose names are "Abraham Lincoln Johnson" and "Martha Washington Johnson." However disparate these racial stereotypes, they do emerge at crucial moments in the deployment of irony and performance. In each case, the racial stereotype appears when the sexual hierarchy of the look is deflected or otherwise problematized. The black performers at the beginning of the film are defined securely within the parameters of objectification when it is apparent—much to Bubbles's irritation and eventual attendant desire—that Jimmie Harris, one of the spectators in the audience, is totally unengaged in the spectacle on stage. The appearance of the white couple in blackface occurs when the centrality of Judy's desire, as defined by her longing gaze at the performance, is affirmed. In the courtroom scene, Judy aggressively and enthusiastically assumes the court as her stage, and the racial stereotype of "Mr. and Mrs. Johnson" appears only when the rivalry between the two women is on the verge of resolution.

In each of these instances, the racial stereotype affirms the distinction between white subject and black object just when the distinction between male subject and female object is being put into question. Though there is nothing in *Dance, Girl, Dance* that approximates a sustained discourse on race, these brief allusions to racial stereotypes are eruptions that cannot be dismissed or disregarded as mere background or as unconscious reflections of a dominant cinematic practice that was racist. The marks of authorship in *Dance, Girl, Dance* include these extremely problematic racist clichés as well as the ironic inflection of the heterosexual contract. I want to stress that female irony is not just a function of sexual hierarchy, but that virtually all forms of narrative and visual opposition are potentially significant. To ignore, in Arzner's case, the intertwining of sexual and racial codes of performance is to claim female authorship as a white preserve. The racial stereotypes that serve as an anchor of distinct otherness in *Dance, Girl, Dance* speak to a more general problem in female authorship. Although Arzner's films suggest other forms of cinematic pleasure that have been relatively untheorized within film studies, these forms cannot be posited in any simple way as "alternatives." I think it is a mistake to assume that the racist clichés are symptomatic of the compromises that inevitably occur with any attempt to create different visions within the classical Hollywood cinema. Such clichés are possible within virtually any kind of film practice.

Dorothy Arzner has come to represent both a textual practice (consciously) and an image (less consciously) in feminist film theory. The textual practice has been described as if there were no determinations—such as those in *Dance, Girl, Dance* having to do with race—besides those of gender. In other words, Arzner's reception foregrounds the extent to which feminist film theory has disavowed the significance of race, particularly when racist codes contradict or complicate the disruption of gender hierarchies. The relationship between the textual practice and the image suggests an area of fascination, if not love, that dare not speak its (her) name. The preferred term *sexual difference* in feminist film theory slides from the tension between masculinity and femininity into a crude determinism whereby there is no representation without heterosexuality. Lesbianism raises some crucial questions concerning identification and desire in the cinema, questions with particular relevance to female cinematic authorship. Cinema offers

simultaneous affirmation and dissolution of the binary oppositions upon which our most fundamental notions of self and
other are based. In feminist film theory, one of the most basic
working assumptions has been that in the classical cinema, at
least, there is an unproblematic fit between the hierarchies of
masculinity and femininity on the one hand, and activity and passivity on the other. If disrupting and disturbing that fit is a major
task for filmmakers and theorists, then lesbianism would seem
to have a strategically important function. For one of the "problems" that lesbianism poses, insofar as representation is concerned, is precisely the fit between the paradigms of sex and
agency, the alignment of masculinity with activity and femininity
with passivity.

It is undoubtedly one of those legendary "no coincidences"
that one discourse in which the "problem" of lesbianism is thus
posed most acutely is psychoanalysis. For reasons both historical
and theoretical, the most persuasive, as well as controversial,
accounts of cinematic identification and desire have been influenced by psychoanalysis. Laura Mulvey's classic account of sexual
hierarchy in narrative cinema established the by-now familiar re-
frain that the ideal spectator of the classical cinema—whatever
his or her biological sex or cultural gender—is male. Many
critics have challenged or extended the implications of Mulvey's
account, most frequently arguing that for women (and sometimes for men as well), cinematic identification occurs at the
very least across gender lines, whether in transvestite or bisexual terms.[23] However complex such accounts, they tend to
leave unexamined another basic assumption common both to
Mulvey's account and to contemporary psychoanalytic accounts
of identification, and that is that cinematic identification not only
functions to affirm heterosexual norms, but also finds its most
basic condition of possibility in the heterosexual division of the
universe. Although feminist film theory and criticism have devoted remarkably extensive attention to the function of the

23
See David
Rodowick, "The Difficulty
of Difference," *Wide Angle*
5, no. 1 (1982), 4–15; Teresa
de Lauretis, *Alice Doesn't:
Feminism, Semiotics, Cin-
ema* (Bloomington: Indiana
University Press, 1984), ch.
5; Miriam Hansen, "Plea-
sure, Ambivalence, Identification: Valentino and
Female Spectatorship," *Cinema Journal* 25, no. 4
(Summer 1986), 6–32; Gay-
lyn Studlar, *In the Realm of
Pleasure: Von Sternberg,
Dietrich, and the Masochistic Aesthetic* (Urbana: University of Illinois Press,
1988). Mulvey herself has
contributed to the discussion; see "Afterthoughts on
'Visual Pleasure and Narrative Cinema' inspired by
King Vidor's *Duel in the Sun*
(1946)," in *Visual and Other
Pleasures* (Bloomington: Indiana University Press,
1989), 29–38.

male gaze in film, the accompanying heterosexual scenario has not received much attention, except for the occasional nod to what seems to be more the realm of the obvious than the explorable or questionable.

An impressive body of feminist writing has been devoted to the exploration of how—following Luce Irigaray—heterosexuality functions as a ruse, a decoy relation to mask male homosocial and homosexual bonds. "Reigning everywhere, although prohibited in practice," Irigaray writes, "hom(m)osexuality is played out through the bodies of women, matter, or sign, and heterosexuality has been up to now just an alibi for the smooth workings of man's relations with himself."[24] Comparatively little attention has been paid to how heterosexual economies work to assure that any exchange between women remains firmly ensconced within that "hom(m)osexual" economy. To be sure, male and female homosexualities occupy quite different positions, and given the logic of the masculine "same" that dominates the patriarchal order, female homosexuality cannot be ascribed functions that are similar to male homosexuality. However, the two homosexualities share the potential to disrupt, in however different ways, the reign of the "hom(m)osexual." Irigaray speaks of the "fault, the infraction, the misconduct, and the challenge that female homosexuality entails." For lesbianism threatens to upset the alignment between masculinity and activity, and femininity and passivity. Hence, writes Irigaray, "[t]he problem can be minimized if female homosexuality is regarded merely as an imitation of male behavior."[25]

Irigaray's discussion of the disruptive potential of female homosexuality emerges from her symptomatic reading and rewriting of Freud. In the Freudian text that occasions Irigaray's remarks on the "problem" of female homosexuality within psychoanalysis, "The Psychogenesis of a Case of Homosexuality in a Woman" (1920), questions of narration and identification, masculinity and femininity, and dominant and alternative practice are

24
Luce Irigaray, "Women on the Market," *This Sex Which Is Not One,* trans. Catherine Porter with Carolyn Burke (Ithaca, N.Y.: Cornell University Press, 1985), 172.

25
Luce Irigaray, "Commodities among Themselves," *This Sex Which Is Not One.*

posed in ways that are particularly relevant to lesbian author-ship in the cinema. Jacqueline Rose has said of the case history that, here, Freud "is in a way at his most radical, rejecting the concept of cure, insisting that the most psychoanalysis can do is restore the original bisexual disposition of the patient, defining homosexuality as nonneurotic."[26]

In the case history, Freud describes the brief analysis of a young woman who was brought to him by her parents after her unsuccessful suicide attempt. This "beautiful and clever girl of eighteen" pursued with great enthusiasm her attraction to a woman ten years older than herself, and her parents (her father in particular) were particularly distressed by her simultaneous brazenness ("she did not scruple to appear in the most fre-quented streets in the company of her questionable friend") and deception ("she disdained no means of deception, no excuses and no lies that would make meetings with her possible and cover them").[27]

The suicide attempt occurred when these two factors that so distressed her parents coincided in full view of her fa-ther. After the young woman and her female companion were greeted by the woman's father with extreme displeasure as his path crossed theirs on the street one day (as Freud notes, the scene had all the elements of a *mise en scène* planned by the young woman), the young woman threw herself in desperation over a railway fence. Despite the apparent gravity of the suicide attempt, Freud saw little hope for successful analysis, for the woman was brought to analysis of a will other than her own.[28] In addition, Freud saw little actual illness in the young woman, at least as far as her sexuality was concerned; rather than resolving a neurotic conflict, Freud was being asked to assist in "convert-ing one variety of the genital organization of sexuality into the other" (137).

As Freud proceeds to untangle the various threads of the young woman's lesbian attachment, a somewhat confusing and

26
Jacqueline Rose, "Dora: Fragment of an Analysis," in *In Dora's Case*, ed. Charles Bernheimer and Claire Kahane (New York: Columbia University Press, 1985), 135.

27
Sigmund Freud, "The Psychogenesis of a Case of Homosexuality in a Woman (1920)," in *Sexu-ality and the Psychology of Love*, ed. Philip Rieff (New York: Collier Books, 1963), 134. Subsequent page num-bers will be indicated in parentheses in the text.

28
See Jacqueline Rose, "Dora: Fragment of an Analysis"; and Suzanne Gearhart, "The Scene of Psychoanalysis: The Un-answered Questions of Dora," in *In Dora's Case*, 105–27.

Mandy Merck dis-
cusses the peculiar portrait
of homosexuality in the
case history; she notes in
particular that there is a
sharp break between the
young woman's homosexual
and heterosexual pasts as
described by Freud, sug-
gesting that despite what
Rose describes as a "non-
neurotic" definition of homosexuality, there remains
nonetheless the desire to
read heterosexuality as the
privileged source of all desire. See "The Train of
Thought in Freud's 'Case of
Homosexuality in a Wo-
man,'" *m/f,* nos. 11–12
(1986), 37, 39.

often contradictory portrait of homosexuality emerges.[29] The woman's sexuality is read through a variety of oppositions that form the territory of psychoanalysis—body and mind ("in both sexes the degree of physical hermaphroditism is to a great ex- tent independent of the psychical hermaphroditism" [140]); masculine and feminine desire ("She had thus not only chosen a feminine love-object, but had also developed a masculine atti- tude towards this object." [141]); and maternal and paternal identification (written before Freud hypothesized more exten- sively about the importance of the pre-oedipal phase for wo- men, the case history nonetheless acknowledges the maternal object as, if not on the same level of importance as the oedipal scenario, then at the very least constitutive of the subject's sex- ual identity). The case history is written within the field of these opposing terms, but there are shades of a breakdown of opposition, and the subsequent interdependence of the oppo- sing terms. Hence, Freud speculates that the woman to whom the analysand was so intensely attracted evoked two love ob- jects, her mother and her brother.

Her latest choice corresponded, therefore, not only with her fem- inine but also with her masculine ideal; it combined gratifica- tion of the homosexual tendency with that of the heterosexual one. It is well known that analysis of male homosexuals has in numerous cases revealed the same combination, which should warn us not to form too simple a conception of the nature and genesis of inversion, and to keep in mind the extensive influence of the bisexuality of mankind [143].

Indeed, this case history occasions some of Freud's most famous pronouncements on the importance of bisexuality. Spec- ulating that rage toward her father caused the young woman to turn away from men altogether, Freud notes that "[in] all of us, throughout life, the libido normally oscillates between male and female objects; the bachelor gives up his men friends when he marries and returns to club-life when married life has lost its savour" (144).

But the "bisexuality of mankind" posited in the case history takes two distinctly different forms. On the one hand, it is posited as an originary force, a kind of biological given from which a variety of factors—Freud sometimes privileges predisposition, and sometimes environment—will determine one's choice of sexual aim and sexual object. On the other, bisexuality emerges in a much more challenging and disturbing way as the violent play of warring forces, as evidenced most particularly in the young woman's suicide attempt. For the desperate jump over the railroad wall is no quivering oscillation, and it is far from the kind of serial bisexuality alluded to in the above quotation about bachelors, marriage, and club life. Rather, in the suicide attempt the battle of maternal and paternal objects attains crisis proportions and provokes a parallel crisis in representation. There are two divergent conceptions of bisexuality in the case history—one that assures that the young woman is either really like a man (in her choice of role) or really like a heterosexual (in her choice of love object), and the other, which suggests, rather, a much more profound tension between the desire to be seen by the father and the desire to construct an alternative scenario of desire altogether.

Despite its reputation as a more successful exploration of questions so problematically posed in the case history of Dora, "The Psychogenesis of a Case of Homosexuality in a Woman" does not read as a particularly convincing narrative in its own right. The "problem" of the case history centers on the woman's self-representation, on her desire, not simply for the loved object, but for a certain staging of that desire. What is not entirely clear is the extent to which the attempted suicide was an unconscious attempt to put an end to parental—and particularly paternal—disapproval by literal self-annihilation, or

rather an equally unconscious attempt to dramatize her conflicting allegiances by creating a scene where she is at once active subject and passive object (Freud notes frequently that the
young woman's amorous feelings took a "masculine" form). The
suicide attempt is best described as both of these simultaneously—one, a desire for resolution, the other a desire for another language altogether to represent her conflicted desires.[30]

30
    I believe what I am
describing as the desire for
another representation of
desire is quite close to
Mandy Merck's discussion
of the young woman's con-
flict about "masculine identification." See "The Train
of Thought," 40.

Put another way, the suicide attempt crystalizes the position of "homosexuality in a woman" as a problem of representation and of narrative. Freud discusses the young woman's case in
ways that suggest quite strongly the pressure of lesbianism
against a system of explanation and representation. Throughout
the case history, the young woman's "masculinity" is the inevitable frame of reference. Masculinity acquires a variety of definitions in the course of the essay, at times associated with the
biological characteristics of men (the young woman favored her
father in appearance) and at others equated with the mere fact
of agency or activity (she displayed a preference for being
"lover rather than beloved" [141]). But "masculinity" never
really "takes" as an explanation, since throughout the case history the woman remains an embodiment of conflicting desires.
The suicide attempt turns upon what has become, in the cinema, a classic account of the activation of desire, the folding of
spectacle into narrative. However, in the standard account, woman leans more toward the spectacle, with man defined as the
active agent. Here, it is the woman's desires to narrate and to
be seen that collide, leading her to make quite a spectacle of
herself, but without a narrative of her own to contextualize
that spectacle. According to the young woman's account, the
disapproving gaze from her father led her to tell her female
companion of the father's disapproval and her companion then
adopted the opinion of the father, saying that they should not
see each other again. The sudden collapse, the identity between
lover and father, the erasure of tension, seem to precipitate

the woman's quite literal fall. The woman's desire for self-annihilation occurs, in other words, when her desire becomes fully representable within conventional terms.

What I am suggesting, then, is that the conditions of the representability of the lesbian scenario in this case history are simultaneously those of a tension, a conflict (which is "readable" in other than homosexual terms), *and* those of a pressure exerted against the overwhelmingly heterosexual assumptions of the language of psychoanalysis, a desire for *another* representation of desire. Or as Monique Wittig puts it, "Homosexuality is the desire for one's own sex. But it is also the desire for something else that is not connoted. This desire is resistance to the norm."[31] Expanding on Irigaray, Teresa de Lauretis writes: "Lesbian representation, or rather, its condition of possibility, depends on separating out the two contrary undertows that constitute the paradox of sexual (in)difference, on isolating but maintaining the two senses of homosexuality and hommosexuality."[32] The lesbian irony in Arzner's signature suggests that division to which de Lauretis refers, a division between a representation of female communities and an inscription of marginality. That irony stands in (ironic) contrast to feminist film theory's division of Arzner into a textual hommo-sexual (in print) and a visible homosexual (in pictures).

Given Arzner's career in Hollywood, and the realist plots central to her films, her influence would seem to be most apparent among those filmmakers who have appropriated the forms of Hollywood cinema to feminist or even lesbian ends—for example, Susan Seidelman (*Desperately Seeking Susan,* 1985) and Donna Deitch (*Desert Hearts,* 1985). A more striking connection, however, exists with those contemporary women filmmakers whose films extend the possibilities of lesbian irony, while revising the components of the classical cinema and inventing new cinematic forms simultaneously. Despite the rigid distinction between dominant and alternative film that has

31
Monique Wittig, "Paradigm," in *Homosexualities and French Literature: Cultural Contexts/ Critical Texts,* ed. George Stambolian and Elaine Marks (Ithaca, N.Y.: Cornell University Press, 1979), 114.

32
Teresa de Lauretis, "Sexual Indifference and Lesbian Representation," *Theatre Journal* 40, no. 2 (May 1988), 159.

remained a foregone conclusion in feminist film theory, the articulation of lesbian authorship in Arzner's work finds a contemporary echo in films that may be more "obviously" lesbian than *Dance, Girl, Dance* or *Craig's Wife,* but whose authorial strategies have been either unreadable or misread in the terms of feminist film theory. Films like Chantal Akerman's *Je tu il elle* (1974), Ulrike Ottinger's *Ticket of No Return [Portrait of a Woman Drinker]* (1979), or Midi Onodera's *Ten Cents a Dance* (1985) are remarkable explorations of the desire to see and to be seen, to detach and to fuse, to narrate one's own desire and to exceed or otherwise complicate the very terms of that narration.

Less optimistically, the disturbing fit between sexual and racial codes of performance, between different modes of irony, finds a contemporary echo in those women's films in which lesbian desire and race collide. The results may not be so clearly racist as in *Dance, Girl, Dance,* but they raise equally important questions for feminist readings based on the implicit assumption that all women are white and heterosexual. In several films that have become classics of feminist film theory—Sally Potter's *Thriller* (1977) and *The Gold Diggers* (1983), and Laura Mulvey's and Peter Wollen's *Riddles of the Sphinx* (1977)—an attraction between two women is central in visual and narrative terms, and in each case the attraction occurs between a white woman and a black woman. Now, these films do not evoke lesbianism and race in identical ways, and my point is not to conclude with a blanket condemnation of them. Rather I want to suggest that the disturbing questions they raise beyond the staples of feminist theory, like mothering, female friendship, and reading against the grain (whether of psychoanalysis or of opera), have not been discussed. The tensions and contradictions so dear to contemporary feminist theory stop at the point that an investigation of sexual difference would require exploration of the *other* sexual difference, or that an examination of female identity as the negative of man would require consideration of white privilege.

Lesbian authorship in Arzner's work constantly assumes the irony of incompatible truths. This irony is not, however, necessarily contestatory or free of the rigid dualisms of white patriarchal film practice. Although I think feminist film theory might do well to explore its own investment in the pleasures of irony, Arzner's case is crucial for a history of lesbian desire and film practice. My own desire, in exploring the way in which Arzner and her films have been read in feminist film theory, has been to make a connection between the lesbian image and the narrative text, while resisting the lure of a seamless narrative, in which the spectacular lesbianism of the photographs of Arzner would fit comfortably and unproblematically with her films, in which spectacle and narrative would be as idealistically joined for feminism and lesbianism as they presumably are in patriarchal film practice.

Discussion

Diana Fuss

I agree with your reading of feminist theory as, collectively, a defense against the erotic structure of the look—women consuming images of other women, if not voyeuristically, then at least "vampiristically." I also agree with the point that theories of female spectatorship—and that would include, I assume, theories of narcissism, masochism, double identification or bisexuality, and transvestism—because they bracket lesbian desire, are inadequate. But though your paper points very persuasively to the need for a theory of lesbian spectatorship, it seems to stop short of elaborating the specifics of such a theory. I wonder if you could suggest some psychical mechanisms that might assist in our understanding of how a lesbian look would operate.

Judith Mayne

Quite honestly, I have some ambivalence about a theory of lesbian spectatorship. The models of female spectatorship that have been elaborated in feminist film theory disturb me on two counts. First, female spectatorship becomes the process of displacement itself: contradiction, oscillation, mobility. Though I'm as interested in contradiction as the next person, there is too great a tendency to valorize contradiction for its own sake. So, second, the female spectator becomes the site at which contradiction itself is embodied, and it begins to appear that the female spectator functions very much like the Woman in classical cinema—as the figure upon whom are projected all the messy, troublesome, complicated things that don't fit elsewhere. I would rather start from the assumption that all spectatorship is potentially contradictory, so that contradiction doesn't have to carry this utopian burden as proof of some kind of resistant force.

At the same time, I'm obviously saying that there is a gay component in everything that involves identification and that this is precisely what has been bracketed off in critical studies of cinema. And although I don't want to say that films made by lesbians are of interest only to lesbians, I'm hesitant to elaborate an overall theory of cinematic identification that would make easy connections between things that I don't think are easily connected. Rather than offer some sort of theoretical prescription, what I would like to stress more strongly at this point is the importance of exploring the investment of lesbian filmmakers in the forming and creating of lesbian spectatorship.

This brings me back to the point I stressed throughout my paper, namely the necessity of a sense of irony. For, on the one hand, there are many aspects of gay and lesbian spectatorship that apply to what I suppose you might call heterosexual spectatorship, but there are numerous places where no such easy alignments can be made. And it seems to me that if you don't keep these two dynamics of sameness and difference in some kind of tension, either you end up affirming some notion of a wishy-washy bisexual human subject—"wishy-washy" in the sense that such a subject-position carries very little political impact in our present society—or you are accused of essentialism. (And in terms of the latter, there is yet another irony, since you can be sure that as soon as you say the word *lesbian* in certain feminist, theoretical circles, the epithet *essentialist* will automatically be applied!)

Teresa de Lauretis Stuart Marshall remarked in his presentation that there should be no global or all-encompassing representation of AIDS because no such thing is possible, and I think in this instance, and at this moment in history, exactly the same thing applies to lesbian spectatorship. That is, I think you are right to insist on addressing only very specific circumstances that exist within certain historical contingencies.

Tom Waugh I had always thought that during the early seventies, when feminists avoided the issue of Dorothy Arzner's lesbianism, it was partially out of courtesy or respect to Arzner, who was still alive and not only in the closet but also disavowing feminism. I'm wondering if, perhaps, the closet as a concept—however crudely biographical—might still be of some value in the analysis of Arzner's work.

For example, the violence of the various disavowals in her films—killing off Basilova in *Dance, Girl, Dance,* the tremendous contradictions from one image of Hepburn to the next in *Christopher Strong*—seems to point toward the closet as a tool of analysis. Certainly one can imagine the denials, disavowals, and contradictory codings necessitated for a lesbian working within the studio system.

Mayne The first part of your comment presumably refers to the interview with Arzner by Gerald Peary and Karyn Kay [in Claire Johnston, ed., *The Work of Dorothy Arzner: Towards a Feminist Cinema* (London, British Film Institute, 1975), 19-29], which is the interview everyone refers to as revealing the "truth" of Arzner's sense of herself as a woman working in Hollywood. I think that critics have been a little too quick to assume that this can be read as representative of all of Arzner's work, or as a window onto her psychic life. This one interview is always used as evidence of Arzner as an extremely closeted director. Certainly there is much defensiveness in this interview, but I'm not convinced that it represents the perspective from which to judge Arzner's entire career. To begin with, it was conducted in the 1970s. Arzner may have had an extremely complex, ambivalent, or ambiguous relationship to feminism as it was then defined. In fact, though, the interviewers never raise the topic of lesbianism; they discuss feminism and ask questions about Arzner's work with a particular actor, or a particular director, and so forth. All of this is to say that there are several levels on which the interview can and should be read. People often cite Arzner as an example of someone who was "in the closet." Although I realize that many women who dressed like Arzner were in the closet, the very fact that she made a public display of her desire through the codes of fashion problematizes enormously the very notion of the closet.

The second part of your question raises the larger issue of the personal and political viability of being able to say one is either "in" or "out of" the closet. I think the alternative reading of Arzner's lesbianism that you're suggesting is important, to the extent that, whereas I might find the death of Madame Basilova an insistence on lesbian marginality vis-à-vis Hollywood, you're suggesting, rather, that her death is a kind of refusal of lesbian coding. But I don't think grounding either or both of these readings in Arzner's supposed closeted status is useful. I simply don't find it possible to make those kinds of absolute divisions— either she was in the closet or she was out—across her work and life.

Mandy Merck   I'm interested in something you broached in the beginning of your paper, a sort of historiography of wish-fulfillment in film theory. If you recall, Pam Cook and Claire Johnston wrote not only about Arzner, but about Raoul Walsh as well, in particular about his film *The Revolt of Mamie Stover* [1956]. In their essay on that film ["The Place of Woman in the Cinema of Raoul Walsh," in *Raoul Walsh*, ed. Phil Hardy (Edinburgh: Edinburgh Film Festival publication, 1974)], they repressed not only possible homosexual meanings, but also the existence of the woman altogether. The famous point of their criticism was that the woman did not exist in the film, that Mamie Stover, the rebellious bar queen, was only an effect of patriarchal projection, a sign produced by male fantasy. Now, I'm interested in the way Lacanian film theory of the seventies policed not only homosexual wishes, but also the desire for feminine figuration. I think it was Ruby Rich who pointed out that in Laura Mulvey's theory there is no woman in the audience, while in Cook and Johnston's theory there is no woman on the screen either—which didn't leave any place for her to go! [Michelle Citron et al., "Women and Film: A Discussion of Feminist Aesthetics," *New German Critique* 13 (Winter 1978)] Yet it does seem that within the terms of a rigorous Lacanian theory—and "rigor" was the requirement then—that that estimation was about right.

During that time, I would agree with heterosexual Lacanians that we weren't going to be voluntaristic. We weren't going to wish any female or homosexual figuration into being that wasn't really there. We were first going to describe what was there, and then later we could create what wasn't there. I don't recall quite how we were going to accomplish this, but we were going to do it somehow.

You cited Andrew Britton, a gay critic who strikes me as being incredibly voluntaristic. Sometimes I go along with his readings and sometimes—I'm thinking of an unpublished paper he wrote on melodrama—I think he's simply producing a wish-fulfillment. Jackie Stacey's essay in *Screen* on *Desperately Seeking Susan* and *All About Eve* also has that quality of wishing lesbian desire onto the screen in ways that make me uneasy.

What I'm therefore curious about is how you negotiate these extremes of rigor, on the one hand, and wish-fulfillment, on the other.

Constance Penley wrote a very interesting essay about apparatus theory, describing that aspect of seventies film criticism as a "bachelor machine," not a scientific description of film production, but a theory that itself perpetuates masculine desire ["Feminism, Film Theory, and the Bachelor Machines," in Constance Penley, *The Future of an Illusion* (Minneapolis: University of Minnesota Press, 1989), 57–80]. But she didn't include this essay in her anthology *Feminism and Film Theory* [New York: Routledge, 1988]. She prefaced that book instead by saying "Some feminists see a textuality in films that I don't see, and this is not a collection of wish-fulfilling criticism." And when Stephen Heath tried to break out of this theoretical impasse in 1978 [Stephen Heath, "Difference," *Screen* 19, no. 3 (Autumn 1978), 51–112], he pointed to Luce Irigaray's writing and to Chantal Akerman's film *Jeanne Dielman* [1975] as raising problems for Lacanian film theory. He didn't address Akerman's homosexuality, didn't discuss *Je tu il elle*, but he raised issues of auteurism; he was fascinated by how Akerman's short stature might have influenced her low camera angles.

Mayne

First, it seems to me rather obvious that there is no such thing as a theory that's not wish-fulfilling in some way or in some instance. You mention Constance Penley, who has been one of the primary spokespersons for the view that the classical cinema is a system of great homogeneity, defined absolutely by patriarchal law and heterosexual order. Feminist or gay critics' desires to see productive conflicts within Hollywood plots as speaking to contradictions that are irresolvable under patriarchy thus become, according to that point of view, "wrong" or naive. The problem, as you make clear, is that in some cases excessive or wrongheaded claims are made in the name of feminism or lesbianism or gay sexuality. But too often the position from which the accusation of error comes equates theoretical sophistication with compulsory heterosexuality.

The essay by Penley to which you refer was first published with a discussion following it in *m/f* [no. 10 (1985), 59]. There, Penley describes the feminist investment in productive gaps within dominant cinema as follows: "they are saying yes, [classical Hollywood narrative] is a machine and no, it isn't. It's a perfect fetishistic position." Fetishism is one of many terms that's gotten an undeserved bad reputation, certainly more so than has voyeurism. Feminist film critics are far more prepared to defend a female investment in voyeurism than in fetishism, as if fetishism were indeed the supreme form of male patriarchal desire. Now, I think Penley's criticism is well taken, up to a point; the feminist claims for heterogeneity in classical cinema often *do* proceed from a vague—unrigorous, as you say—sense of wanting the object you love to have some kind of feminist value. Irony *is* a kind of fetishism, and I think that should be acknowledged. Too often it's assumed not only that women cannot identify with fetishism but also that they *should* not.

There is an unfortunate tendency to be dualistic about these issues: if you criticize psychoanalytic theory, you're resisting, denying; if you affirm the productive potential of alternative readings, you're engaging in wishful thinking. Then, the equally unfortunate flip side of this is to cling to those contradictions in a defensive way, without really examining the issues. All of which goes back to the point Teresa raised earlier about the necessity to think more specifically—in very detailed, delimited ways—rather than always in terms of a global theory that attempts to explain everything.

Peter Bowen I think your reading of Arzner was particularly helpful in its challenge to totalizing theories of spectatorship, their preclusion of even the possibility of a lesbian spectator by positing a hegemonic male spectator. Your paper reminds me of other work that attempts to articulate the possibility of female spectatorship—

for example, Miriam Hansen's essay on Valentino ["Pleasure, Ambivalence, Identification: Valentino and Female Spectatorship," *Cinema Journal* 25, no. 4 (Summer 1986), 6–32]. Hansen attempts to historicize the question of the gaze in Hollywood cinema and to identify a "double female gaze" in Valentino's films. Her reading discovers a female spectatorship that the films themselves ultimately disavow. Valentino exists in the films as a spectacularized male body looked at salaciously by a female character. But that look is displaced by the narrative when Valentino rejects the desire of the "bad girl" and usurps the look in order to objectify and legitimize the demure "good girl," the one who doesn't look. But the problem of the male body as the object of the gaze extends the "scandal" of the female spectator to the "scandal" of the eroticized male body. The consequent narrative disavowal is also a disavowal of the homosexualization of the male gaze, or, to put it another way, the possibility of a gay male spectator.

Mayne

I also like Miriam Hansen's essay on Valentino very much. But, like other feminist revisions of the question of spectatorship, Hansen's essay emphasizes a bisexual oscillation, a constant movement across supposedly opposing positions. Clearly, there's much to be said for such an understanding of bisexuality, but I'm not completely convinced that the rigid dichotomous thinking characteristic of compulsory heterosexuality has been replaced so much as displaced. In other words, I see the potential problem of this position as one of displacing a heterosexual essentialism onto a kind of bisexual essentialism.

Ruby Rich

A comment and a question. You started out by talking about Arzner's dress and the way it's been used to try to tease out an identity for her, and you went on to discuss the dress of women in Arzner's films. I think this produced an interesting and coherent argument for fashion as sexual identity—you've given a whole new meaning to the term *closet!*

I was thinking about Isaac Julien's film *Looking for Langston* [1988] in relation to your paper, and it suggested a sort of parallel idea of "Looking for Dorothy." Given the reaction to Isaac's film—the hysteria about "protecting" the image of Langston Hughes from the "contamination" of homosexuality— do you see the issue you raised—feminist theory's fascination with Arzner's image and simultaneous disavowal of her homosexuality—do you see this as a manifestation of hysteria? Why do you think people are drawn repeatedly to that which they refuse to name?

Mayne   For the longest time, I think I naively accepted that theorists weren't addressing the kinds of issues I have addressed because they weren't personally interested in them—you know, a basic liberal approach to the field. But looking at the way in which Arzner is so obsessively pictured, looking at the extremely dykey images of her that are most often reproduced, it's obvious that there is an aspect of that fascination that has been denied. The particular repressions I have noted in relation to analyses of Arzner's work are, in a sense, typical of more insidious, general types of conscious refusals within film theory to acknowledge the lesbian or gay other.

Looking for My Penis
The Eroticized Asian in Gay Video Porn

Richard Fung

Several scientists have begun to examine the relation between personality and human reproductive behaviour from a gene-based evolutionary perspective. . . . In this vein we reported a study of racial difference in sexual restraint such that Orientals > whites > blacks. Restraint was indexed in numerous ways, having in common a lowered allocation of bodily energy to sexual functioning. We found the same racial pattern occurred on gamete production (dizygotic birthing frequency per 100: Mongoloids, 4; Caucasoids, 8; Negroids, 16), intercourse frequencies (premarital, marital, extramarital), developmental precocity (age at first intercourse, age at first pregnancy, number of pregnancies), primary sexual characteristics (size of penis, vagina, testis, ovaries), secondary sexual characteristics (salient voice, muscularity, buttocks, breasts), and biologic control of behaviour (periodicity of sexual response, predictability of life history from onset of puberty), as well as in androgen levels and sexual attitudes.[1]

[1] J. Philippe Rushton and Anthony F. Bogaert, University of Western Ontario, "Race versus Social Class Difference in Sexual Behaviour: A Follow-up Test of the r/K Dimension," *Journal of Research in Personality* 22 (1988), 259.

This passage from the *Journal of Research in Personality* was written by University of Western Ontario psychologist Philippe Rushton, who enjoys considerable controversy in Canadian academic circles and in the popular media. His thesis, articulated throughout his work, appropriates biological studies of the continuum of reproductive strategies of oysters through to chimpanzees and posits that degree of "sexuality"—interpreted as penis and vagina size, frequency of intercourse, buttock and lip size—correlates positively with criminality and sociopathic behavior and inversely with intelligence, health, and longevity. Rushton sees race as *the* determining factor and places East Asians (Rushton uses the word *Orientals*) on one end of the spectrum and blacks on the other. Since whites fall squarely in the middle, the position of perfect balance, there is no need for analysis, and they remain free of scrutiny.

Notwithstanding its profound scientific shortcomings, Rushton's work serves as an excellent articulation of a dominant discourse on race and sexuality in Western society—a system of ideas and reciprocal practices that originated in Europe simultaneously with (some argue as a conscious justification for[2]) colonial expansion and slavery. In the nineteenth century these ideas took on a scientific gloss with social Darwinism and eugenics. Now they reappear, somewhat altered, in psychology journals from the likes of Rushton. It is important to add that these ideas have also permeated the global popular consciousness. Anyone who has been exposed to Western television or advertising images, which is much of the world, will have absorbed this particular constellation of stereotyping and racial hierarchy. In Trinidad in the 1960s, on the outer reaches of the empire, everyone in my schoolyard was thoroughly versed in these "truths" about the races.

Historically, most organizing against racism has concentrated on fighting discrimination that stems from the intelligence–social behavior variable assumed by Rushton's scale. Discrimination based on perceived intellectual ability does, after all, have direct ramifications in terms of education and employment, and therefore for survival. Until recently, issues of gender and sexuality remained a low priority for those who claimed to speak for the communities.[3] But antiracist strategies that fail to subvert the race-gender status quo are of seriously limited value. Racism cannot be narrowly defined in terms of race hatred. Race is a factor in even our most intimate relationships.

The contemporary construction of race and sex as exemplified by Rushton has endowed black people, both men and women, with a threatening hypersexuality. Asians, on the other hand, are collectively seen as undersexed.[4] But here I want to make some crucial distinctions. First, in North America, stereo-

2
See Eric Williams, *Capitalism and Slavery* (New York: Capricorn, 1966).

3
Feminists of color have long pointed out that racism is phrased differently for men and women. Nevertheless, since it is usually heterosexual (and often middle-class) males whose voices are validated by the power structure, it is their interests that are taken up as "representing" the communities. See Barbara Smith, "Toward a Black Feminist Criticism," in *All the Women Are White, All the Blacks Are Men, But Some of Us Are Brave: Black Women's Studies* (Old Westbury, N.Y.: The Feminist Press, 1982), 162.

4
The mainstream "leadership" within Asian communities often colludes with the myth of the model minority and the reassuring desexualization of Asian people.

typing has focused almost exclusively on what recent colonial language designates as "Orientals"—that is East and Southeast Asian peoples—as opposed to the "Orientalism" discussed by Edward Said, which concerns the Middle East. This current, popular usage is based more on a perception of similar physical features—black hair, "slanted" eyes, high cheek bones, and so on—than through a reference to common cultural traits. South Asians, people whose backgrounds are in the Indian subcontinent and Sri Lanka, hardly figure at all in North American popular representations, and those few images are ostensibly devoid of sexual connotation.[5]

Second, within the totalizing stereotype of the "Oriental," there are competing and sometimes contradictory sexual associations based on nationality. So, for example, a person could be seen as Japanese and somewhat kinky, or Filipino and "available." The very same person could also be seen as "Oriental" and therefore sexless. In addition, the racial hierarchy revamped by Rushton is itself in tension with an earlier and only partially eclipsed depiction of *all* Asians as having an undisciplined and dangerous libido. I am referring to the writings of the early European explorers and missionaries, but also to antimiscegenation laws and such specific legislation as the 1912 Saskatchewan law that barred white women from employment in Chinese-owned businesses.

Finally, East Asian women figure differently from men both in reality and in representation. In "Lotus Blossoms Don't Bleed," Renee Tajima points out that in Hollywood films:

There are two basic types: the Lotus Blossom Baby (a.k.a. China Doll, Geisha Girl, shy Polynesian beauty, et al.) and the Dragon Lady (Fu Manchu's various female relations, prostitutes, devious madames). . . . Asian women in film are, for the most part, passive figures who exist to serve men—as love interests for white men (re: Lotus Blossoms) or as partners in crime for men of their own kind (re: Dragon Ladies).[6]

5
In Britain, however, more race-sex stereotypes of South Asians exist. Led by artists such as Pratibha Parmar, Sunil Gupta, and Hanif Kureishi, there is also a growing and already significant body of work by South Asians themselves which takes up questions of sexuality.

6
Renee Tajima, "Lotus Blossoms Don't Bleed: Images of Asian Women," *Anthologies of Asian American Film and Video* (New York: A distribution project of Third World Newsreel, 1984), 28.

Further:

Dutiful creatures that they are, Asian women are often assigned the task of expendability in a situation of illicit love. . . . Noticeably lacking is the portrayal of love relationships between Asian women and Asian men, particularly as lead characters.[7]

Because of their supposed passivity and sexual compliance, Asian women have been fetishized in dominant representation, and there is a large and growing body of literature by Asian women on the oppressiveness of these images. Asian men, however—at least since Sessue Hayakawa, who made a Hollywood career in the 1920s of representing the Asian man as sexual threat[8]—have been consigned to one of two categories: the egghead/wimp, or—in what may be analogous to the lotus blossom—dragon lady dichotomy—the kung fu master/ninja/samurai. He is sometimes dangerous, sometimes friendly, but almost always characterized by a desexualized Zen asceticism. So whereas, as Fanon tells us, "the Negro is eclipsed. He is turned into a penis. He *is* a penis,"[9] the Asian man is defined by a striking absence down there. And if Asian men have no sexuality, how can we have homosexuality?

Even as recently as the early 1980s, I remember having to prove my queer credentials before being admitted with other Asian men into a Toronto gay club. I do not believe it was a question of a color barrier. Rather, my friends and I felt that the doorman was genuinely unsure about our sexual orientation. We also felt that had we been white and dressed similarly, our entrance would have been automatic.[10]

Although a motto for the lesbian and gay movements has been "we are everywhere," Asians are largely absent from the images produced by both the political and the commercial sectors of the mainstream gay and lesbian communities. From the earliest articulation of the Asian gay and lesbian movements, a principal concern has therefore been visibility. In political organizing, the demand for a voice, or rather the demand to be

7
Ibid, 29.

8
See Stephen Gong, "Zen Warrior of the Celluloid (Silent) Years: The Art of Sessue Hayakawa," *Bridge* 8, no. 2 (Winter 1982–83), 37–41.

9
Frantz Fanon, *Black Skin White Masks* (London: Paladin, 1970), 120. For a reconsideration of this statement in the light of contemporary black gay issues, see Kobena Mercer, "Imaging the Black Man's Sex," in *Photography/ Politics: Two*, ed. Pat Holland, Jo Spence, and Simon Watney (London: Comedia/ Methuen, 1987); reprinted in *Male Order: Unwrapping Masculinity*, ed. Rowena Chapman and Jonathan Rutherford (London: Lawrence and Wishart, 1988), 141.

10
I do not think that this could happen in today's Toronto, which now has the second largest Chinese community on the continent. Perhaps it would not have happened in San Francisco. But I still believe that there is an onus on gay Asians and other gay people of color to prove our homosexuality.

The term *minority* is misleading. Racism is not a matter of numbers but of power. This is especially clear in situations where people of color constitute actual majorities, as in most former European colonies. At the same time, I feel that none of the current terms are really satisfactory and that too much time spent on the politics of "naming" can in the end be diversionary.

12
To organize effectively with lesbian and gay Asians, we must reject self-righteous condemnation of "closetedness" and see coming out more as a process or a goal, rather than as a prerequisite for participation in the movement.

13
Racism is available to be used by anyone. The conclusion that—because racism = power + prejudice—only white people can be racist is Eurocentric and simply wrong. Individuals have varying degrees and different sources of power, depending on the given moment in a shifting context. This does not contradict the fact that, in contemporary North American society, racism is generally organized around white supremacy.

14
From simple observation, I feel safe in saying that most gay Asian men in North America hold white men as their idealized sexual partners. However, I am not trying to construct an argument for determinism, and there are a number of outstanding problems that are not easily answered by current analy-

heard, has largely been responded to by the problematic practice of "minority" representation on panels and boards.[11] But since racism is a question of power and not of numbers, this strategy has often led to a dead-end tokenistic integration, failing to address the real imbalances.

Creating a space for Asian gay and lesbian representation has meant, among other things, deepening an understanding of what is at stake for Asians in coming out publicly.[12] As is the case for many other people of color and especially immigrants, our families and our ethnic communities are a rare source of affirmation in a racist society. In coming out, we risk (or feel that we risk) losing this support, though the ever-growing organizations of lesbian and gay Asians have worked against this process of cultural exile. In my own experience, the existence of a gay Asian community broke down the cultural schizophrenia in which I related on the one hand to a heterosexual family that affirmed my ethnic culture and, on the other, to a gay community that was predominantly white. Knowing that there was support also helped me come out to my family and further bridge the gap.

If we look at commercial gay sexual representation, it appears that the antiracist movements have had little impact: the images of men and male beauty are still of *white* men and *white* male beauty. These are the standards against which we compare both ourselves and often our brothers—Asian, black, native, and Latino.[13] Although other people's rejection (or fetishization) of us according to the established racial hierarchies may be experienced as oppressive, we are not necessarily moved to scrutinize our own desire and its relationship to the hegemonic image of the white man.[14]

In my lifelong vocation of looking for my penis, trying to fill in the visual void, I have come across only a handful of primary and secondary references to Asian male sexuality in North Ameri-

ses of power. What of the experience of Asians who are attracted to men of color, including other Asians? What about white men who prefer Asians sexually? How and to what extent is desire articulated in terms of race as opposed to body type or other attributes? To what extent is sexual attraction exclusive and/or changeable, and can it be consciously programmed? These questions are all politically loaded, as they parallel and impact the debates between essentialists and social constructionists on the nature of homosexuality itself. They are also emotionally charged, in that sexual choice involving race has been a basis for moral judgment.

15
See Richard Dyer, *Heavenly Bodies: Film Stars and Society* (New York: St. Martin's Press, 1986). In his chapter on Marilyn Monroe, Dyer writes extensively on the relationship between blondness, whiteness, and desirability.

can representation. Even in my own video work, the stress has been on deconstructing sexual representation and only marginally on creating erotica. So I was very excited at the discovery of a Vietnamese American working in gay porn.

Having acted in six videotapes, Sum Yung Mahn is perhaps the only Asian to qualify as a gay porn "star." Variously known as Brad Troung or Sam or Sum Yung Mahn, he has worked for a number of different production studios. All of the tapes in which he appears are distributed through International Wavelength, a San Francisco–based mail order company whose catalog entries feature Asians in American, Thai, and Japanese productions. According to the owner of International Wavelength, about 90 percent of the Asian tapes are bought by white men, and the remaining 10 percent are purchased by Asians. But the number of Asian buyers is growing.

In examining Sum Yung Mahn's work, it is important to recognize the different strategies used for fitting an Asian actor into the traditionally white world of gay porn and how the terms of entry are determined by the perceived demands of an intended audience. Three tapes, each geared toward a specific erotic interest, illustrate these strategies.

Below the Belt (1985, directed by Philip St. John, California Dream Machine Productions), like most porn tapes, has an episodic structure. All the sequences involve the students and *sensei* of an all-male karate *dojo*. The authenticity of the setting is proclaimed with the opening shots of a gym full of *gi*-clad, serious-faced young men going through their weapons exercises. Each of the main actors is introduced in turn; with the exception of the teacher, who has dark hair, all fit into the current porn conventions of Aryan, blond, shaved, good looks.[15] Moreover, since Sum Yung Mahn is not even listed in the opening credits, we can surmise that this tape is not targeted to an audience with any particular erotic interest in Asian men. Most gay video porn exclusively uses white actors; those tapes having

16
Print porn is somewhat more racially integrated, as are the new safe sex tapes—by the Gay Men's Health Crisis, for example—produced in a political and pedagogical rather than a commercial context.

the least bit of racial integration are pitched to the speciality market through outlets such as International Wavelength.[16] This visual apartheid stems, I assume, from an erroneous perception that the sexual appetites of gay men are exclusive and unchangeable.

A Karate dojo offers a rich opportunity to introduce Asian actors. One might imagine it as the gay Orientalist's dream project. But given the intended audience for this video, the erotic appeal of the dojo, except for the costumes and a few misplaced props (Taiwanese and Korean flags for a Japanese art form?) are completely appropriated into a white world.

The tape's action occurs in a gym, in the students' apartments, and in a garden. The one scene with Sum Yung Mahn is a dream sequence. Two students, Robbie and Stevie, are sitting in a locker room. Robbie confesses that he has been having strange dreams about Greg, their teacher. Cut to the dream sequence, which is coded by clouds of green smoke. Robbie is wearing a red headband with black markings suggesting script (if indeed they belong to an Asian language, they are not the Japanese or Chinese characters that one would expect). He is trapped in an elaborate snare. Enter a character in a black *ninja* mask, wielding a *nanchaku*. Robbie narrates: "I knew this evil samurai would kill me." The masked figure is menacingly running the nanchaku chain under Robbie's genitals when Greg, the teacher, appears and disposes of him. Robbie explains to Stevie in the locker room: "I knew that I owed him my life, and I knew I had to please him [long pause] in any way that he wanted." During that pause we cut back to the dream. Amid more puffs of smoke, Greg, carrying a man in his arms, approaches a low platform. Although Greg's back is toward the camera, we can see that the man is wearing the red headband that identifies him as Robbie. As Greg lays him down, we see that Robbie has "turned Japanese"! It's Sum Yung Mahn.

Greg fucks Sum Yung Mahn, who is always face down.

Philip St. John, *Below the Belt*, California Dream Machine Productions, 1985.

Looking for My Penis

The scene constructs anal intercourse for the Asian Robbie as an act of submission, not of pleasure: unlike other scenes of anal intercourse in the tape, for example, there is no dubbed dialogue on the order of "Oh yeah . . . fuck me harder!" but merely ambiguous groans. Without coming, Greg leaves. A group of (white) men wearing Japanese outfits encircle the platform, and Asian Robbie, or "the Oriental boy," as he is listed in the final credits, turns to lie on his back. He sucks a cock, licks someone's balls. The other men come all over his body; he comes. The final shot of the sequence zooms in to a close-up of Sum Yung Mahn's headband, which dissolves to a similar close-up of Robbie wearing the same headband, emphasizing that the two actors represent one character.

We now cut back to the locker room. Robbie's story has made Stevie horny. He reaches into Robbie's pants, pulls out his penis, and sex follows. In his Asian manifestation, Robbie is fucked and sucks others off (Greek passive/French active/ bottom). His passivity is pronounced, and he is never shown other than prone. As a white man, his role is completely reversed: he is at first sucked off by Stevie, and then he fucks him (Greek active/French passive/top). Neither of Robbie's manifestations veers from his prescribed role.

To a greater extent than most other gay porn tapes, *Below the Belt* is directly about power. The hierarchical dojo setting is milked for its evocation of dominance and submission. With the exception of one very romantic sequence midway through the tape, most of the actors stick to their defined roles of top or bottom. Sex, especially anal sex, as punishment is a recurrent image. In this genre of gay pornography, the role-playing in the dream sequence is perfectly apt. What is significant, however, is how race figures into the equation. In a tape that appropriates emblems of Asian power (karate), the only place for a real Asian actor is as a caricature of passivity. Sum Yung Mahn does not portray an Asian, but rather the literalization of a metaphor, so that by being passive, Robbie actually becomes "Oriental." At a more practical level, the device of the dream also allows the producers to introduce an element of the mysterious, the exotic, without disrupting the racial status quo of the rest of the tape. Even in the dream sequence, Sum Yung Mahn is at the center of the frame as spectacle, having minimal physical involvement with the men around him. Although the sequence ends with his climax, he exists for the pleasure of others.

Richard Dyer, writing about gay porn, states that although the pleasure of anal sex (that is, of being anally fucked) is represented, the narrative is never organized around the desire to be fucked, but around the desire to ejaculate (whether or not following from anal intercourse). Thus, although at a level of public representation gay men may be thought of as deviant and disruptive of masculine norms because we assert the pleasure of being fucked and the eroticism of the anus, in our pornography this takes a back seat.[17]

Although Tom Waugh's amendment to this argument—that anal pleasure is represented in individual sequences[18]—also holds true for *Below the Belt,* as a whole the power of the penis and the pleasure of ejaculation are clearly the narrative's organizing principles. As with the vast majority of North American tapes featuring Asians, the problem is not the representation of anal pleasure per se, but rather that the narratives privilege the penis while always assigning the Asian the role of bottom; Asian and anus are conflated. In the case of Sum Yung Mahn, being fucked may well be his personal sexual preference. But the fact remains that there are very few occasions in North American video porn in which an Asian fucks a white man, so few, in fact, that International Wavelength promotes the tape *Studio X* (1986) with the blurb "Sum Yung Mahn makes history as the first Asian who fucks a non-Asian."[19]

Although I agree with Waugh that in gay as opposed to

17
Richard Dyer, "Coming to Terms," *Jump Cut,* no. 30 (March 1985), 28.

18
Tom Waugh, "Men's Pornography, Gay vs. Straight," *Jump Cut,* no. 30 (March 1985), 31.

19
International Wavelength News 2, no. 1 (January 1991).

20
Tom Waugh,
"Men's Pornography, Gay vs.
Straight," 33.

straight porn "the spectator's positions in relation to the representations are open and in flux,"[20] this observation applies only when all the participants are white. Race introduces another dimension that may serve to close down some of this mobility. This is not to suggest that the experience of gay men of color with this kind of sexual representation is the same as that of heterosexual women with regard to the gendered gaze of straight porn. For one thing, Asian gay men are men. We can therefore physically experience the pleasures depicted on the screen, since we too have erections and ejaculations and can experience anal penetration. A shifting identification may occur despite the racially defined roles, and most gay Asian men in North America are used to obtaining pleasure from all-white pornography. This, of course, goes hand in hand with many problems of self-image and sexual identity. Still, I have been struck by the unanimity with which gay Asian men I have met, from all over this continent as well as from Asia, immediately identify and resist these representations. Whenever I mention the topic of Asian actors in American porn, the first question I am asked is whether the Asian is simply shown getting fucked.

Asian Knights (1985, directed by Ed Sung, William Richhe Productions), the second tape I want to consider, has an Asian producer-director and a predominantly Asian cast. In its first scenario, two Asian men, Brad and Rick, are seeing a white psychiatrist because they are unable to have sex with each other:

Rick: We never have sex with other Asians. We usually have sex with Caucasian guys.

Counselor: Have you had the opportunity to have sex together?

Rick: Yes, a coupla times, but we never get going.

Homophobia, like other forms of oppression, is seldom dealt with in gay video porn. With the exception of safe sex tapes that attempt a rare blend of the pedagogical with the pornographic, social or political issues are not generally associated with the erotic. It is therefore unusual to see one of the favored discussion topics for gay Asian consciousness-raising groups employed as a sex fantasy in *Asian Knights*. The desexualized image of Asian men that I have described has seriously affected our relationships with one another, and often gay Asian men find it difficult to see each other beyond the terms of platonic friendship or competition, to consider other Asian men as lovers.

True to the conventions of porn, minimal counseling from the psychiatrist convinces Rick and Brad to shed their clothes. Immediately sprouting erections, they proceed to have sex. But what appears to be an assertion of gay Asian desire is quickly derailed. As Brad and Rick make love on the couch, the camera cross-cuts to the psychiatrist looking on from an armchair. The rhetoric of the editing suggests that we are observing the two Asian men from his point of view. Soon the white man takes off his clothes and joins in. He immediately takes up a position at the center of the action—and at the center of the frame. What appeared to be a "conversion fantasy" for gay Asian desire was merely a ruse. Brad and Rick's temporary mutual absorption really occurs to establish the superior sexual draw of the white psychiatrist, a stand-in for the white male viewer, who is the real sexual subject of the tape. And the question of Asian-Asian desire, though presented as the main narrative force of the sequence, is deflected, or rather reframed from a white perspective.

Sex between the two Asian men in this sequence can be related somewhat to heterosexual sex in some gay porn films, such as those produced by the Gage brothers. In *Heatstroke* (1982), for example, sex with a woman is used to establish the authenticity of the straight man who is about to be seduced into gay sex. It dramatizes the significance of the conversion from the sanctioned object of desire, underscoring the power of the gay man to incite desire in his socially defined superior. It is also tied up with the fantasies of (female) virginity and con-

Ed Sung, *Asian Knights*, William Richhe Productions, 1985.

Looking for My Penis

quest in Judeo-Christian and other patriarchal societies. The therapy-session sequence of *Asian Knights* also suggests parallels to representations of lesbians in straight porn, representations that are not meant to eroticize women loving women, but rather to titillate and empower the sexual ego of the heterosexual male viewer.

Asian Knights is organized to sell representations of Asians to white men. Unlike Sum Yung Mahn in *Below the Belt,* the actors are therefore more expressive and sexually assertive, as often the seducers as the seduced. But though the roles shift during the predominantly oral sex, the Asians remain passive in anal intercourse, except that they are now shown to want it! How much this assertion of agency represents a step forward remains a question.

Even in the one sequence of *Asian Knights* in which the Asian actor fucks the white man, the scenario privileges the pleasure of the white man over that of the Asian. The sequence begins with the Asian reading a magazine. When the white man (played by porn star Eric Stryker) returns home from a hard day at the office, the waiting Asian asks how his day went, undresses him (even taking off his socks), and proceeds to massage his back.[21] The Asian man acts the role of the mythologized geisha or "the good wife" as fantasized in the mail-order bride business. And, in fact, the "house boy" is one of the most persistent white fantasies about Asian men. The fantasy is also a reality in many Asian countries where economic imperialism gives foreigners, whatever their race, the pick of handsome men in financial need. The accompanying cultural imperialism grants status to those Asians with white lovers. White men who for various reasons, especially age, are deemed unattractive in their own countries, suddenly find themselves elevated and desired.

From the opening shot of painted lotus blossoms on a screen to the shot of a Japanese garden that separates the episodes, from the Chinese pop music to the chinoiserie in the

Ed Sung, *Asian Knights,* William Richhe Productions, 1985.

21
It seems to me that the undressing here is organized around the pleasure of the white man in being served. This is in contrast to the undressing scenes in, say, James Bond films, in which the narrative is organized around undressing as an act of revealing the woman's body, an indicator of sexual conquest.

Interestingly, the gay video porn from Japan and Thailand that I have seen has none of this Oriental coding. Asianness is not taken up as a sign but is taken for granted as a setting for the narrative.

apartment, there is a conscious attempt in *Asian Knights* to evoke a particular atmosphere.[22] Self-conscious "Oriental" signifiers are part and parcel of a colonial fantasy—and reality—that empowers one kind of gay man over another. Though I have known Asian men in dependent relations with older, wealthier white men, as an erotic fantasy the house boy scenario tends to work one way. I know of no scenarios of Asian men and white house boys. It is not the representation of the fantasy that offends, or even the fantasy itself, rather the uniformity with which these narratives reappear and the uncomfortable relationship they have to real social conditions.

International Skin (1985, directed by William Richhe, N'wayvo Richhe Productions), as its name suggests, features a Latino, a black man, Sum Yung Mahn, and a number of white actors. Unlike the other tapes I have discussed, there are no "Oriental" devices. And although Sum Yung Mahn and all the men of color are inevitably fucked (without reciprocating), there is mutual sexual engagement between the white and nonwhite characters.

William Richhe, International Skin, N'wayvo Richhe Productions, 1985.

In this tape Sum Yung Mahn is Brad, a film student making a movie for his class. Brad is the narrator, and the film begins with a self-reflexive "head and shoulders" shot of Sum Yung Mahn explaining the scenario. The film we are watching supposedly represents Brad's point of view. But here again the tape is not targeted to black, Asian, or Latino men; though Brad introduces all of these men as his friends, no two men of color ever meet on screen. Men of color are not invited to participate in the internationalism that is being sold, except through identification with white characters. This tape illustrates how an agenda of integration becomes problematic if it frames the issue solely in terms of black-white, Asian-white mixing: it perpetuates a system of white-centeredness.

The gay Asian viewer is not constructed as sexual subject in any of this work—not on the screen, not as a viewer. I may find Sum Yung Mahn attractive, I may desire his body, but I am always aware that he is not meant for me. I may lust after Eric Stryker and imagine myself as the Asian who is having sex with him, but the role the Asian plays in the scene with him is demeaning. It is not that there is anything wrong with the image of servitude per se, but rather that it is one of the few fantasy scenarios in which we figure, and we are always in the role of servant.

Are there then no pleasures for an Asian viewer? The answer to this question is extremely complex. There is first of all no essential Asian viewer. The race of the person viewing says nothing about how race figures in his or her own desires. Uniracial white representations in porn may not in themselves present a problem in addressing many gay Asian men's desires. But the issue is not simply that porn may deny pleasures to some gay Asian men. We also need to examine what role the pleasure of porn plays in securing a consensus about race and desirability that ultimately works to our disadvantage.

Though the sequences I have focused on in the preceding examples are those in which the discourses about Asian sexuality are most clearly articulated, they do not define the totality of depiction in these tapes. Much of the time the actors merely reproduce or attempt to reproduce the conventions of pornography. The fact that, with the exception of Sum Yung Mahn, they rarely succeed—because of their body type, because Midwestern-cowboy-porn dialect with Vietnamese intonation is just a bit incongruous, because they groan or gyrate just a bit too much—more than anything brings home the relative rigidity of the genre's codes. There is little seamlessness here. There are times, however, when the actors appear neither as simulated whites nor as symbolic others. There are several moments in *International Skin,* for example, in which the focus shifts from the genitals to hands caressing a body; these moments feel to me more "genuine." I do not mean this in the sense of an essential Asian sexuality, but rather a moment is captured in which the actor stops pretending. He does not stop acting, but he stops pretending to be a white porn star. I find myself focusing on moments like these, in which the racist ideology of the text seems to be temporarily suspended or rather eclipsed by the erotic power of the moment.

In "Pornography and the Doubleness of Sex for Women," Joanna Russ writes

Sex is ecstatic, autonomous and lovely for women. Sex is violent, dangerous and unpleasant for women. I don't mean a dichotomy (i.e., two kinds of women or even two kinds of sex) but rather a continuum in which no one's experience is wholly positive or negative.[23]

Gay Asian men are men and therefore not normally victims of the rape, incest, or other sexual harassment to which Russ is referring. However, there is a kind of doubleness, of ambivalence, in the way that Asian men experience contemporary North American gay communities. The "ghetto," the mainstream gay movement, can be a place of freedom and sexual identity. But it is also a site of racial, cultural, *and* sexual alienation sometimes more pronounced than that in straight society. For me sex is a source of pleasure, but also a site of humiliation and pain. Released from the social constraints against expressing overt racism in public, the intimacy of sex can provide my (non-Asian) partner an opening for letting me know my place—sometimes literally, as when after we come, he turns over and asks where I come from.[24] Most gay Asian men I know have similar experiences.

This is just one reality that differentiates the experiences and therefore the political priorities of gay Asians and, I think, other gay men of color from those of white men. For one thing we cannot afford to take a libertarian approach. Porn can be an

23
Joanna Russ, "Pornography and the Doubleness of Sex for Women," *Jump Cut*, no. 32 (April 1986), 39.

24
Though this is a common enough question in our postcolonial, urban environments, when asked of Asians it often reveals two agendas: first, the assumption that all Asians are newly arrived immigrants and, second, a fascination with difference and sameness. Although we (Asians) all supposedly look alike, there are specific characteristics and stereotypes associated with each particular ethnic group. The inability to tell us apart underlies the inscrutability attributed to Asians. This "inscrutability" took on sadly ridiculous proportions when during World War II the Chinese were issued badges so that white Canadians could distinguish them from "the enemy."

active agent in representing *and* reproducing a sex-race status quo. We cannot attain a healthy alliance without coming to terms with these differences.

The barriers that impede pornography from providing representations of Asian men that are erotic and politically palatable (as opposed to correct) are similar to those that inhibit the Asian documentary, the Asian feature, the Asian experimental film and videotape. We are seen as too peripheral, not commercially viable—not the general audience. *Looking for Langston* (1988),[25] which is the first film I have seen that affirms rather than appropriates the sexuality of black gay men, was produced under exceptional economic circumstances that freed it from the constraints of the marketplace.[26] Should we call for an independent gay Asian pornography? Perhaps I am, in a utopian sort of way, though I feel that the problems in North America's porn conventions are manifold and go beyond the question of race. There is such a limited vision of what constitutes the erotic.

In Canada, the major debate about race and representation has shifted from an emphasis on the image to a discussion of appropriation and control of production and distribution— who gets to produce the work. But as we have seen in the case of *Asian Knights,* the race of the producer is no automatic guarantee of "consciousness" about these issues or of a different product. Much depends on who is constructed as the audience for the work. In any case, it is not surprising that under capitalism, finding my penis may ultimately be a matter of dollars and cents.

25
Isaac Julien (director), *Looking for Langston* (United Kingdom: Sankofa Film and Video, 1988).

26
For more on the origins of the black film and video workshops in Britain, see Jim Pines, "The Cultural Context of Black British Cinema," in *Black-frames: Critical Perspectives on Black Independent Cinema,* ed. Mybe B. Cham and Claire Andrade-Watkins (Cambridge, Mass.: MIT Press, 1988), 26.

I would like to thank Tim McCaskell and Helen Lee for their ongoing criticism and comments, as well as Jeff Nunokawa and Douglas Crimp for their invaluable suggestions in converting the original spoken presentation into a written text. Finally, I would like to extend my gratitude to Bad Object-Choices for inviting me to participate in "How Do I Look?"

Discussion

Audience member	You made a comment about perceived distinctions between Chinese and Japanese sexuality. I have no idea what you mean.
Richard Fung	In the West, there are specific sexual ambiences associated with the different Asian nationalities, sometimes based on cultural artifacts, sometimes on mere conjecture. These discourses exist simultaneously, even though in conflict with, totalizing notions of "Oriental" sexuality. Japanese male sexuality has come to be identified with strength, virility, perhaps a certain kinkiness, as signified for example by the clothing and gestures in *Below the Belt*. Japanese sexuality is seen as more "potent" than Chinese sexuality, which is generally represented as more passive and languorous. At the same time, there is the cliché that "all Orientals look alike." So in this paradox of the invisibility of difference lies the fascination. If he can ascertain where I'm from, he feels that he knows what he can expect from me. In response to this query about "ethnic origins," a friend of mine answers, "Where would you like me to be from?" I like this response because it gently confronts the question while maintaining the erotic possibilities of the moment.
Simon Watney	I wanted to point out that the first film you showed, *Below the Belt,* presents us with a classic anxiety dream image. In it there is someone whose identity is that of a top man, but that identity is established in relation to a competing identity that allows him to enjoy sexual passivity, which is represented as a racial identity. It's as if he were in racial drag. I thought this film was extraordinary. Under what other conditions are Caucasian men invited to fantasize ourselves as racially other? And it seems to me that the only condition that would allow the visibility of that fantasy to be acted out in this way is the prior anxiety about a desired role, about top and bottom positions. This film is incredibly transparent and unconscious about how it construes or confuses sexual role-playing in relation to race. And the thrust

of it all seems to be the construction of the Asian body as a kind of conciliatory pseudoheterosexuality for the white "top," who has anus envy, as it were.

Fung I completely agree. The film says too much for its own good by making this racist agenda so clear.

Ray Navarro I think your presentation was really important, and it parallels research I'm doing with regard to the image of Latino men in gay male porn. I wondered if you might comment a bit more, however, about the class relations you find within this kind of work. For example, I've found a consistent theme running throughout gay white male porn of Latino men represented as either *campesino* or criminal. That is, it focuses less on body type—masculine, slight, or whatever—than on signifiers of class. It appears to be a class fantasy collapsed with a race fantasy, and in a way it parallels the actual power relations between the Latino stars and the producers and distributors, most of whom are white.

Fung There are ways in which your comments can also apply to Asians. Unlike whites and blacks, most Asians featured in gay erotica are younger men. Since youth generally implies less economic power, class-race hierarchies appear in most of the work. In the tapes I've been looking at, the occupations of the white actors are usually specified, while those of the Asians are not. The white actors are assigned fantasy appeal based on profession, whereas for the Asians, the sexual cachet of race is deemed sufficient. In *Asian Knights* there are also sequences in which the characters' lack of "work" carries connotations of the housewife or, more particularly, the house boy.

But there is at least one other way to look at this discrepancy. The lack of a specified occupation may be taken to suggest that the Asian actor is the subject of the fantasy, a surrogate for the Asian viewer, and therefore does not need to be coded with specific attributes.

Tom Waugh	I think your comparison of the way the Asian male body is used in gay white porn to the way lesbiansim is employed in heterosexual pornography is very interesting. You also suggested that racial markers in gay porn tend to close down its potential for openness and flux in identifications. Do you think we can take it further and say that racial markers in gay porn replicate, or function in the same way as, gender markers do in heterosexual pornography?
Fung	What, in fact, I intended to say with my comparison of the use of lesbians in heterosexual porn and that of Asian male bodies in white gay male porn was that they're similar but also very different. I think that certain comparisons of gender with race are appropriate, but there are also profound differences. The fact that Asian gay men are *men* means that, as viewers, our responses to this work are grounded in our gender and the way gender functions in this society. Lesbians are *women,* with all that that entails. I suspect that although most Asian gay men experience ambivalence with white gay porn, the issues for women in relation to heterosexual pornography are more fundamental.
Waugh	The same rigidity of roles seems to be present in most situations.
Fung	Yes, that's true. If you notice the way the Asian body is spoken of in Rushton's work, the terms he uses are otherwise used when speaking of women. But it is too easy to discredit these arguments. I have tried instead to show how Rushton's conclusions are commensurate with the assumptions everywhere present in education and popular thought.
Audience member	I'm going to play devil's advocate. Don't you think gay Asian men who are interested in watching gay porn involving Asian actors will get ahold of the racially unmarked porn that is produced in Thailand or Japan? And if your answer is yes, then why should a white producer of gay porn go to the trouble of mak-

ing tapes that cater to a relatively small gay Asian market? This is about dollars and cents. It seems obvious that the industry will cater to the white man's fantasy.

Fung   On the last point I partially agree. That's why I'm calling for an independent porn in which the gay Asian man is producer, actor, and intended viewer. I say this somewhat halfheartedly, because personally I am not very interested in producing porn, though I do want to continue working with sexually explicit material. But I also feel that one cannot assume, as the porn industry apparently does, that the desires of even white men are so fixed and exclusive.

Regarding the first part of your question, however, I must insist that Asian Americans and Asian Canadians are Americans and Canadians. I myself am a fourth-generation Trinidadian and have only a tenuous link with Chinese culture and aesthetics, except for what I have consciously searched after and learned. I purposely chose not to talk about Japanese or Thai productions because they come from cultural contexts about which I am incapable of commenting. In addition, the fact that porn from those countries is sometimes unmarked racially does not mean that it speaks to my experience or desires, my own culture of sexuality.

Isaac Julien   With regard to race representation or racial signifiers in the context of porn, your presentation elaborated a problem that came up in some of the safe sex tapes that were shown earlier. In them one could see a kind of trope that traces a circular pattern—a repetition that leads a black or Asian spectator to a specific realm of fantasy.

I wonder if you could talk a bit more about the role of fantasy, or the fantasy one sees in porn tapes produced predominantly by white producers. I see a fixing of different black subjects in recognizable stereotypes rather than a more dialectical representation of black identities, where a number of options or fantasy positions would be made available.

Fung	Your last film, *Looking for Langston*, is one of the few films I know of that has placed the sexuality of the black gay subject at its center. As I said earlier, my own work, especially *Chinese Characters* [1986], is more concerned with pulling apart the tropes you refer to than in constructing an alternative erotics. At the same time I feel that this latter task is imperative, and I hope that it is taken up more. It is in this context that I think the current attack on the National Endowment for the Arts and arts funding in the United States supports the racist status quo. If it succeeds, it effectively squelches the possibility of articulating counterhegemonic views of sexuality.

Just before I left Toronto, I attended an event called "Cum Talk," organized by two people from Gay Asians Toronto and from Khush, the group for South Asian lesbians and gay men. We looked at porn and talked about the images people had of us, the role of "bottom" that we are constantly cast in. Then we spoke of what actually happened when we had sex with white men. What became clear was that we don't play out that role and are very rarely asked to. So there is a discrepancy between the ideology of sexuality and its practice, between sexual representation and sexual reality.

Gregg Bordowitz When Jean Carlomusto and I began working on the porn project at Gay Men's Health Crisis, we had big ideas of challenging many of the roles and positionings involved in the dominant industry. But as I've worked more with porn, I find that it's really not an efficient arena in which to make such challenges. There is some room to question assumptions, but there are not many ways to challenge the codes of porn, except to question the conditions of production, which was an important point raised at the end of your talk. It seems to me that the only real way to picture more possibilities is, again, to create self-determining groups, make resources available for people of color and lesbians and other groups so that they can produce porn for themselves.

Fung	I only partly agree with you, because I think, so far as is possible, we have to take responsibility for the kinds of images we create, or re-create. *Asian Knights* had a Chinese producer, after all. But, yes, of course, the crucial thing is to activate more voices, which would establish the conditions for something else to happen. The liberal response to racism is that we need to integrate everyone—people should all become coffee-colored, or everyone should have sex with everyone else. But such an agenda doesn't often account for the specificity of our desires. I have seen very little porn produced from such an integrationist mentality that actually affirms my desire. It's so easy to find my fantasies appropriated for the pleasures of a white viewer. In that sense, porn is most useful for revealing relationships of power.
José Arroyo	You've been talking critically about a certain kind of colonial imagery. Isaac's film *Looking for Langston* contains not only a deconstruction of this imagery in its critique of the Mapplethorpe photographs, but also a new construction of black desire. What kind of strategies do you see for a similar reconstructing of erotic Asian imagery?
Fung	One of the first things that needs to be done is to construct Asians as viewing subjects. My first videotape, *Orientations* [1984], had that as a primary goal. I thought of Asians as sexual subjects, but also as viewing subjects to whom the work should be geared. Many of us, whether we're watching news or pornography or looking at advertising, see that the image or message is not really being directed at us. For example, the sexism and heterosexism of a disk jockey's attitudes become obvious when he or she says, "When you and your girlfriend go out tonight. . . ." Even though that's meant to address a general audience, it's clear that this audience is presumed not to have any women (not to mention lesbians!) in it. The general audience, as I analyze *him,* is white, male, heterosexual, middle-class, and center-right

politically. So we have to understand this presumption first, to see that only very specific people are being addressed.

When I make my videotapes, I know that I am addressing Asians. That means that I can take certain things for granted and introduce other things in a completely different context. But there are still other questions of audience. When we make outreach films directed at the straight community—the "general public"—in an effort to make lesbian and gay issues visible, we often sacrifice many of the themes that are important to how we express our sexualities: drag, issues of promiscuity, and so on. But when I made a tape for a gay audience, I talked about those same issues very differently. For one thing, I *talked* about those issues. And I tried to image them in ways that were very different from the way the dominant media image them. In *Orientations* I had one guy talk about park and washroom sex—about being a slut, basically—in a park at midday with front lighting. He talked very straightforwardly about it, which is only to say that there are many possibilities for doing this.

I think, however, that to talk about gay Asian desire is very difficult, because we need to swim through so much muck to get to it. It is very difficult (if even desirable) to do in purely positive terms, and I think it's necessary to do a lot of deconstruction along the way. I have no ready-made strategies; I feel it's a hit-and-miss sort of project.

Lei Chou I want to bring back the issue of class. One of the gay Asian stereotypes that you mentioned was the Asian house boy. The reality is that many of these people are immigrants: English is a second language for them, and they are thus economically disenfranchised through being socially and culturally displaced. So when you talk about finding the Asian penis in pornography, how will this project work for such people? Since pornography is basically white and middle-class, what kind of tool is it? Who really is your target audience?

Fung

If I understand your question correctly, you are asking about the prognosis for new and different representations within commercial porn. And I don't think the prognosis is very good: changes will probably happen very slowly. At the same time, I think that pornography is an especially important site of struggle precisely for those Asians who are, as you say, economically and socially at a disadvantage. For those who are most isolated, whether in families or rural areas, print pornography is often the first introduction to gay sexuality—before, for example, the gay and lesbian press or gay Asian support groups. But this porn provides mixed messages: it affirms gay identity articulated almost exclusively as white. Whether we like it or not, mainstream gay porn is more available to most gay Asian men than any independent work you or I might produce. That is why pornography is a subject of such concern for me.

Skin Head Sex Thing
Racial Difference and the Homoerotic Imaginary

Kobena Mercer

In this article I want to explore the experience of aesthetic ambivalence in visual representations of the black male nude. The photographs of Robert Mapplethorpe provide a salient point of entry into this complex "structure of feeling" as they embody such ambivalence experienced at its most intense.[1]

1
References are made primarily to *Black Males*, with introduction by Edmund White (Amsterdam: Gallerie Jurka, 1982) and *The Black Book*, with foreword by Ntozake Shange (New York: St. Martin's Press, 1986).

My interest in this aspect of Mapplethorpe's work began in 1982, when a friend lent me his copy of *Black Males*. It circulated between us as a kind of illicit object of desire, albeit a highly problematic one. We were fascinated by the beautiful bodies, as we went over the repertoire of images again and again, drawn in by the desire to look and enjoy what was given to be seen. We wanted to look, but we didn't always find what we wanted to see: we were shocked and disturbed by the racial discourse of the imagery, and above all, we were angered by the aesthetic equation that reduced these black male bodies to abstract visual "things," silenced in their own right as subjects, serving only to enhance the name and reputation of the author in the rarefied world of art photography. But still we were stuck, unable to make sense of our own implication in the emotions brought into play by Mapplethorpe's imaginary.

I've chosen to situate the issue of ambivalence in relation to these experiences because I am now involved in a partial revision of arguments made in an earlier reading of Mapplethorpe's work.[2] This revision arises not because those

2
Kobena Mercer, "Imaging the Black Man's Sex," in *Photography/Politics: Two*, ed. Pat Holland, Jo Spence, and Simon Watney (London: Comedia/Methuen, 1987), 61–69.

arguments were wrong, but because I've changed my mind, or rather I should say that I still can't make up my mind about Mapplethorpe. In returning to my earlier essay I want to suggest an approach to ambivalence not as something that occurs "inside" the text (as if cultural texts were hermetically sealed or self-sufficient), but as something that is experienced across the relations between authors, texts, and readers, relations that are always contingent, context-bound, and historically specific.

Posing the problem of ambivalence and undecidability in this way not only underlines the role of the reader, but also draws attention to the important, and equally undecidable, role of context in determining the range of different readings that can be produced from the same text. In this respect, it is impossible to ignore the crucial changes in context that frame the readings currently negotiated around Mapplethorpe and his work. Mapplethorpe's death in 1989 from AIDS, a major retrospective of his work at the Whitney Museum in New York, the political "controversy" over federal arts policy initiated by the fundamentalist Right in response to a second Mapplethorpe exhibition organized by the Institute of Contemporary Art in Philadelphia—these events have irrevocably altered the context in which we perceive, argue about, and evaluate Mapplethorpe's most explicitly homoerotic work.

The context has also changed as a result of another set of contemporary developments: the emergence of new aesthetic practices among black lesbian and gay artists in Britain and the United States. Across a range of media, such work problematizes earlier conceptions of identity in black cultural practices. This is accomplished by entering into the ambivalent and overdetermined spaces where race, class, gender, sexuality, and ethnicity intersect in the social construction and lived experiences of individual and collective subjectivities. Such developments demand acknowledgment of the historical contingency of context and in turn raise significant questions about the universalist character of some of the grand aesthetic and political claims once made in the name of cultural theory. Beginning with a summary of my earlier argument, I want to identify some of the uses and limitations of psychoanalytic concepts in cultural theory before mapping a more historical trajectory within which to examine the constitutive ambivalence of the identifications we actually inhabit in living with difference.

Revising　　　　The overriding theme of my earlier reading of Mapplethorpe's photographs was that they inscribe a process of objectification in which individual black male bodies are aestheticized and eroticized as objects of the gaze. Framed within the artistic conventions of the nude, the bodies are sculpted and shaped into artifacts that offer an erotic source of pleasure in the act of looking. Insofar as what is represented in the pictorial space of the photograph is a "look," or a certain "way of looking," the pictures say more about the white male subject behind the camera than they do about the black men whose beautiful bodies we see depicted. This is because the invisible or absent subject is the actual agent of the look, at the center and in control of the apparatus of representation, the I/eye at the imaginary origin of the perspective that marks out the empty space to which the viewer is invited as spectator. This argument was based on a formal analysis of the codes and conventions brought to bear on the pictorial space of the photographs, and, equally important, on an analogy with feminist analyses of the erotic objectification of the image of women in Western traditions of visual representation.

Three formal conventions interweave across the photographic text to organize and direct the viewer's gaze into its pictorial space: a sculptural code, concerning the posing and posture of the body in the studio enclosure; a code of portraiture concentrated on the face; and a code of lighting and framing, fragmenting bodies in textured formal abstractions. All of these help to construct the *mise en scène* of fantasy and desire that structures the spectator's disposition toward the image. As all references to a social or historical context are effaced by the cool distance of the detached gaze, the text enables the projec-

Robert Mapplethorpe, *Jimmy Freeman,* **1982.**
The Estate of Robert Mapplethorpe.

Robert Mapplethorpe, *Roedel Middleton*, 1986.

The Estate of Robert Mapplethorpe.

Skin Head Sex Thing

tion of a fantasy that saturates the black male body in sexual predicates.

These codes draw from aspects of Mapplethorpe's oeuvre as a whole and have become the signs by which we recognize his authorial signature. Their specific combination, moreover, is punctuated by the technical perfection—especially marked in the printing process—that also distinguishes Mapplethorpe's presence as an author. Considering the way in which the glossy allure of the photographic print becomes consubstantial with the shiny texture of black skin, I argued that a significant element in the pleasures the photographs make available consists in the fetishism they bring into play. Such fetishism not only eroticizes the visible difference the black male nude embodies, it also lubricates the ideological reproduction of racial otherness as the fascination of the image articulates a fantasy of power and mastery over the other.

Before introducing a revision of this view of racial fetishism in Mapplethorpe's photographs, I want to emphasize its dependence on the framework of feminist theory initially developed in relation to cinematic representation by Laura Mulvey.[3] Crudely put, Mulvey showed that men look and women are looked at. The position of "woman" in the dominant regimes of visual representation says little or nothing about the historical experiences of women as such, because the female subject functions predominantly as a mirror image of what the masculine subject wants to see. The visual depiction of women in the mise en scène of heterosexual desire serves to stabilize and reproduce the narcissistic scenario of a phallocentric fantasy in which the omnipotent male gaze sees but is never seen. What is important about this framework of analysis is the way it reveals the symbolic relations of power and subordination at work in the binary relations that structure dominant codes and conventions of visual representations of the body. The field of visibility is thus organized by the subject-object dichotomy that associ-

3
Laura Mulvey, "Visual Pleasure and Narrative Cinema," in *Feminism and Film Theory*, ed. Constance Penley (New York: Routledge, 1988), 57–68.

ates masculinity with the activity of looking and femininity with the subordinate, passive role of being that which is looked at.

In extrapolating such terms to Mapplethorpe's black nudes, I suggested that because both artist and models are male, a tension arises that transfers the frisson of difference to the metaphorically polarized terms of racial identity. The black-white duality overdetermines the subject-object dichotomy of seeing and being seen. This metaphorical transfer underlines the erotic investment of the gaze in the most visible element of racial difference—the fetishization of black skin. The dynamics of this tension are apparently stabilized within the pictorial space of the photographs by the ironic appropriation of commonplace stereotypes—the black man as athlete, as savage, as mugger. These stereotypes in turn serve to regulate and fix the representational presence of the black subject, who is thereby "put into his place" by the power of Mapplethorpe's gaze.

The formal work of the codes essentializes each model into the homogenized embodiment of an ideal type. This logic of typification in dominant regimes of racial representation has been emphasized by Homi Bhabha, who argues that "an important feature of colonial discourse is its dependence on the concept of 'fixity' in the ideological construction of otherness."[4] The scopic fixation on black skin thus implies a kind of "negrophilia," an aesthetic idealization and eroticized investment in the racial other that inverts and reverses the binary axis of the fears and anxieties invested in or projected onto the other in "negrophobia." Both positions, whether they devalue or overvalue the signs of racial difference, inhabit the representational space of what Bhabha calls colonial fantasy. Although I would now qualify the theoretical analogies on which this analysis of Mapplethorpe's work was based, I would still want to defend the terms of a psychoanalytic reading of racial fetishism, a fetishism that can be most tangibly grasped in a photograph such as *Man in a Polyester Suit* (1980).

4
Homi Bhabha, "The Other Question: The Stereotype and Colonial Discourse," *Screen* 24, no. 6 (November–December 1983), 18–36.

Skin Head Sex Thing

Robert Mapplethorpe, *Man in Polyester Suit,* 1980.
The Estate of Robert Mapplethorpe.

Mercer

The scale and framing of this picture emphasizes the sheer size of the black dick. Apart from the hands, the penis and the penis alone identifies the model as a black man. As Frantz Fanon said, diagnosing the figure of "the Negro" in the fantasies of his white psychiatric patients, "One is no longer aware of the Negro, but only of a penis: the Negro is eclipsed. He is turned into a penis. He *is* a penis."[5] The element of scale thus summons up one of the deepest mythological fears and anxieties in the racist imagination, namely that all black men have huge willies. In the fantasmatic space of the supremacist imaginary, the big black phallus is a threat not only to the white master (who shrinks in impotence from the thought that the subordinate black male is more potent and sexually powerful than he), but also to civilization itself, since the "bad object" represents a danger to white womanhood and therefore miscegenation and racial degeneration.

The binarisms of classical racial discourse are emphasized in Mapplethorpe's photograph by the jokey irony of the contrast between the black man's private parts and the public respectability signified by the business suit. The oppositions exposed/hidden and denuded/clothed play upon the binary oppositions nature/culture and savage/civilized to bring about a condensation of libidinal investment, fear, and wish-fulfillment in the fantasmatic presence of the other. The binarisms repeat the assumption that sex is the essential "nature" of black masculinity, while the cheap, tacky polyester suit confirms the black man's failure to gain access to "culture." The camouflage of respectability cannot conceal the fact that, in essence, he originates, like his prick, from somewhere anterior to civilization. What is dramatized in the picture is the splitting of levels of belief, which Freud regarded as the key feature of the logic of disavowal in fetishism.[6] Hence, the implication: "*I know* it's not true that all black men have big penises, *but still,* in my photographs they do."

5
Frantz Fanon, *Black Skin, White Masks* (London: Paladin, 1970), 120.

6
Sigmund Freud, "Fetishism" (1927), *The Standard Edition of the Complete Psychological Works of Sigmund Freud,* ed. James Strachey (London: Hogarth Press, 1953–74), vol. 21 (1961), 147–57.

Skin Head Sex Thing

It is precisely at this point, however, that the concept of fetishism threatens to conceal more than it reveals about the ambivalence the spectator experiences in relation to the "shock effect" of Mapplethorpe's work. Freud saw the castration anxiety in the little boy's shock at discovering the absence of a penis in the little girl (acknowledged and disavowed in the fetish) as constitutive of sexual difference. The clinical pathology or perversion of the fetishist, like a neurotic symptom, unravels for classical psychoanalysis the "normal" developmental path of oedipal heterosexual identity: it is the point at which the norm is rendered visible by the pathological. The concept of fetishism was profoundly enabling for feminist film theory because it uncovered the logic of substitution at work in all regimes of representation, which make present for the subject what is absent in the real. But although analogies facilitate cognitive connections with important cultural and political implications, there is also the risk that they repress and flatten out the messy spaces in between. As Jane Gaines has pointed out concerning feminist film theory, the inadvertent reproduction of the heterosexual presumption in the orthodox theorization of sexual difference also assumed a homogeneous racial and ethnic context, with the result that racial and ethnic differences were erased from or marginalized within the analysis.[7] Analogies between race and gender in representation reveal similar ideological patterns of objectification, exclusion, and "othering." In Mapplethorpe's nudes, however, there is a subversive homoerotic dimension in the substitution of the black male subject for the traditional female archetype. This subversive dimension was underplayed in my earlier analysis: my use of the theoretical analogy minimized the homosexual specificity of Mapplethorpe's eroticism, which rubs against the grain of the generic high art status of the traditional female nude.

To pose the problem in another way, one could approach the issue of ambivalence by simply asking: do photographs like

7
Jane Gaines, "White Privilege and Looking Relations: Race and Gender in Feminist Film Theory," *Screen* 29, no. 4 (Autumn 1988), 12–27.

Man in a Polyester Suit reinscribe the fixed beliefs of racist ideology, or do they problematize them by foregrounding the intersections of difference where race and gender cut across the representation of sexuality? An unequivocal answer is impossible or undecidable, it seems to me, because the image throws the question back onto the spectator, for whom it is experienced precisely as the shock effect. What is at issue is not primarily whether the question can be decided by appealing to authorial intentions, but rather the equally important question of the role of the reader and how he or she attributes intentionality to the author. The elision of homoerotic specificity in my earlier reading thus refracts an ambivalence not so much on the part of Mapplethorpe the author, or on the part of the text, but on my part as a reader. More specifically, it refracted the ambivalent "structure of feeling" that I inhabit as a black gay male reader in relation to the text. Indeed, I've only recently become aware of the logical slippage in my earlier reading, which assumed an equivalence between Mapplethorpe as the individual agent of the image and the empty, anonymous, and impersonal ideological category I described as "the white male subject" to which the spectator is interpellated. Paradoxically, this conflation undermined the very distinction between author-function and ideological subject-position that I drew from Michel Foucault's antinaturalist account of authorship.[8]

8
Michel Foucault, "What Is an Author?" in *Language, Counter-Memory, Practice,* ed. Donald F. Bouchard (Ithaca, N.Y.: Cornell University Press, 1977), 113–38; see also Roland Barthes, "The Death of the Author," in *Image-Music-Text* (New York: Hill and Wang, 1977), 142–48.

In retrospect I feel this logical flaw arose as a result of my own ambivalent positioning as a black gay spectator. To call something fetishistic implies a negative judgment, to say the least. I want to take back the unavoidably moralistic connotation of the term, because I think what was at issue in the rhetoric of my previous argument was the encoding of an ambivalent structure of feeling, in which anger and envy divided the identifications that placed me somewhere always already inside the text. On the one hand, I emphasized objectification because I felt identified with the black males in the field of vision, an identi-

Skin Head Sex Thing

fication with the other that might best be described in Fanon's terms as a feeling that "I am laid bare. I am overdetermined from without. I am a slave not of the 'idea' that others have of me but of my own appearance. I am being dissected under white eyes. I am *fixed*. . . . Look, it's a Negro."[9] But on the other hand, and more difficult to disclose, I was also implicated in the fantasy scenario as a gay subject. That is to say, I was identified with the author insofar as the objectified black male was also an image of the object chosen by my own fantasies and erotic investments. Thus, sharing the same desire to look as the author-agent of the gaze, I would actually occupy the position that I said was that of the "white male subject."

I now wonder whether the anger in that earlier reading was not also the expression and projection of a certain envy. Was it not, in this sense, an effect of a homosexual identification on the basis of a similar object-choice that invoked an aggressive rivalry over the same unattainable object of desire, depicted and represented in the visual field of the other? According to Jacques Lacan, the mirror-stage constitutes the "I" in an alienated relation to its own image, as the image of the infant's body is "unified" by the prior investment that comes from the look of the mother, always already in the field of the other.[10] In this sense, the element of aggressivity involved in textual analysis—the act of taking things apart—might merely have concealed my own narcissistic participation in the pleasures of Mapplethorpe's texts. Taking the two elements together, I would say that my ambivalent positioning as a black gay male reader stemmed from the way in which I inhabited two contradictory identifications at one and the same time. Insofar as the anger and envy were an effect of my identifications with both object and subject of the gaze, the rhetorical closure of my earlier reading simply displaced the ambivalence onto the text by attributing it to the author.

9
Fanon, *Black Skin, White Masks*, 82.

10
Jacques Lacan, "The mirror stage as formative of the function of the I," in *Ecrits: A Selection* (London: Tavistock, 1977), 1–7.

Rereading

If this brings us to the threshold of the kind of ambivalence that is historically specific to the context, positions, and experiences of the reader, it also demonstrates the radically polyvocal quality of Mapplethorpe's photographs and the way in which contradictory readings can be derived from the same body of work. I want to suggest, therefore, an alternative reading that demonstrates this textual reversibility by revising the assumption that fetishism is necessarily a bad thing.

By making a 180-degree turn, I want to suggest that the articulation of ambivalence in Mapplethorpe's work can be seen as a subversive deconstruction of the hidden racial and gendered axioms of the nude in dominant traditions of representation. This alternative reading also arises out of a reconsideration of poststructuralist theories of authorship. Although Romantic notions of authorial creativity cannot be returned to the central role they once played in criticism and interpretation, the question of agency in cultural practices that contest the canon and its cultural dominance suggests that it really *does* matter who is speaking.

The question of enunciation—who is speaking, who is spoken to, what codes do they share to communicate?—implies a whole range of important political issues about who is empowered and who is disempowered in the representation of difference. It is enunciation that circumscribes the marginalized positions of subjects historically misrepresented or underrepresented in dominant systems of representation. To be marginalized is to have no place from which to speak, since the subject positioned in the margins is silenced and invisible. The contestation of marginality in black, gay, and feminist politics thus inevitably brings the issue of authorship back into play, not as the centered origin that determines or guarantees the aesthetic and political value of a text, but as a question about agency in the cultural struggle to "find a voice" and "give voice" to subordinate experiences, identities, and subjectivities. A rela-

tivization of authoritative poststructuralist claims about decentering the subject means making sense of the biographical
and autobiographical dimension of the context-bound relations
between authors, texts, and readers without falling back on liberal humanist or empiricist common sense. Quite specifically,
the "death of the author" thesis demands revision because the
death of the author in *our* case inevitably makes a difference to
the kinds of readings we make.

Comments by Mapplethorpe, and by some of the black
models with whom he collaborated, offer a perspective on the
questions of authorship, identification, and enunciation. The first
of these concerns the specificity of Mapplethorpe's authorial
identity as a gay artist and the importance of a metropolitan gay
male culture as a context for the homoeroticism of the black
male nudes.

In a British Broadcasting Corporation documentary in
1988, Lynne Franks pointed out that Mapplethorpe's work is remarkable for its absence of voyeurism. A brief comparison with
the avowedly heterosexual scenario in the work of photographers such as Edward Weston and Helmut Newton would
suggest similar aesthetic conventions at the level of visual fetishization; but it would also highlight the significant differences that
arise in Mapplethorpe's homoeroticism. Under Mapplethorpe's
authorial gaze there is a tension within the cool distance between subject and object. The gaze certainly involves an element of erotic objectification, but like a point-of-view shot in
gay male pornography, it is reversible. The gendered hierarchy
of seeing/being seen is not so rigidly coded in homoerotic representations, since sexual sameness liquidates the associative
opposition between active subject and passive object. This element of reversibility at the level of the gaze is marked elsewhere in Mapplethorpe's oeuvre, most notably in the numerous
self-portraits, including the one of him with a bullwhip up his
bum, in which the artist posits himself as the object of the look.

In relation to the black male nudes and the s&m pictures that preceded them, this reversibility creates an ambivalent distance measured by the direct look of the models, which is another salient feature of gay male pornography. In effect, Mapplethorpe implicates himself in his field of vision by a kind of participatory observation, an ironic ethnography whose descriptive clarity suggests a reversible relation of equivalence, or identification, between the author and the social actors whose world is described. In this view, Mapplethorpe's homoeroticism can be read as a form of stylized reportage that documented aspects of the urban gay subcultural milieu of the 1970s. One can reread Mapplethorpe's homoerotica as a kind of photographic documentary of a world that has profoundly changed as a result of AIDS. This reinterpretation is something Mapplethorpe drew attention to in the BBC television interview:

I was part of it. And that's where most of the photographers who move in that direction are at a disadvantage, in that they're not part of it. They're voyeurs moving in. With me it was quite different. Often I had experienced some of those experiences which I later recorded, myself, firsthand, without a camera. . . . It was a certain moment, and I was in a perfect situation in that most of the people in the photographs were friends of mine and they trusted me. I felt almost an obligation to record those things. It was an obligation for me to do it, to make images that nobody's seen before and to do it in a way that's *aesthetic*.

In this respect, especially in the light of the moral and ethical emphasis by which Mapplethorpe locates himself as a member of an elective community, it is important to acknowledge the ambivalence of authorial motivation suggested in his rationale for the black male nude studies:

At some point I started photographing black men. It was an area that hadn't been explored intensively. If you went through the history of nude male photography, there were very few black subjects. I found that I could take pictures of black men that were so subtle, and the form was so photographical.

On the one hand, this could be interpreted as the discovery and conquest of "virgin territory" in the field of art history; but alternatively, Mapplethorpe's acknowledgment of the exclusion and absence of the black subject from the canonical realm of the fine art nude can be interpreted as the elementary starting point of an implicit critique of racism and ethnocentrism in Western aesthetics.

Once we consider Mapplethorpe's own marginality as a gay artist, placed in a subordinate relation to the canonical tradition of the nude, his implicitly critical position on the presence/absence of the race in dominant regimes of representation enables a reappraisal of the intersubjective collaboration between artist and model. Whereas my previous reading emphasized the apparent inequality between the famous, author-named white artist and the anonymous and interchangeable black models, the biographical dimension reveals an important element of mutuality. In a magazine interview that appeared after his death in 1989, Mapplethorpe's comments about the models suggest an intersubjective relation based on a shared social identity: "Most of the blacks don't have health insurance and therefore can't afford AZT. They all died quickly, the blacks. If I go through my *Black Book,* half of them are dead."[11] In his mourning, there is something horribly accurate about the truism that death is the great leveler, because his pictures have now become *memento mori,* documentary evidence of a style of life and a sexual ethics in the metropolitan gay culture of the 1970s and early 1980s that no longer exist in the way they used to. As a contribution to the historical formation of urban gay culture, Mapplethorpe's homoeroticism is invested with memory, with the intense emotional residue Barthes described when he wrote about the photographs of his mother.[12]

The element of mutual identification between artist and models undermines the view that the relation was necessarily

11
"The Long Goodbye," interview by Dominick Dunne, *Blitz,* London, May 1989, 67–68.

12
Roland Barthes, *Camera Lucida* (New York: Hill and Wang, 1981).

exploitive simply because it was interracial. Comments by Ken Moody, one of the models in the *Black Book,* suggest a degree of reciprocity. When asked in the BBC television interview whether he recognized himself in Mapplethorpe's pictures, he said, "Not always, not most of the time. . . . When I look at it as me, and not just a piece of art, I think I look like a freak. I don't find that person in the photograph necessarily attractive, and it's not something I would like to own." The alienation of not even owning your own image might be taken as evidence of objectification, of being reduced to a "piece of art"; but at the same time Moody rejects the view that it was an unequivocal relation, suggesting instead a reciprocal gift relationship that further underlines the theme of mutuality:

I don't honestly think of it as exploitation. . . . It's almost as if— and this is the conclusion I've come to now, because I really haven't thought about it up to now—it's almost as if he wants to give a gift to this particular group. He wants to create something very beautiful and give it to them. . . . And he is actually very giving.

I don't want to over- or underinterpret such evidence, but I do think this biographical dimension to the issues of authorship and enunciation enables a rereading of the textual ambivalence in Mapplethorpe's artistic practice. Taking the question of identification into account, as that which inscribes ambivalent relations of mutuality and reversibility in the gaze, enables a reconsideration of the cultural politics of Mapplethorpe's black male nudes.

Once grounded in the context of contemporary urban gay male culture in the United States, the shocking modernism that informs the ironic juxtaposition of elements drawn from the repository of high culture—where the nude is indeed one of the most valued genres in Western art history—can be read as a subversive recoding of the normative aesthetic ideal. In this view, it becomes possible to reverse the reading of racial fetish-

Robert Mapplethorpe, *Ken Moody*, 1983.
The Estate of Robert Mapplethorpe.

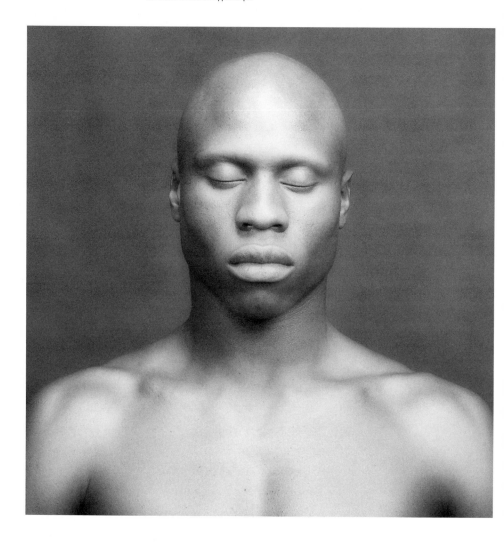

ism in Mapplethorpe's work, not as a repetition of racist fantasies but as a deconstructive strategy that lays bare psychic and
social relations of ambivalence in the representation of race and
sexuality. This deconstructive aspect of his homoeroticism is experienced, at the level of audience reception, as the disturbing
shock effect.

The Eurocentric character of the liberal humanist values
invested in classical Greek sculpture as the originary model of
human beauty in Western aesthetics is paradoxically revealed by
the promiscuous intertextuality whereby the filthy and degraded form of the commonplace racist stereotype is brought
into the domain of aesthetic purity circumscribed by the privileged place of the fine art nude. This doubling within the pictorial space of Mapplethorpe's black nudes does not reproduce
either term of the binary relation between "high culture" and
"low culture" as it is: it radically decenters and destabilizes the
hierarchy of racial and sexual difference in dominant systems of
representation by folding the two together within the same
frame. It is this ambivalent intermixing of textual references,
achieved through the appropriation and articulation of elements
from the "purified" realm of the transcendental aesthetic ideal
and from the debased and "polluted" world of the commonplace racist stereotype, that disturbs the fixed positioning of the
spectator. One might say that what is staged in Mapplethorpe's
black male nudes is the return of the repressed in the ethnocentric imaginary. The psychic-social boundary that separates
"high culture" and "low culture" is transgressed, crossed and
disrupted precisely by the superimposition of two ways of seeing, which thus throws the spectator into uncertainty and undecidability, precisely the experience of ambivalence as a structure
of feeling in which one's subject-position is called into question.

In my previous argument, I suggested that the regulative
function of the stereotype had the upper hand, as it were, and
helped to "fix" the spectator in the ideological subject-position

of the "white male subject." Now I'm not so sure. Once we recognize the historical and political specificity of Mapplethorpe's practice as a contemporary gay artist, the aesthetic irony that informs the juxtaposition of elements in his work can be seen as the trace of a subversive strategy that disrupts the stability of the binary oppositions into which difference is coded. In social, economic, and political terms, black men in the United States constitute one of the "lowest" social classes: disenfranchised, disadvantaged, and disempowered as a distinct collective subject in the late capitalist underclass. Yet in Mapplethorpe's photographs, men who in all probability came from this class are elevated onto the pedestal of the transcendental Western aesthetic ideal. Far from reinforcing the fixed beliefs of the white supremacist imaginary, such a deconstructive move begins to undermine the foundational myths of the pedestal itself.

The subaltern black social subject, who was historically excluded from dominant regimes of representation—"invisible men" in Ralph Ellison's phrase—is made visible within the codes and conventions of the dominant culture whose ethnocentrism is thereby exposed as a result. The mythological figure of "the Negro," who was always excluded from the good, the true, and the beautiful in Western aesthetics on account of his otherness, comes to embody the image of physical perfection and aesthetic idealization in which, in the canonical figure of the nude, Western culture constructed its own self-image. Far from confirming the hegemonic white, heterosexual subject in his centered position of mastery and power, the deconstructive aspects of Mapplethorpe's black male nude photographs loosen up and unfix the common-sense sensibilities of the spectator, who thereby experiences the shock effect precisely as the affective displacement of given ideological subject-positions.

To shock was always the key verb of the avant-garde in modernist art history. In Mapplethorpe's work, the shock effected by the promiscuous textual intercourse between ele-

ments drawn from opposite ends of the hierarchy of cultural value decenters and destabilizes the ideological fixity of the spectator. In this sense, his work begins to reveal the political unconscious of white ethnicity. It lays bare the constitutive ambivalence that structures whiteness as a cultural identity whose hegemony lies, as Richard Dyer suggests, precisely in its "invisibility."[13]

The splitting of the subject in the construction of white identity, entailed in the affirmation and denial of racial difference in Western humanism, is traced in racist perception. Blacks are looked down upon and despised as worthless, ugly, and ultimately unhuman creatures. But in the blink of an eye, whites look up to and revere the black body, lost in awe and envy as the black subject is idolized as the embodiment of the whites' ideal. This schism in white subjectivity is replayed daily in the different ways black men become visible on the front and back

13
Richard Dyer,
"White," *Screen* 29, no. 4
(Autumn 1988), 44–64.

pages of tabloid newspapers, seen as undesirable in one frame—the mugger, the terrorist, the rapist—and highly desirable in the other—the athlete, the sports hero, the entertainer. Mapplethorpe undercuts this conventional separation to show the recto-verso relation between these contradictory "ways of seeing" as constitutive aspects of white identity. Like a mark that is legible on both sides of a sheet of paper, Mapplethorpe's aesthetic strategy places the splitting in white subjectivity under erasure: it is crossed out but still visible. In this sense, the anxieties aroused in the exhibition history of Mapplethorpe's homoerotica not only demonstrate the disturbance and decentering of dominant versions of white identity, but also confront whiteness with the otherness that enables it to be constituted as an identity as such.

In suggesting that this ambivalent racial fetishization of difference actually enables a potential deconstruction of whiteness, I think Mapplethorpe's use of irony can be recontextualized in relation to Pop Art practices of the 1960s. The undecidable question that is thrown back on the spectator—do the images undermine or reinforce racial stereotypes?—can be compared to the highly ambivalent aura of fetishism that frames the female body in the paintings of Allen Jones. Considering the issues of sexism and misogyny at stake, Laura Mulvey's reading, from 1972, suggests a contextual approach to the political analysis of fetishism's "shocking" undecidability:

By revealing the way in which fetishistic images pervade not just specialist publications but the whole of mass media, Allen Jones throws a new light on woman as spectacle. Women are constantly confronted with their own image . . . yet, in a real sense, women are not there at all. The parade has nothing to do with woman, everything to do with man. The true exhibit is always the phallus. . . . The time has come for us to take over the show and exhibit our own fears and desires.[14]

This reading has a salutary resonance in the renewal of de-

14
Laura Mulvey, "Fears, Fantasies and the Male Unconscious, or 'You don't know what is happening, do you, Mr Jones?'" in *Visual and other Pleasures* (London: Macmillan, 1989), 13.

bates on black aesthetics insofar as contemporary practices that contest the marginality of the black subject in dominant regimes of representation have gone beyond the unhelpful binarism of so-called positive and negative images. We are now more aware of the identities, fantasies, and desires that are coerced, simplified, and reduced by the rhetorical closure that flows from that kind of critique. But Mulvey's reading also entails a clarification of what we need from theory as black artists and intellectuals. The critique of stereotypes was crucial in the women's and gay movements of the 1960s and 1970s, just as it was in the black movements that produced aesthetic-political performative statements such as Black Is Beautiful. As the various movements have fragmented politically, however, their combined and uneven development suggests that analogies across race, gender, and sexuality may be useful only insofar as we historicize them and what they make possible. Appropriations of psychoanalytic theory arose at a turning point in the cultural politics of feminism; in thinking about the enabling possibilities this has opened up for the study of black representation, I feel we also need to acknowledge the other side of ambivalence in contemporary cultural struggles, the dark side of the political predicament that ambivalence engenders.

In contrast to the claims of academic deconstruction, the moment of undecidability is rarely experienced as a purely textual event; rather it is the point where politics and the contestation of power are felt to be at their most intense. According to V. N. Volosinov, the social multiaccentuality of the ideological sign has an "inner dialectical quality [that] comes out only in times of social crises or revolutionary changes," because "in ordinary circumstances . . . an established dominant ideology . . . always tries, as it were, to stabilize the dialectical flux."[15] Indeterminacy means that multiaccentual or polyvalent signs have no necessary belonging and can be articulated and appropriated into the political discourse of the Right as easily as they can into

15
V. N. Volosinov,
Marxism and the Philoso-
phy of Language, Cam-
bridge, Mass.: Harvard
University Press, 1973), 24.

Skin Head Sex Thing

that of the Left. Antagonistic efforts to fix the multiple connotations arising from the ambivalence of the key signs of ideological struggle demonstrate what in Gramsci's terms would be
described as a war of position whose outcome is *never* guaran-
teed in advance one way or the other.

We have seen how, despite their emancipatory objectives,
certain radical feminist antipornography arguments have been
taken up and translated into the neoconservative cultural and
political agenda of the Right. For my part, I want to emphasize
that I've reversed my reading of racial signification in Mapplethorpe not for the fun of it, but because I do *not* want a black
gay critique to be appropriated to the purposes of the Right's
antidemocratic cultural offensive. Jesse Helms's amendment to
public funding policies in the arts—which was orchestrated in
relation to Mapplethorpe's homoerotic work—forbids the public funding of art deemed "obscene or indecent." But it is crucial
to note that a broader remit for censorship was originally articulated on the grounds of a moral objection to art that "deni-
grates, debases, or reviles a person, group, or class of citizens
on the basis of race, creed, sex, handicap, or national origin."[16]
In other words, the discourse of liberal and social democratic
antidiscrimination legislation is being appropriated and rearticulated into a right-wing position that promotes a discriminatory
politics of cultural censorship and ideological coercion.

Without a degree of self-reflexivity, black critiques of
Mapplethorpe's work can be easily assimilated into a politics of
homophobia. Which is to say, coming back to the photographs,
that precisely on account of their ambivalence, Mapplethorpe's
photographs are open to a range of contradictory readings
whose political character depends on the social identity that different audiences bring to bear on them. The photographs can
confirm a racist reading as easily as they can produce an antiracist one. Or again, they can elicit a homophobic reading as
easily as they can confirm a homoerotic one. Once ambivalence

16
*The New York
Times*, 27 July 1989, A1.

and undecidability are situated in the contextual relations between author, text, and readers, a cultural struggle ensues in which antagonistic efforts seek to articulate the meaning and value of Mapplethorpe's work.

What is at issue in this "politics of enunciation" can be clarified by a linguistic analogy, since certain kinds of performative statements produce different meanings not so much because of what is said but because of who is saying it. As a verbal equivalent of Mapplethorpe's visual image, the statement "the black man is beautiful" takes on different meanings depending on the identity of the social subject who enunciates it. Does the same statement mean the same thing when uttered by a white woman, a black woman, a white man, or a black man? Does it mean the same thing whether the speaker is straight or gay? In my view, it cannot possibly mean the same thing in each instance because the racial and gendered identity of the enunciator inevitably "makes a difference" to the social construction of meaning and value.

Today we are adept at the all too familiar concatenation of identity politics, as if by merely rehearsing the mantra of "race, class, gender" (and all other intervening variables) we have somehow acknowledged the diversified and pluralized differences at work in contemporary culture, politics, and society. Yet the complexity of what actually happens "between" the contingent spaces where each variable intersects with the others is something only now coming into view theoretically, and this is partly the result of the new antagonistic cultural practices by hitherto marginalized artists. Instead of analogies, which tend to flatten out these intermediate spaces, I think we need to explore theories that enable new forms of dialogue. In this way we might be able to imagine a dialogic or relational conception of the differences we actually inhabit in our lived experiences of identity and identification. The observation that different readers produce different readings of the same cultural texts is not as circular as it seems: I want to suggest that it provides an outlet onto the dialogic character of the political imaginary of difference. To open up this area for theoretical investigation, I want to point to two ways in which such relational differences of race, gender, and sexuality do indeed "make a difference."

Different Readers Make Different Readings

Here, I simply want to itemize a range of issues concerning readership and authorship that arise across the intertextual field in which Mapplethorpe "plays." To return to *Man in a Polyester Suit,* one can see that an anonymous greeting card produced and marketed in a specifically gay cultural context works on similar fantasies of black sexuality. The greeting card depicts a black man in a business suit alongside the caption "Everything you ever heard about black men . . . is true"—at which point one unfolds the card to reveal the black man's penis. The same savage-civilized binarism that I noted in Mapplethorpe's photograph is signified here by the contrast between the body clothed in a business suit, then denuded to reveal the penis (with some potted plants in the background to emphasize the point about the nature-culture distinction). Indeed, the card replays the fetishistic splitting of levels of belief as it is opened: the image of the big black penis serves as the punchline of the little joke. But because the card is authorless, the issue of attributing racist or antiracist intentions is effectively secondary to the context in which it is exchanged and circulated, the context of an urban, commercial, gay male subculture. My point is that gay readers in this vernacular sign-community may share access to a range of intertextual references in Mapplethorpe's work that other readers may not be aware of.

Returning to the "enigma" of the black models in Mapplethorpe's work: the appearance of black gay video porn star Joe Simmons (referred to as Thomas in *The Black Book*) on magazine covers from *Artscribe* to *Advocate Men* offers a source of intertextual pleasure to those "in the know" that accentuates

Skin Head Sex Thing

Robert Mapplethorpe, *Thomas*, 1986.

The Estate of Robert Mapplethorpe.

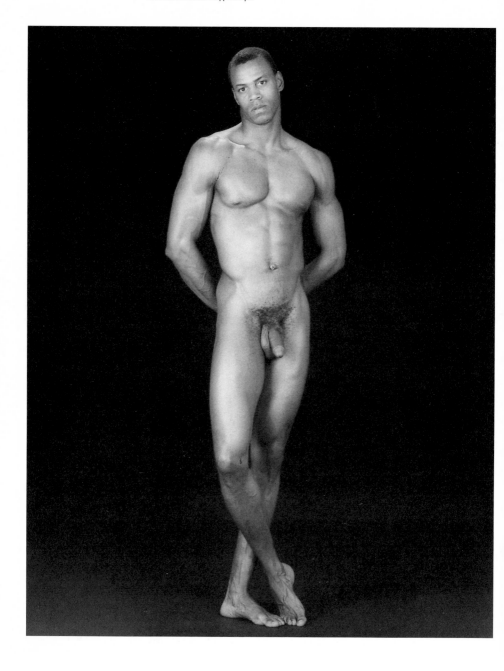

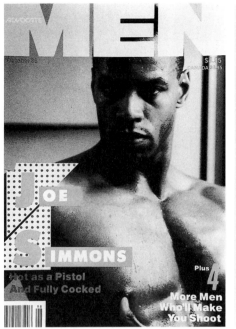

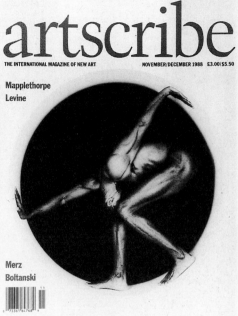

and inflects Mapplethorpe's depiction of the same person. Repetition has become one of the salient pleasures of gay male pornography, as photographic reproduction and video piracy encourage the accelerated flow by which models and scenarios constantly reappear in new intertextual combinations. By extending this process into "high art," circulating imagery between the streets and the galleries, Mapplethorpe's promiscuous textuality has a sense of humor that might otherwise escape the sensibilities of nongay or antigay viewers.

The mobility of such intertextual moves cannot be arrested by recourse to binary oppositions. The sculpted pose of Joe Simmons in one frame immediately recalls the celebrated nude studies of Paul Robeson by Nicholas Murray in 1926. Once the photograph is situated in this historical context, which may or may not be familiar to black readers in particular, one might compare Mapplethorpe to Carl Van Vechten, the white photographer of black literati in the Harlem Renaissance. In this context, Richard Dyer has retrieved a revealing instance of overwhelming ambivalence in racial-sexual representations. In the 1920s, wealthy white patrons in the Philadelphia Art Alliance commissioned a sculpture of Robeson by Antonio Salemme. Although they wanted it to embody Robeson's "pure" beauty in bronze, they rejected the sculpture because its aesthetic sensuality overpowered their moral preconceptions.[17]

The historical specificity of this reference has a particular relevance in the light of renewed interest in the Harlem Renaissance in contemporary black cultural practices. This rediscovery of the past has served to thematize questions of identity and desire in the work of black gay artists such as Isaac Julien. In _Looking for Langston_ (1988), Julien undertakes an archeological inquiry into the enigma of Langston Hughes's sexual identity. Insofar as the aesthetic strategy of the film eschews the conventions of documentary realism in favor of a dialogic combination of poetry, music, and archival imagery, it does not claim to discover an authentic or essential homosexual identity (for Langston Hughes or anyone else). Rather, the issue of authorial identity is invested with fantasy, memory, and desire and serves as an imaginative point of departure for speculation and reflection on the social and historical relations in which black gay male identity is lived and experienced in disapora societies such as Britain and the United States. In this sense, the criticism that the film is not about Langston Hughes misses the point. By showing the extent to which our identities as black gay men are historically constructed in and through representations, Julien's film interrogates aspects of social relations that silence and repress the representability of black gay identities and desires. The search for iconic heroes and heroines has been an important element in lesbian, gay, and feminist cultural politics, and the process of uncovering identities previously "hidden from his-

17
Richard Dyer,
"Paul Robeson: Crossing
Over," in _Heavenly Bodies:
Film Stars and Society_
(New York: St. Martin's
Press, 1986), 67–139.

tory" has had empowering effects in culture and society at large. Julien is involved in a similar project, but his film refuses, through its dialogic strategy, to essentialize Hughes into a black gay cultural icon. This strategy focuses on the question of power at issue in the ability to make and wield representations. Above all, it focuses on who has the "right to look" by emphasizing both interracial and intraracial looking relations that complicate the subject-object dichotomy of seeing and being seen.

Hence, in one key scene, we see the white male protagonist leisurely leafing through *The Black Book*. Issues of voyeurism, objectification, and fetishization are brought into view not in a didactic confrontation with Mapplethorpe, but through a seductive invitation into the messy spaces in between the binary oppositions that dominate the representation of difference. Alongside visual quotations from Jean Cocteau, Jean Genet, and Derek Jarman, the voices of James Baldwin, Toni Morrison, and Amiri Baraka combine to emphasize the relational conception of "identity" that Julien's dialogic strategy makes possible. It is through this relational approach that the film reopens the issue of racial fetishism. An exchange of looks between "Langston" and his mythic object of desire, a black man called "Beauty," provokes a hostile glare from Beauty's white partner. In the daydream that follows, Langston imagines himself coupled with Beauty, their bodies intertwined on a bed in an image reappropriated and reaccentuated from the homoerotic photography of George Platt-Lynes. It is here that the trope of visual fetishization makes a subversive return. Close-up sequences lovingly linger on the sensuous mouth of the actor portraying Beauty, with the rest of his face cast in shadow. As in Mapplethorpe's photographs, the strong emphasis on chiaroscuro lighting invests the fetishized fragment with a powerful erotic charge in which the "thick lips" of the Negro are hypervalorized as the emblem of Beauty's impossible desirability. In other words, Julien takes the artistic risk of replicating the

stereotype of the "thick-lipped Negro" in order to revalorize
that which has historically been devalorized as emblematic of
the other's ugliness. It is only by operating "in and against" such
tropes of racial fetishism that Julien lays bare the ambivalence of
the psychic and social relations at stake in the relay of looks between the three men.

Historically, black people have been the objects of representation rather than its subjects and creators because racism
often determines who gets access to the means of representation in the first place. Through his dialogic textual strategy,
Julien overturns this double-bind as the black subject "looks
back" to ask the audience who or what *they* are looking for. The
motif of the "direct look" appeared in Julien's first film with the
Sankofa Collective, *Territories* (1984), which involved an "epis-

temological break" with the realist documentary tradition in black art. Similarly, what distinguishes current work by black lesbian and gay artists—such as the film and video of Pratibha Parmar or the photography of Rotimi Fani-Kayode—is the break with static and essentialist conceptions of identity. The salient feature of such work is its hybridity; it operates on the borderlines of race, class, gender, nationality, and sexuality, investigating the complex overdetermination of subjective experiences and desires as they are historically constituted in the ambivalent spaces in between.

Elsewhere I suggested that, in relation to black British film, such hybridized practices articulate a critical dialogue about the constructed character of black British identities and experiences.[18] Something similar informs the hybridized homoerotica of Nigerian British photographer Rotimi Fani-Kayode. The very title of his first publication, *Black Male/White Male*,[19] suggests an explicitly intertextual relationship with Mapplethorpe. However, salient similarities in Fani-Kayode's construction of pictorial space—the elaborate body postures enclosed within the studio space, the use of visual props to stage theatrical effects, and the glossy monochrome texture of the photographic print—underline the important differences in his refiguration of the black male nude. In contrast to Mapplethorpe's isolation-effect, whereby only one black man occupies the field of vision at any one time, in Fani-Kayode's photographs bodies are coupled and contextualized. In pictures such as *Technique of Ecstasy,* the erotic conjunction of two black men suggests an Afrocentric imaginary in which the implied power relations of the subject-object dichotomy are complicated by racial sameness. In *Bronze Head,* what looks like a Benin mask appears beneath a black man's splayed buttocks. This shocking contextualization places the image in an ambivalent space, at once an instance of contemporary African art, referring specifically to Yoruba iconography, and an example of homoerotic art

18
Kobena Mercer, "Diaspora Culture and the Dialogic Imagination: The Aesthetics of Black Independent Film in Britain," in *Blackframes: Critical Perspectives on Black Independent Cinema,* ed. Mbye B. Cham and Claire Andrade-Watkins (Cambridge, Mass.: MIT Press, 1988), 50–61.

19
Rotimi Fani-Kayode, *Black Male/White Male* (London: Gay Men's Press, 1987); see also Rotimi Fani-Kayode, "Traces of Ecstasy," *Ten.8,* no. 28 (Summer 1988), 36–43.

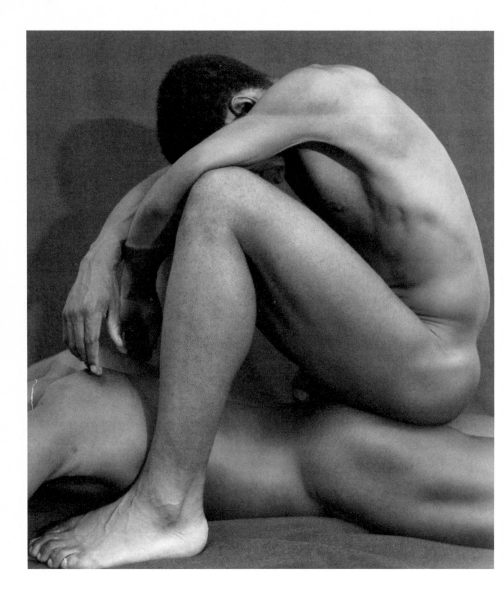

Rotimi Fani-Kayode, *Bronze Head,* 1987.

Skin Head Sex Thing

photography that recalls Mapplethorpe's portrait of Derrick Cross, in which the black man's bum resembles a Brancusi.

If such dialogic strategies do indeed "make a difference" to our understanding of the cultural politics of identity and diversity, does this mean the work is different *because* its authors are black? No, not necessarily. What is at issue is not an essentialist argument that the ethnic identity of the artist guarantees the aesthetic or political value of the text, but on the contrary, how common-sense conceptions of authorship and readership are challenged by practices that acknowledge the diversity and heterogeneity of the relations in which identities are socially constructed. Stuart Hall helped to clarify what is at stake in this shift when he argued that such acknowledgment of difference and diversity in black cultural practices has brought the innocent notion of the essential black subject to an end. Once we recognize blackness as a category of social, psychic, and political relations that have no fixed guarantees in nature but only the contingent forms in which they are constructed in culture, the questions of value cannot be decided by recourse to empirical common sense about "color" or melanin. As Stuart Hall put it, "Films are not necessarily good because black people make them. They are not necessarily 'right on' by virtue of the fact that they deal with the black experience.[20]

20
Stuart Hall, "New Ethnicities," in *Black Film/British Cinema*, ICA Document 7 (London: Institute of Contemporary Art/British Film Institute, 1988), 28.

In this view, I would argue that black gay and lesbian artists are producing exciting and important work not because they happen to be black lesbians and gay men but because they have made cultural and political choices out of their experiences of marginality that situate them at the interface between different traditions. Insofar as they speak *from* the specificity of such experiences, they overturn the assumption that minority artists speak *for* the entire community from which they come. This is an important distinction in the relations of enunciation because it bears upon the politics of representation that pertain to all subjects in marginalized or minoritized situations, whether

Mercer

black, feminist, lesbian, or gay. In a material context of restricted access to the means of representation, minoritized subjects are charged with an impossible "burden of representation." Where subordinate subjects acquire the right to speak only one at a time, their discourse is circumscribed by the assumption that they speak as "representatives" of the entire community from which they come.

It is logically impossible for any one individual to bear such a burden, not only because it denies variety and heterogeneity within minority communities, but also because it demands an intolerable submission to the iron law of the stereotype, namely the view from the majority culture that every minority subject is "the same." In the master codes of the dominant culture, the assumption that "all black people are the same" reinforces the view that black communities are monolithic and homogeneous and that black subjectivity is defined exclusively by race and nothing but race. The dialogic element in contemporary black artistic practices begins to interrupt this restricted economy of representation by making it possible to imagine a democratic politics of difference and diversity. The work of black gay and lesbian artists participates in what has been called "postmodernism" in terms of practices that pluralize available representations in the public sphere. To the extent that their aesthetic of critical dialogism underlines their contribution to the "new cultural politics of difference," as Cornel West has put it,[21] it seems to me that rather than mere "celebration," their work calls for a critical response that reopens issues and questions we thought had been closed.

As I suggested in rereading Mapplethorpe, one of the key questions on the contemporary agenda concerns the cultural construction of whiteness. One of the signs of the times is that we really don't know what "white" is. The implicitly ethnocentric agenda of cultural criticism, since the proliferation of poststructuralist theories in the 1970s, not only obscured the

21
Cornel West, "The New Cultural Politics of Difference," in *Out There: Marginalization and Contemporary Cultures*, ed. Russell Ferguson, Martha Gever, Trinh T. Minh-ha, and Cornel West (Cambridge, Mass.: MIT Press, 1990), 19–36.

Skin Head Sex Thing

range of issues concerning black authorship, black spectatorship, and black intertextuality that black artists have been grappling with, but also served to render invisible the constructed, and contested, character of "whiteness" as a racial/ethnic identity. Richard Dyer has shown how difficult it is to theorize whiteness, precisely because it is so thoroughly naturalized in dominant ideologies as to be invisible as an ethnic identity: it simply goes without saying. Paradoxically then, for all our rhetoric about "making ourselves visible," the real challenge in the new cultural politics of difference is to make "whiteness" visible for the first time, as a culturally constructed ethnic identity historically contingent upon the disavowal and violent denial of difference. Gayatri Spivak has shown that it was only through the "epistemic violence" of such denial that the centered subject of Western philosophy posited itself as the universalized subject— "Man"—in relation to whom others were not simply different but somehow less than human, dehumanized objects of oppression. Women, children, savages, slaves, and criminals were all alike insofar as their otherness affirmed "his" identity as the subject at the center of logocentrism and indeed all the other centrisms—ethnocentrism and phallocentrism—in which "he" constructed his representations of reality.[22] But who is "he"? The identity of the hegemonic white male subject is an enigma in contemporary cultural politics.

22
Gayatri Chakravorty Spivak, "Feminism and Critical Theory," in *In Other Worlds: Essays in Cultural Politics* (New York and London: Methuen, 1987), 77–92.

Different Degrees of Othering

Coming back to Mapplethorpe's photographs, in the light of this task of making "whiteness" visible as a problem for cultural theory, I want to suggest that the positioning of gay (white) people in the margins of Western culture may serve as a perversely privileged place from which to reexamine the political unconscious of modernity. By negotiating an alternative interpretation of Mapplethorpe's authorial position, I argued that his aesthetic strategy lays bare and makes visible the "splitting" in white subjectivity that is anchored, by homology, in the split between "high culture" and "low culture." The perverse interaction between visual elements drawn from both sources begins to subvert the hierarchy of cultural value, and such subversion of fixed categories is experienced precisely as the characteristic shock effect.

Broadening this theme, one can see that representations of race in Western culture entail different degrees of othering. Or, to put it the other way around: different practices of racial representation imply different positions of identification on the part of the white subject. Hollywood's iconic image of the "nigger minstrel" in cinema history, for example, concerns a deeply ambivalent mixture of othering and identification. The creation of the minstrel mask in cinema, and in popular theater and the music hall before it, was really the work of white men in blackface. What is taking place in the psychic structures of such historical representations? What is going on when whites assimilate and introject the degraded and devalorized signifiers of racial otherness into the cultural construction of their own identity? If imitation implies identification, in the psychoanalytic sense of the word, then what is it about whiteness that makes the white subject want to be black?

"I Wanna Be Black," sang Lou Reed on the album *Street Hassle* (1979), which was a parody of a certain attitude in postwar youth culture in which the cultural signs of blackness—in music, clothes, and idioms of speech—were the mark of "cool." In the American context, such a sensibility predicated on the ambivalent identification with the other was enacted in the bohemian beatnik subculture and became embodied in Norman Mailer's literary image of "the White Negro" stalking the jazz clubs in search of sex, speed, and psychosis. Like a photographic negative, the white negro was an inverted image of otherness, in which attributes devalorized by the dominant culture were simply revalorized or hypervalorized as emblems of alienation and outsiderness, a kind of strategic self-othering in relation to dominant cultural norms. In the museum without walls, Mailer's white negro, who went in search of the systematic derangement of the senses, merely retraced an imaginary pathway in the cultural history of modernity previously traveled by Arthur Rimbaud and Eugène Delacroix in nineteenth-century Europe. There is a whole modernist position of "racial romanticism" that involves a fundamental ambivalence of identifications. At what point do such identifications result in an imitative masquerade of white ethnicity? At what point do they result in ethical and political alliances? How can we tell the difference?[23]

My point is that white ethnicity constitutes an "unknown" in contemporary cultural theory: a dark continent that has not yet been explored. One way of opening it up is to look at the ambivalent coexistence of the two types of identification, as they figure in the work of (white) gay artists such as Mapplethorpe and Jean Genet. In *Un Chant d'amour* (1950), Genet's only foray into cinema, there is a great deal of ambivalence, to say the least, about the black man, the frenzied and maniacal negro seen in the masturbatory dance through the scopophilic gaze of the prison guard. In another context, I wrote "The black man in Genet's film is fixed like a stereotype in the fetishistic axis of the look. . . . , subjected to a pornographic exercise of colonial power."[24] Yes, I know . . . but. There is something else going on as well, not on the margins but at the very center of Genet's film. The romantic escape into the woods, which is the liberated zone of freedom in which the lover's utopian fantasy of coupling is enacted, is organized around the role of the "dark" actor, the Tunisian, the one who is not quite white. In this view, the ambivalence of ethnicity has a central role to play in the way that Genet uses race to figure the desire for political freedom beyond the prisonhouse of marginality. Once located in relation to his plays, such as *The Balcony* and *The Blacks,* Genet's textual practice must be seen as his mode of participation in the "liberation" struggles of the postwar era.

23

See Norman Mailer, "The White Negro: Superficial Reflections on the Hipster," in *Advertisements for Myself* (New York: Putnam, 1959), 337–58. The fantasy of wanting to be black is discussed as a masculinist fantasy in Suzanne Moore, "Getting a Bit of the Other: The Pimps of Postmodernism," in *Male Order: Unwrapping Masculinity,* ed. Rowena Chapman and Jonathan Rutherford, (London: Lawrence and Wishart, 1988), 165–92.

24

See "Sexual Identities: Questions of Difference," a panel discussion with Kobena Mercer, Gayatri Spivak, Jacqueline Rose, and Angela McRobbie, *Undercut,* no. 17 (Spring 1988), 19–30.

The word *liberation* tends to stick in our throats these days because it sounds so deeply unfashionable; but we might also recall that in the 1950s and 1960s it was precisely the connections between movements for the liberation from colonialism and movements for the liberation from the dominant sex and gender system that underlined their radical democratic character. In the contemporary situation, the essentialist rhetoric of categorical identity politics threatens to erase the connectedness of our different struggles. At its worst, such forms of identity politics play into the hands of the Right as the fundamentalist belief in the essential and immutable character of identity keeps us locked into the prisonhouse of marginality in which oppressions of race, class, and gender would have us live. By historicizing the imaginary identifications that enable democratic agency, we might rather find a way of escaping this ideological bantustan.

Instead of giving an answer to the questions that have been raised about the ambivalence of ethnicity as a site of identification and enunciation, I conclude by recalling Genet's wild and adventurous story about being smuggled across the Canadian border by David Hilliard and other members of the Black Panther Party in 1968. He arrived at Yale University to give a May Day speech, along with Allen Ginsberg and others, in defense of imprisoned activist Bobby Seale. Genet talks about this episode in *Prisoner of Love,* where it appears as a memory brought to consciousness by the narration of another memory, about the beautiful fedayyin, in whose desert camps Genet lived between 1969 and 1972. The memory of his participation in the elective community of the Palestinian freedom fighters precipitates the memory of the Black Panther "brotherhood," into which he was adopted—this wretched, orphaned, nomadic homosexual thief. I am drawn to this kind of ambivalence, sexual and political, that shows through, like a stain, in his telling:[25]

In white America the Blacks are the characters in which history

25
Jean Genet, *Prisoner of Love* (London: Picador, 1989), 213.

Skin Head Sex Thing

is written. They are the ink that gives the white page its meaning. . . . [The Black Panthers' Party] built the black race on a white America that was splitting. . . . The Black Panthers' Party wasn't an isolated phenomenon. It was one of many revolutionary outcrops. What made it stand out in white America was its black skin, its frizzy hair and, despite a kind of uniform black leather jacket, an extravagant but elegant way of dressing. They wore multicoloured caps only just resting on their springy hair; scraggy moustaches, sometimes beards; blue or pink or gold trousers made of satin or velvet, and cut so that even the most shortsighted passer-by couldn't miss their manly vigour.

Under what conditions does eroticism mingle with political solidarity? When does it produce an effect of empowerment? And when does it produce an effect of disempowerment? When does identification imply objectification, and when does it imply equality? I am intrigued by the ambivalent but quite happy coexistence of the fetishized big black dick beneath the satin trousers and the ethical equivalence in the struggle for postcolonial subjectivity. Genet's affective participation in the political construction of imagined communities suggests that the struggle for democratic agency and subjectivity always entails the negotiation of ambivalence. Mapplethorpe worked in a different context, albeit one shaped by the democratic revolutions of the 1960s, but his work similarly draws us back into the difficult questions that Genet chose to explore, on the "dark side" of the political unconscious of the postcolonial world. The death of the author doesn't necessarily mean mourning and melancholia, but rather mobilizing a commitment to countermemory. In the dialogue that black gay and lesbian artists have created in contemporary cultural politics, the exemplary political modernism of Mapplethorpe and Genet, "niggers with attitude" if there ever were, is certainly worth remembering as we begin thinking about our pitiful "postmodern" condition.

Discussion

Robert Garcia

At this conference much has been said about cultural theory in relation to issues of concern to gays and lesbians of color. And since gays and lesbians of color are also producers and consumers of such theory, it's been truly a cause for celebration to see the work of Richard Fung, Isaac Julien, and yourself extensively referred to throughout this conference. My question is, what do you see as the most crucial tools to be given back to the Latino, African-American, and Asian communities to get them out of, as you put it, the prisonhouse of marginality? What does cultural theory offer most immediately in terms of access to the information and power that the white, middle-class, and predominately male culture has in our society?

Kobena Mercer

I think exemplary tools are already provided by films such as *Looking for Langston,* which, like other films by Isaac Julien and the Sankofa Collective, is informed by a range of theoretical work from film theory and feminism to cultural studies. What has been crucial, though, with the creative upsurge in work by black lesbians and gay men in the eighties, is the *practice,* actually gaining access to the means of production. When you consider artists as diverse as Rotimi Fani-Kayode, Pratibha Parmar, and Sunil Gupta in Britain, or Michelle Parkerson, Marlon Riggs, and Essex Hemphill in the U.S., what is exciting is that their work challenges assumptions not only in white lesbian and gay communities, but in our own black communities as well. I would therefore argue that, instead of the theory-practice distinction, it would be more useful to look at what kinds of critical dialogue are provoked, whether by a film, a poem, or a cultural theory.

    Looking for Langston is exemplary in this respect because the issue of censorship has been raised; the version of the film that is being shown in the U.S. has Hughes's voice silenced for copyright reasons. In my view, such a response by the

Hughes estate means the film has touched a nerve concerning homosexuality in black society. Similarly, Sankofa's film *The Passion of Remembrance* [1986] provoked angry responses from the black community when it was shown on television in Britain. The important thing is that the films have provoked discussion, debate, and dialogue about issues such as black homophobia. So even if black audiences have expressed displeasure, they are participating in the dialogue. I'm not sure whether theory can ever be a direct means of empowerment, but insofar as it informs cultural practices, it can help provoke critical dialogues in which issues previously denied or repressed are brought out into the open.

Having said that, however, I would add that the new wave of black aesthetic strategies has raised complex issues for which cultural theory has no ready answers. There has been a break with the didacticism of avant-garde film in the seventies, which relativizes the universalist and absolutist claims once made in the name of theory. I discussed this in the introduction to the special issue of *Screen* that I coedited with Isaac Julien [*The Last 'Special Issue' on Race*, 29, no. 4 (Autumn 1988)]. When I was at college in the late seventies, *Screen* had an authoritative presence as a "center" of film theory, but questions of race and ethnicity were invisible or marginal at best. During the period when theory became *Theory* with a capital *T*, there was a kind of intellectual authoritarianism about having the "correct line," a theoretical superego telling filmmakers what they should or shouldn't do. I think it's great that those attitudes have faded away and that issues of race are now on the intellectual agenda. This doesn't mean, on the other hand, that we can simply abandon theory and say that anything goes. I'm an "anticelebrationist" in this respect. Work by black artists needs to be recognized and valued, but I think it's a bit of an insult to do nothing more than celebrate, in which case criticism is replaced by cathartic feel-good therapy. If we simply celebrate, without critical appraisal, we end up in the essentialist trap, which says, "If a black person makes a film it must be good, because it's made by a black person." That circular position gets us nowhere.

Ada Griffin But if you don't celebrate the work of blacks, you have a situation such as that of Mapplethorpe's work of black men made beautiful. They appeal on a direct, visceral level—and not only to gay men or to black gay men—and no one asks the questions you've asked—about who the author is, for example, and what his relation to the men photographed is. So when it's done by a black man, and done differently, you do want to celebrate that difference. I was struck by your reference to the way the white artist positions himself as black in order to appropriate the black image for his art.

Regarding your comments about controlling imagery, recently a group of us were shooting a video in Bedford-Stuyvesant about the conflicts between blacks and Koreans. A group of black men surrounded us and tried to cut the cord of our equipment because we did not ask if we could have their image. It struck me that people are no longer willing to allow their images to circulate in ways that they don't control. I wondered what your thoughts are about this militant position—the subjects' relationship to their own images.

Mercer I think the issue of who controls the image is crucial. We have all become more aware of the importance of the media in shaping our everyday social reality. The critique of the dominant images in circulation has always been an integral element of black struggles for access to the means of representation, of the historical formation of black independent media as alternative sources of images. But the underlying issues of power and control are very complex. The very fact that your video equipment was attacked by a group of black men shows that the question can't be reduced to a binary opposition of black versus white.

Taking our question in a broader frame, I would say the experience you've described highlights an aspect of the decentering of the subject that we've been told about ad nauseam in postmodern discourse. Decentering—the fragmentation of social relations, the loss of identity, *differance*—has often been presented as an inherently "groovy" thing. But it should be clear that there is nothing groovy about the political predicament of postmodernism. There are a lot of anxieties that well up in the experience of being decentered. The crisis of authority in late capitalist societies means the proliferation of conflicts to more and more areas of social life, which generates uncertainty for everyone.

The cultural production of images has become an area of permanent contestation and is no longer seen as peripheral to politics. People like Margaret Thatcher and Ronald Reagan fully appreciated the importance of the media. That is why I would say we cannot afford merely to celebrate the achievements of radical black artists, because that avoids the difficult political question of the antagonisms that exist *within* black communities and the conflicts *between* different identities within black society. Previously, because of a certain kind of cultural nationalism, it was said that we should not air our differences publicly, in other words, that we should practice self-censorship and stay in the closet. What is courageous about black gay artists today is that they take artistic and political risks in order to address the divisions within the black community. Moreover, by confronting the hypocrisy of the idea that gayness is a "white thing," for example, their work not only challenges homophobia, but brings these divisions out into the open, for political debate, thus showing that there is no such thing as a homogeneous and unitary black community, but only *communities,* in the plural, made up of interdependent, and sometimes contradictory, identities.

Once we recognize that the feeling of "unity" associated with belonging to a community is not something to be taken for granted, but something that has to be struggled for, actively constructed, then we have to take up the challenge of ambivalence in an overtly political sense. One's identity, as a black person, as a gay person, whatever, does not guarantee a progressive political position. Let's not forget that some black people and some gay people have supported the antidemocratic policies of Reagan and Thatcher over the past decade. If we can no longer think of identity as a fixed category, then we have to recognize the different kinds of *identifications* that we are capable of as social actors. That means thinking about alliances in the name of radical democracy, which is an area of deep political ambivalence because, as Malcolm X said, "Sometimes it's hard to tell the difference between your friends and your enemies." In any political struggle, you need friends as much as you need enemies. That is why I focussed on the ambivalence of white identifications with black people. Even someone as radical as Genet objectified and fetishized black men at the same time that he was participating—in the context of the war to end colonialism in Algeria and later in relation to the Panthers and the Palestine Liberation Organization—as an equal member of the imagined communities he chose to join.

Cora Kaplan   I wonder whether, though, you really want to put Jean Genet and Norman Mailer in the same political frame of ambivalence. It seems to me that Mailer, in the period of the "white Negro," is so demonstratively racist and homophobic that he really belongs with other figures on the Right. And I think that to distinguish those two kinds of appropriation is really important in rereading the radical history of the fifties and early sixties.

Mercer   I agree with you. It's exactly that: how to distinguish an exploitative appropriation of black culture from an enabling or empowering identification. Mapplethorpe's work touches on this difficult question. What is at issue in the Freudian concept of identification is the nature of the emotional bond. When we acknowledge the role of identifications in politics—in the alliances we choose to make and in the way we name our opponents, adversaries, or enemies—the question of relations between the psychic and the social becomes considerably more complex. This seems especially true with regard to the alliances white people made with black civil rights struggles. Racial inequality and injustice were central to the mobilization of the New Left, and one sees extensions of this in the countercultural politics of feminism and gay liberation in the sixties, when black pride was translated into gay pride or "sisterhood is powerful." Norman Mailer's positions in this context were deeply reactionary, and I find the whole fantasy of "the white Negro" repulsive in many ways; but it is worth remembering, whether we like it or not, that Mailer was a member of the New Left intelligentsia when he published that article in *Dissent* in 1957. He was attempting to articulate a critique of sexual and social norms. One can't resolve the matter by simply saying Mailer = bad/Genet = good, because such binary thinking ends up with the static concept of identity rather than the more volatile concept of identification.

Gregg Bordowitz   I want to ask for clarification on one point. What I heard—and of course this will be a paraphrase—was that we should resist reducing many of the concerns you've been talking about to the simple Marxist formula that change can be effected only by causing change at the base, that is, at the level of modes of production. But you also spoke of the burden of responsibility placed on disenfranchised practitioners because of their lack of access to the means of producing representations. First, I'd like to know if I'm representing what you said accurately, and then I'd like to ask if you would explain more fully what you meant by the burden of responsibility and, practically, how it can be lifted from disenfranchised producers.

Mercer   I didn't actually mention the base-superstructure model, but it is relevant in that economics form part of the material context in which cultural work is produced. In this sense, your question bears on the issue that Ada raised of who controls the image and under what conditions.

What I wanted to suggest in talking about the burden of

representation is the way in which the reproduction of racism depends on the regulation and control of black people's access to the apparatuses of image-making in our society. In a situation where only one black person is allowed to speak, as it were—a situation where there is only one black filmmaker who is talked about, or only one black person on the panel in a conference, for example—there is an assumption that that person is speaking on behalf of the black community as a whole. This is the problem of tokenism. If there is only one black person in any given public or institutional space, he or she is positioned as "representative." This gives rise to a political problem of representation. On the one hand, the idea that an individual black person could be totally representative of his or her community reinforces the racist stereotype that all blacks are the same and that the black community is a homogeneous and undifferentiated entity. On the other hand, against the experience of being misrepresented or underrepresented, of not having a voice, when black subjects do take part in public discourse, there is also a risk that they will deny or disavow differences and divisions within black society. That is the political economy of enunciation in dominant regimes of representation. It remains a problematic issue in the discourse of black left politics because, in the movements of the 1960s, the interests of black women and gay men were often negated when community "leaders" took on the role of public spokesmen. This was the predicament that Sankofa's *The Passion of Remembrance* sought to address.

What is the solution? I think that if people's democratic right of access to representation were something we could take for granted, then the problem would probably not arise. The struggle to gain access to representation is cultural and political at one and the same time and therefore cannot be separated into base and superstructure. If all media practitioners were to acknowledge difference in their work instead of paying tokenistic lip service to the bureaucratic formula of "race, class, and

	gender," then we might see further progress in the political deconstruction of dominant regimes of minority-majority representation. One can lift the burden off so-called minority practitioners by spreading responsibility for the representation of difference.
Douglas Crimp	I'd like to relate this to the discussion about Jean Carlomusto's lesbian porn videotape, *Current Flow* [1989]. It should perhaps be pointed out that this is the only existing safe sex tape made for lesbians, and this singleness places on it the burden of representation you're referring to. That this single tape should be so carefully scrutinized for the ways it deals with butch-femme roles, with race, and so on, seems unfair, especially since it is also assuming the difficult task of combining safe sex instruction with pornography.
Mercer	Yes, it's true that because it was the only lesbian safe sex tape that Cindy showed in her presentation, there was an implicit assumption that it is representative and must speak for the diversity of efforts in that particular area. Nevertheless, I think the comments made about it are legitimate, and in that respect I wouldn't agree that a burden was placed on Jean. I think it is necessary to question the coding, the kind of vernacular languages that one has to use in work of that sort.
Crimp	I don't think the "burden" and the "questions" are quite the same thing. I'm not saying that the questions were illegitimate, but simply that the questions partially arose out of the fact that it was taken to be representative.
Mercer	Yes, I agree.
Michelle Parkerson	I wonder if you can mention any black lesbians who do the kind of theoretical work you do?
Mercer	Pratibha Parmar is an Indian, British, lesbian-feminist writer and videomaker working in Britain. Both she and Hazel Carby made black feminist contributions to *The Empire Strikes Back,* an extremely important book published in the early eighties by the Centre for Contemporary Cultural Studies in Birmingham

that influenced the new cultural practices. In her writings on photography, Pratibha has emphasized a critique of essentialist discourse within black women's image-making. In her video *Memory Pictures* [1989], a biographical portrait of the London-based gay Indian photographer Sunil Gupta, she translates theory into practice by showing the diverse identities of lesbians and gay men in the Asian diaspora. More recently, in a piece that appeared in *Feminist Review* [Inge Blackman and Kathryn Perry, "Skirting the Issue: Lesbian Fashion for the 1990s, no. 34 (Spring 1990), 67–78], Inge Blackman coauthored a critical reading of lesbian style and fashion from a black perspective. About a year ago, Inge and I took part, with Joan Nestle, in a panel discussion on "Putting sex back into sexual politics," organized by Sheba Feminist Publishers. It was a very controversial discussion because it addressed pornography; and it was exciting as a political dialogue because it was one of the rare opportunities for lesbians and gay men, white and black alike, to talk about our differences.

Robert Mignott **Regarding the mythical, awesome black phallus, what are your feelings regarding an internalization of this ideology? In other words, what are your thoughts about black men who subscribe to this and objectify other black men?**

Mercer That is a really important question; it's difficult to know where to start. Yes, black men objectify, fetishize, and get off on other black men, sometimes acting out the roles that racist stereotypes prescribe. Perhaps it's because we have internalized the myth of the big black dick. The first thing to say is: at least we can talk about it now! There is so much moralism and self-censorship when it comes to talking about sex and sexuality that is attributable to the imperative of being ideologically "right on." Paradoxically, many people who say they're involved in sexual politics seem to be afraid of talking about sex for fear of not being "politically correct." This seems to be a strong element in separatist ideologies, and it underpins the moralistic finger-wagging of fundamentalist versions of sexual-identity politics. We can all live without that kind of authoritarian policing of desire, not simply because it inhibits dialogue, but because it replicates the very ideologies we are trying to break away from, namely the logocentric demand that you can have only one "authentic" identity. The replicating of authoritarianism within liberation movements is a political paradox that needs to be explored, because it's similar to the way in which aspects of black masculinity replicate some of the oppressive dimensions of male power throughout our societies.

To get down to your question specifically, I think the question of internalizing sexual myths needs to be seen historically. Sociologists like Robert Staples have shown that the construction of black masculinity as a gender role cannot be separated from its dialectical interaction with white masculinity and the power relations of slave and post-slave societies. In order to gain some degree of power within the conditions of powerlessness that slavery entailed, black men "internalized" aspects of white patriarchy, such as the attempt to master and control others as indicative of one's masculinity. Black macho, which develops out of this model of subordinate masculinity, reproduces oppression by displacing it onto others. One cannot understand "internalized oppression," which is manifest in, say, black-on-black crime, without considering gender to be as important as race and class. In my view, the subjective dimension of the lived experience of oppression is magnified in the domain of sexuality—in acts of sexual violence such as rape—which activists like Eldridge Cleaver valorized politically in the sixties as part of the "liberation" of black men.

What is problematic in this, though, is the very dichotomy between self and society, between inside and outside, which the notion of internalization presupposes. This is where I feel psychoanalytic concepts might offer a better way of dealing with the subjective dimension of desire and fantasy that we live through, as black men, at the level of the political unconscious. If oppressive, and self-oppressive, aspects of black masculinity depend on an unconscious identification with aspects of the white-master model, then there is no clear division between inside and outside, self and social, but rather an overdetermined relation in which the innermost aspects of our lives, our sex and sexual fantasies, are connected with the historical structures in which we live.

José Arroyo   I would like to return to the question of the burden of representation. We generally talk about the burden placed on film-makers or other cultural producers. I have heard you speak on other occasions about these people's consciousness of being positioned as representative and of feeling a tremendous responsibility toward their communities. I'd like you to extend the discussion to the role of the black critic. From what I know of the criticism of black British cinema, you have been doing quite a lot of it. Do you feel there is a burden on you?

Mercer   Yes, it's about making a difference under circumstances not of your own choosing. I think the burden of representation is something we have all experienced at one time or another. The problems it creates, the pressures and constraints, are particularly magnified in relation to race and the cultural politics of black representation, but the burden of representation can affect anyone who is marginalized or "minoritized." For example, at work or in the office, when the subject runs to homosexuality, people will turn to you for your opinion, positioning you as the authentic gay subject who speaks for the entire gay male community. Foucault and Deleuze talked about the "indignity of speaking for others," which I take to mean that politics is fundamentally about representation. Struggles for dignity and democracy are about the right of everyone to speak.

In this sense, there is no place for the critic as the "universal intellectual" who has to answer for everything; rather what is called for is the "specific intellectual," who speaks from a specific context and situation with the aim of making connections. Instead of analogies, which imply that gay people, black people, women, whoever, all live in separate essentialist spaces, the idea of criticism as public dialogue aims to extend the democratization of public discourse, in the struggle to "find a voice," as bell hooks puts it.

In my own case, I like the idea of "traveling theory," in the sense that it suggests casting off the burden of representation through displacement and movement across boundaries and barriers, whether imaginary, symbolic, or real. Traveling theory is germane for artists and intellectuals in the black diaspora, I suppose, because our cultural histories are about movement, migration, displacement, which any of us can experience just walking around Manhattan. In New York, when you travel from Christopher Street to Harlem, for example, you negotiate imaginary boundaries between the Third World and the First World in one and the same social space.

Film and the Visible

Teresa de Lauretis

1
See Kobena Mercer, guest editor, *Black Film/British Cinema*, ICA Document 7 (London: Institute of Contemporary Arts, 1988); Paul Willemen, "The Third Cinema Question: Notes and Reflections," *Framework*, issue dedicated to the memory of Claire Johnston, no. 34 (1987), 4–38; and Jim Pines and Paul Willemen, eds., *Questions of Third Cinema* (London: British Film Institute, 1989).

Whoever came up with the conference title "How Do I Look? Queer Film and Video" must have meant it not only as a provocation—the coinage of the phrase *queer video and cinema* immediately recalls "women's cinema" and "poor cinema" in the 1970s, or more recently "black cinema" and again "third cinema," all oppositional, militant practices of cinema and cinematic representation[1]—but also as a bait dangled before the likes of me, that is, those in the business of cultural critique, so-called academics (though I would prefer "organic intellectuals," but don't ask me organic to what), enmeshed in the vicissitudes of discourse, the never-ending plots of language. Well, I will take the bait, accept the provocation, the intellectual come-on of that tropical question: how do I look?

The first take is to hear it narcissistically (why not? I am, after all, female and queer), to hear it as an intransitive verb: how do I look—to you, to myself, how do I appear, how am I seen? What are the ways in which I'm seen or can be seen, the conditions of my visibility? The second take is to hear the transitive, active verb, subject to object: how do I look at you, at her, at the film, at myself? How do I see, what are the modes, constraints, and possibilities of my seeing, the terms of vision for me? The next take is to hear the verb as active but not transitive: how do I look *on,* as the film unrolls from reel to reel in the projector, as the images appear and the story unfolds on the screen, as the fantasy scenario unveils and the soundtrack plays on in my head? In short, the questions of the conference seem to be: to see or not to see, to be seen (and how) or not to be seen (at all?). Subjective vision and social visibility, being and passing, representation and spectatorship—the conditions of the visible, what can be *seen,* and eroticized, and on what *scene.*

As I attempt to come to terms with these questions, I refer to something I wrote a couple of years ago on the problem of lesbian self-representation:

The difficulty in defining an autonomous form of female sexuality and desire in the wake of a cultural tradition still Platonic, still grounded in sexual (in)difference, still caught in the tropism of hommo-sexuality, is not to be overlooked or willfully bypassed. It is perhaps even greater than the difficulty in devising strategies of representation which will, in turn, alter the standard of vision, the frame of reference of visibility, of *what can be seen.* For, undoubtedly, that is the project of lesbian performance, theatre and film[:] redefining the conditions of vision, as well as the modes of representing.[2]

2
Teresa de Lauretis, "Sexual Indifference and Lesbian Representation," *Theatre Journal* 40, no. 2 (May 1988), 170–71.

Here I will try to work through those three sentences, to articulate ways of conceptualizing, theorizing, or "putting into discourse" the terms of an autonomous form of lesbian sexuality and desire in relation to filmic representation. I will be arguing that films that portray or are about lesbian and gay subjects may provide sympathetic accounts, "positive images," of those subjects without necessarily producing new ways of seeing or a new inscription of the social subject in representation. Conversely, I will attempt to articulate how a film's work with and against narrative codes and conventional forms of enunciation and address may produce modes of representing that effectively alter the standard frame of reference and visibility, the conditions of the visible, what *can* be seen and represented. I will give examples of films that represent "lesbians" and films that represent the problem of representation; examples of critical writings about the problem of representing lesbian subjectivity and desire, and examples of critical writings that obscure or minimize that problem, taking too much for granted, or not enough.

I take as point of departure Sheila McLaughlin's film *She Must Be Seeing Things* (1987). My purpose is not to do a textual reading, however tempting that may be with a film so rich and so eminently "cinematic," but rather to take the film as the ground from which to pose the question of lesbian representation and spectatorship. Again I will start from the title, since film titles, too, can be provocative or suggestive, in addition to being marketable.[3] At face value, the currency of its narrative image is the "she" who must *be seeing* things, who is imagining things that aren't "real." This could be a "Film About a Woman Who . . . ," to cite perhaps the fundamental text of feminist independent cinema, or it could be yet another film of the genre ironized by Yvonne Rainer—a film about a woman who, like Freud's hysteric who "suffers from reminiscences" or like the paranoiac, at once produces and is assailed by images, hallucinations, "things" that are symptoms of her own mental world or psychic state rather than events in the real world.[4] However, such "things" are never simple, and this is a different sort of film.

To begin with, *She Must Be Seeing Things* is not about one woman but two; one makes movies, the other doesn't. Or doesn't she? In a sense, they both do: both make movies in their minds, as they read novels or diaries and look at various pictures, still photographs, snapshots, and moving pictures; and from that reading and seeing, Jo (played by Lois Weaver) then writes scripts, shoots, and edits her rushes into films, while Agatha (played by Sheila Dabney) makes pictures more like hallucinations. The title *She Must Be Seeing Things,* then, really refers to both. Or, to advance a point I will come back to later on, the two women in the film "inhabit the subject position together," as Sue-Ellen Case suggests of the lesbian roles of butch and femme, which represent a coupled, rather than split, subject and which, by playing "on the phallic economy rather than to it," succeed, as Case puts it, in "replacing the Lacanian slash with a lesbian bar."[5] Second, I propose that the word *must* in McLaughlin's title is not descriptive but provocative and does sustain another meaning: "she" *must* be seeing things, she can't help seeing things the way she does. And I'll come back to this

3
The title of a film together with the publicity stills, posters, trailers, trade magazine blurbs and reviews, and other paraphernalia of cinema as social technology make up a film's "narrative image," as Stephen Heath has called it, "which is a film's presence, how it can be talked about, what it can be sold and bought on, itself represented as" (*Questions of Cinema* [Bloomington: Indiana University Press, 1981], 121).

4
See Yvonne Rainer, "Film Scripts," in *The Films of Yvonne Rainer* (Bloomington: Indiana University Press, 1989), 77–97.

5
Sue-Ellen Case, "Towards a Butch-Femme Aesthetic," *Discourse* 11, no. 1 (Fall–Winter 1988–89), 56–57.

later. For the moment, I want to stress that the title does refer to both and pursue for a while this queer notion of a film about two women who. . . .

If the most immediate reference of the title's "she," conveyed by the narrative and emphasized by the opening shot of Agatha looking off-space, screen-left, in extreme close-up, is undoubtedly Agatha, nevertheless Jo, too, is seeing things in or through her films. First, in directing the actress who plays Catalina (Kyle de Camp), telling her what she will see and how to look at it, and then in cutting the film (all of which we see her do, we see Jo seeing), she constructs a vision of things—events, emotions, relationships, and possibilities. Take the editing room scene toward the end of the film, where Jo cuts the final sequence of her film, *Catalina* (from Thomas De Quincey's *The Spanish Military Nun*), the story of "a seventeenth-century woman who rebelled," as the film tells us.[6] That scene marks the end of the film within the film, which Jo and Agatha watch, as well as the diegetic resolution of the film we watch, and both

6
See Catalina da Erauso, *Historia de la Monja Alferez Dona Catalina de Erauso, escrita por ella misma,* ed. Joaquin Maria de Ferrer (Paris: Julio Didot, 1829), cited in Rudolf Dekker and Lotte van de Pol, *The Tradition of Female Transvestism in Early Modern Europe* (New York: St. Martin's Press, 1989), 96 and 114.

films end with two women leaving together and leaving men behind. Unlike the women in most of the movies we have seen (with very few exceptions, and those mostly in avant-garde or independent women's cinema[7]), Catalina does not die or get married: think, for example, of *Rebecca* (1940) and Mrs. Danforth going up in flames, or of *Jane Eyre*'s quintessential female-narrative ending: "Reader, I married him." Nor does Catalina end up surviving, even victorious, but alone, like Scarlett O'Hara, or like Alex in the recent noir remake *Black Widow* (1986). Instead, she escapes with the other woman, whom she does not hate, compete with, or prove herself "better" than, but whom she . . . desires? loves? is fascinated by? The question is left suspended, despite the film's conventional narrative ending. Moreover, what the film-within-the-film does diegetically (in the world of the story, of what happens in it), the film we watch does cinematically, by means of the apparatus of cinema and what film theory has defined as film language: framing, editing, sound-image mixing, and the deployment of the system of the look, the specific way narrative cinema has of mobilizing the looks of the camera, of the characters within the film, and of the viewer or spectator. That is to say, not only do Jo and Agatha leave the cutting room together, and that's how their story also ends; but also more originally, McLaughlin's film constructs for both spectators and filmmakers a new position of seeing in the movies, a new place of the look: the place of a woman who desires another woman; the place from where each one looks at the other with desire and, more important still, a place from where we see their look and their desire; in other words, a place where the equivalence of look and desire—which sustains spectatorial pleasure and the very power of cinema in constructing and orienting the viewer's identification—is invested in two women.

What I want to argue is this: in thus reframing the oedipal scenario, working through the convention of the film-within-

7
For example, Sally Potter's *Thriller* and *The Gold Diggers* (1983), Chantal Akerman's *Je tu il elle* (1974), Sue Friedrich's *Damned If You Don't* (1987), Ulrike Ottinger's *Madame X* (1977) and *Johanna d'Arc of Mongolia* (1989), Lizzie Borden's *Born in Flames* (1983), or Monika Treut's *The Virgin Machine* (1989). That all these filmmakers are lesbians, or were at the time they made these films, is certainly a queer coincidence.

Film and the Visible

the-film, and rearticulating the function of voyeurism both diegetically and cinematically (in the closing shots of *Catalina* as well as in several other scenes throughout *She Must Be Seeing Things*), McLaughlin foregrounds, precisely, the question of what *can* be seen and the relations of seeing (and imaging) to "seeing" as imagining, the relations of spectatorship to fantasy, of subjectivity and desire to the imaginary—and in particular to the imaginary of cinema. Furthermore, by locating itself in the ambiguous space between seeing and not seeing, and in the play between conventions of seeing and conventions of cinema, her film takes up a different position of enunciation and addresses the spectator in what I will now, rashly, call a lesbian subject-position—reminding you that, of course, address is quite another thing from audience.

She, the spectator who occupies or is addressed in that position, is represented diegetically in Agatha sitting at the cutting table, watching Jo's film, and reacting with intense participation because the film has something to do with her life. And she, the filmmaker, who enunciates that subject-position, is represented in Jo, who is also sitting there, watching the words and images she's put together into a *figure of her desire* for Agatha. For it is clear that Catalina represents Agatha, or better, represents what Jo finds attractive in Agatha—her rebelliousness against a repressive, Catholic upbringing; her jealousy and anger at God's and men's claim of exclusive access to women; her lesbian difference; her pain and her defiance: throughout the film, all the scenes with Catalina are crosscut with shots of Agatha; whether imagined by Jo or actually being shot on location, or finally edited by Jo in the cutting room, all the scenes of the film-within-the-film are intercut with shots of Agatha reading Jo's diary and looking at the pictures in it, or Agatha watching on the shooting stage, or Agatha watching the edited film. In this sense *both* Agatha and Jo, both spectator and filmmaker, are *seeing things*. Yet so far as dominant culture is concerned, both might

as well be "seeing things," that is, imagining them. For indeed some of the things Jo sees through her film—women desiring women, and a film that inscribes that desire in its narrative through an articulation of the system of the look—such things do not exist in dominant representations in our culture. Or, if they do, they exist as something else, usually as the desire of one woman to be like, or to be, another, with positive or negative connotations of narcissistic and role-model identification (cf. *Desperately Seeking Susan* [1985], *Black Widow*), or rivalry (from *All About Eve* [1950] to *Working Girl* [1988]); or else they exist as the impossible, doomed desire of a woman who would desire like a man (the Barbara Stanwyck character in *Walk on the Wild Side* [1962], or the protagonist of the Brazilian film *Vera* [1987]).

For the spectator of *She Must Be Seeing Things,* the film-within-the-film's final sequence models a way of seeing that is not new in its filmic language, strictly speaking, but is quite new in its contextual, discursive placement and affective import. Catalina's looking on the primal scene and, against all odds cinematic and otherwise, entering the oedipal stage as active agent, then actually exiting it victorious in phallic defiance (no femininity for her!) may be no more of a fantasy than most adventure films are, except for the ending and the sex of the hero. But unlike the adventure genre film, calling for a direct spectatorial identification with the hero, and thus too often straining our capacity for willing suspension of disbelief to the breaking point (cf. *Back to the Future* [1985]), the affective, deeply embedded, contextual meaning of Catalina's picture-story is overlaid and heavily inflected by its subjective, identificatory effects on the two more immediately involved spectators, Agatha and Jo, who mediate and complicate our own, purposefully distanced, spectatorial relation to it.

Consider, for comparison, the play-within-the-film sequence in Leontine Sagan's version of *Maedchen in Uniform* (1931), where Manuela, cross-dressing in the role of Schiller's Don Carlos, declares her (his) forbidden love for Elizabeth (the name of both Fraülein von Bernburg and the Queen Mother in *Don Carlos*). As Ruby Rich observes in her detailed reading of the film, "despite the [girls] school's aura of eroticism," it is only when Manuela proclaims her love for Fraülein von Bernburg after the play—"in a coming out that is the opposite of Don Carlos's vow of silence," making explicit and publicly naming what the play-within-the-film only suggests—that the full sense of her trangression hits the audience both of and within the film.[8] In other words, Manuela's message must be conveyed more explicitly for its trangressive meaning to be seen and registered by the audience. What I am proposing by this comparison of two rather similar uses of the play-within-the-film (or film-within-the-film) device is that their different effects in spectatorship derive from the particular specification of the characters who mediate our spectatorial identification, and their capacity to act as figures of spectatorial desire. The school play's

8
B. Ruby Rich, "From Repressive Tolerance to Erotic Liberation: *Maedchen in Uniform,*" in *Re-vision: Essays in Feminist Film Criticism,* ed. Mary Ann Doane, Patricia Mellencamp, and Linda Williams (Frederick, Md.: University Publications of America and The American Film Institute, 1984), 109–10.

audience in *Maedchen* is a general, if mostly female, audience, whereas Agatha and Jo in *She Must Be Seeing Things* are affectively, subjectively involved in what engages them more directly as a fantasy, rather than as a performance or an object of viewing: their capacity to act as figures of spectatorial identification and desire is much greater.

Thus if Catalina's picaresque tale cannot be dismissed as just a tomboy's oedipal fantasy, it is not only because her story is cast deliberately and significantly in those terms, but more particularly because its function in the overall film's mirror construction (*mise en abîme*) is that of an original or primal fantasy (*fantasme originaire, Urphantasie*) in the sense given to this term by Laplanche and Pontalis:

By locating the origin of fantasy in the auto-erotism, we have shown the connection between fantasy and desire. Fantasy, however, *is not the object of desire, but its setting*. In fantasy the subject does not pursue the object or its sign: [s]he appears caught up [her]self in the sequence of images. [S]he forms no representation of the desired object, but is [her]self represented as participating in the scene although, in the earliest forms of fantasy, [s]he cannot be assigned any fixed place in it (hence the danger, in treatment, of interpretations which claim to do so). As a result, the subject, although always present in the fantasy, may be so in a desubjectivized form, that is to say, in the very syntax of the sequence in question.[9]

9
Jean Laplanche and Jean-Bertrand Pontalis, "Fantasy and the Origins of Sexuality," in *Formations of Fantasy*, ed. Victor Burgin, James Donald, and Cora Kaplan (London and New York: Methuen, 1986), 26. Emphasis added, pronominal gender altered.

If such is the case, the Catalina primal fantasy is shared by both Agatha and Jo. That is to say, like the title of McLaughlin's film, it only *apparently* refers to Agatha alone, thematically and in its setting (the Spanish locale, Catholicism, Catalina's cross-dressing). In fact, like the film-within-the-film that serves as its setting, the Catalina primal fantasy is made up by Jo with absorbed, passionate involvement—so passionate that she risks breaking up with her lover during the shooting of the film. If Laplanche and Pontalis are right, then, Jo is as much the subject of the Catalina fantasy, a subject present and participating, if in a "desubjectivized form," as they say, "in the very syntax of the sequence in question." And indeed what better figure of such participation than that of the filmmaker, "caught up [her]self in the sequence of images" (cf. the scenes of the shooting of Catalina, Jo's involvement with the actress, her nervous directorial concentration during rehearsals and the final shoot) and even more emphatically present in "the very syntax of the sequence in question" (the final cut in the editing room).[10] In sum, not only are Jo and Agatha both the subject of that fantasy, but they also share it, and share it together. This is a film about two women who share a common fantasy, a lesbian fantasy, and if "the origin of the subject [her]self" is located "in the field of fantasy" (19), then this very fantasy, which they share, constitutes them as a lesbian subject. Not the least implication of which is that it takes two women, not one, to make a lesbian.

10
    On the relation of montage to what may be called the syntax of film language (the *"grande syntagmatique"* of narrative cinema), see Christian Metz, *Language and Cinema*, trans. Donna Jean Umiker-Sebeok (The Hague: Mouton, 1974).

Shortly before the passage cited above, Laplanche and Pontalis have been concerned to locate the origin of fantasy in autoerotism. Autoerotism, they contend, is not "a stage of libidinal development" but rather "a mythical moment of disjunction between the pacification of need (*Befriedigung*) and the fulfilment of desire (*Wünscherfüllung*), between the two stages represented by real experience and its hallucinatory revival, between the object that satisfies [the real object, the milk] and the sign that describes both the object and its absence [the lost object, the breast]: a mythical moment in which hunger and sexuality meet in a common origin" (24–25). But this "mythical moment," they insist, stressing "its permanence and presence in all adult sexual behavior," is not to be understood in the object-directed sense, as "a first stage, enclosed within itself, from which the subject has to rejoin the world of objects." On the contrary, they argue on the side of Freud, "the drive *becomes* auto-erotic, only after the loss of the object." So that, "if it can be said of auto-erotism that it is objectless, it is in no sense because it may appear before any object relationship," but rather because its origin is in that moment, "more abstract than definable in time, since it is always renewed," when sexuality, "disengaged from any natural object, moves into the field of fantasy *and by that very fact becomes sexuality*" (25; emphasis added). And hence, they suggest, the ideal image of "auto-erotism is 'lips that kiss themselves.' Here, in this apparently self-centred enjoyment, as in the deepest fantasy, in this discourse no longer addressed to anyone, all distinction between subject and object has been lost" (26).

It is striking to refind this image in a text dated 1964, much prior too Irigaray's "When Our Lips Speak Together," which has made the image famous in feminist discourse ("Kiss me. Two lips kissing two lips . . .").[11] Often read as a representation of lesbian love, Irigaray's image has been criticized precisely for its blurring of all distinctions and difference between subject and object, and so confining the lesbian erotic relationship to the imaginary, or to the pre-oedipal, and in either case coming short of the symbolic and of the possibility of articulating lesbian subjectivity and desire therein.[12] Without going into the merits of the criticism of Irigaray's position at this time—a position, in any case, never reiterated or further elaborated in her work, and an image so much less forceful, less convincing as a figure of lesbian eros than the *J/e-tu,* protagonist of Monique Wittig's *The Lesbian Body,* with its/their difference and sameness, its/their violence and tenderness, its/their anaclitic overvaluation and narcissistic reversibility—let us read on to Laplanche and Pontalis's footnote to the image of the "lips that kiss themselves." They write:

Cf. also, in S. Freud, "Instincts and their vicissitudes" [1915], SE, vol. XIV, the analysis of the pairs of opposites, sadism-masochism, voyeurism-exhibitionism. Beneath the active or

11
Luce Irigaray, *This Sex Which Is Not One,* trans. Catherine Porter with Carolyn Burke (Ithaca, N.Y.: Cornell University Press, 1985), 210.

12
For a very useful and generous discussion of Irigaray's theory of sexual difference as "a theory of the *hetero-sexual* rather than the homo-sexual" that is feminist but not lesbian, see E. A. Grosz, "The Hetero and the Homo: The Sexual Ethics of Luce Irigaray," *Gay Information* (Australia), no. 17–18 (March 1988), 37–44.

passive form of the phrase (seeing, being seen, for instance), we must assume a reflexive form (seeing oneself) which, according to Freud, would be primordial. No doubt this primordial degree is to be found when the subject no longer places [her]self in one of the different terms of the fantasy. [34, note 64]

In the vicissitudes of the component instincts, with their oscillation between and copresence of opposites, the subject is caught up in a doubling and a splitting, a reversible pattern of specularization *and* differentiation that presupposes two terms of the fantasy, two bodies, and in the present instance, two female bodies (in this sense, as well, it takes two women, not one, to make a lesbian). The primordial, reflexive form of the instinct, seeing oneself—if primordial is taken in the sense of a constitutive, originary narcissism-voyeurism of the bodily ego[13]—may find a place in cinema in the position of the spectator as subject seeing herself and yet not seeing herself, a subject not placed in either one of the terms of the fantasy, but looking on, outside the fantasy scenario and nonetheless involved, present in it.

To explore this notion further, let us see how Laplanche and Pontalis argue for a homology between different levels of fantasy, from daydreams and reveries to the delusional fears of paranoiacs and the unconscious fantasies of hysterics.

From the unconscious fantasy distorted and yet revealed under the dream-façade, to the form it takes as the secondary elaboration reworks it into a fantasy more acceptable to consciousness, Laplanche and Pontalis maintain, Freud "discovers the same relationship between the deepest unconscious fantasy and the daydream: the fantasy is present at both extremities of the process of dreaming" (20–21). In the daydream, or in Freud's "model fantasy," the reverie, "that form of novelette, both stereotyped and infinitely variable, which the subject composes and relates to [her]self in a waking state,"
the scenario is basically in the first person, and the subject's place clear and invariable. . . . But the original fantasy, on the

13
"For the beginning of its activity the scopophilic instinct is auto-erotic: it has indeed an object, but that object is part of the subject's own body. . . . The only correct statement to make about the scopophilic instinct would be that all stages of its development, its auto-erotic, preliminary stage as well as its final active or passive form, coexist alongside one another" (Sigmund Freud, *The Standard Edition of the Complete Psychological Works of Sigmund Freud*, ed. James Strachey [London: Hogarth Press, 1953–74], vol. 14, 130). All further references to this work are given in the text by the abbreviation *SE* followed by the volume number in Roman numerals and the page number in Arabic numerals.

other hand, is characterized by the absence of subjectivization, and the subject is present in the scene: the child, for instance, is one character amongst many in the fantasy "a child is beaten." Freud insisted on this visualization of the subject on the same level as the other protagonists. [22]

Let us now consider the positions of the subject in the various forms of the beating fantasy analyzed in Freud's paper "A Child Is Being Beaten": its final form, as given in the title, overrides and is a substitute for two earlier ones, namely, "My father is beating the child" and "I am being beaten by my father." The latter form represents a transition from the first, objective form ("my father is beating the child"), in which the subject is altogether absent or unseeing, to the third and final one, in which the subject appears as a spectator, looking on as "a child is being beaten." The transitional form ("I am being beaten by my father"), Freud states, remains unconscious, is never remembered by the subject, and must be postulated as a construction in analysis. This transitional, unconscious form, buried beneath the first, objective form and the final, voyeuristic form of the beating fantasy, would seem to correspond to the reflexive form of the scopophilic instinct, "seeing oneself," which Laplanche and Pontalis posit ("we must assume") beneath the active or passive form, and which also usually remains unconscious in the cinema spectator.

The analogy between the subject of fantasy and the subject in cinematic spectatorship may be extended further: the unconscious beating fantasy is both active and passive ("the form of this fantasy is sadistic; the satisfaction which is derived from it is masochistic" [SE, XVII, 191]), and the subject is directly present and participating in it in a fully subjectivized manner—and hence it remains unconscious. Similarly, the reflexive "seeing oneself" of the subject in cinematic spectatorship is both active and passive, as well as unconscious. If the three forms of the beating fantasy are different manifestations of the structural and imaginary "unity of the fantasy whole," as Laplanche and Pontalis remark (22), it is possible to argue that a similar "unity" could be produced as subject-effect in spectatorship; that is to say, the film would constitute the spectator as subject of its fantasy in its different levels and forms, would provide at once the fantasy and the means of access to it, would make a place for the spectator as subject in its fantasy, by the solicitation of her "primordial" autoerotic and scopophilic instinct in its reflexive form. Hence Freud's insistence on the visualization of the subject in clinical practice acquires relevance for the practice of film viewing, as well as film theory: How do I look at the film? How do I appear in its fantasy? Am I looking on? Can I be seen? Do I see myself in it? Is this my fantasy?

The foregoing discussion is relevant to my argument in two ways. First, to my reading of the film: the significance of its reframing the Catalina fantasy as a film-within-the-film—a fantasy within what is already a fantasmatic regime in spectatorship—and of presenting it to the spectator mediated by the two framing characters of Jo and Agatha, and by the larger frame of the narrative of *She Must Be Seeing Things,* is that the film sets or embeds the primal scene, "the deepest fantasy" (which, as in clinical anamnesis, occurs very late or at the end of the two films), within a situation of adult, postoedipal lesbian sexuality where the symbolic, as well as the imaginary, is conspicuously present and foregrounded (what could be more symbolic or socially marked—technologically, semiotically, and ideologically—than the apparatus of film production?). Thus both autoerotism, which Laplanche and Pontalis locate at the origin of sexuality and subject processes in fantasy, and female object-choice coexist in the subjectivity of the two women who, by this very coexistence, may be identified as lesbians. It is because of such reframing, mediation, and symbolic inscription of lesbian fantasy that the use of the convention of the film-within-the-film is so important to the film's address. By positioning the spectator in the place of the subject—the subject looking on or the desubjectivized subject—of the fantasy it represents, the film does not merely represent a lesbian fantasy but makes it accessible to the spectator, renders it representable for her as self-representation. In other words, in acting as the relay of our spectatorial position(s) in desire, Agatha and Jo provide a *visualization* of the subject and the figure, mise en abîme, of the very processes of spectatorship, namely, identification with the image(s) (of the primal fantasy), production of reference and meaning in the narrative construction (selective [re]arrangement of the images into a secondarized, narrativized scenario), and affective participation at a distance: the spatial and symbolic, representational distance of the spectator from the screen and of the voyeur from the scene looked on, and the psychotemporal distance of the subject from that "other scene," the original fantasy.

Secondly, and somewhat incidentally in the present context, I will advance the thesis of a longer work in progress: lesbian sexuality is neither convergent with heterosexual female sexuality (where autoerotism and narcissism do not coexist with female object-choice), nor pre-oedipal, in the sense of the "mother-child dyad" dear to much of so-called psychoanalytic feminism, nor finally altogether outside or independent of the oedipal fantasy structure, as many would prefer to think. A corollary of this thesis, which I expect to be unpopular in feminist circles, is that the notion of female sexuality as fluid, diffuse, polymorphously perverse, or mobile and unbounded, is applicable to lesbian sexuality only if the above qualifiers are not, as they usually are, taken to be equivalent to bisexual. For it seems to me that this notion of female bisexuality, with its emphasis on androgyny—or a blurring of the boundaries between male-sexed and female-sexed bodies, or of the boundaries of gender that, wishful theorizing notwithstanding, do stick to the sexed body in one way or another—is itself a fantasy. And not a very engaging fantasy for lesbians.

In their essay Laplanche and Pontalis mention three original fantasies, or fantasies of origins, so-called because, "[l]ike myths, they claim to provide a representation of, and a solution to, the major enigmas which confront the child": the primal scene (*Urszene*), which "pictures the origin of the individual" in the child's imaging of parental coitus; seduction, "the origin and upsurge of sexuality"; and castration, "the origin of the difference between the sexes" (19). Since this film is centrally concerned with fantasy in relation to vision and to subjectivity, it is not surprising that the other two primal fantasies are traceable as well. The seduction fantasy I will discuss in some detail later on. As for the castration fantasy, it is recurrently figured from the very beginning of the film, in Agatha's conscious fantasies or daydreams of Jo's sexual encounters with men, in her sadistic fantasies of Jo machine-gunned in the street (reminiscent of the ending of *Bonnie and Clyde* [1967] and Valie Export's *Invisible Adversaries* [1977]) or strangled with the telephone cord (as in *Dial M for Murder* [1954]), as well as in her hallucinations or unconscious fantasies: most forcefully in the scene where, from her office window, Agatha sees Jo walking down the street flirting with a man and kissing him. The film presents this scene, constructed as a series of alternating shot/reverse-shots and jump cuts, specifically as a hallucination: that is, the woman walking in the street, in the first reverse shot and jump cut, is clearly recognizable to the spectator as Jo (Lois Weaver), but suddenly, after the second cut to the reverse shot from Agatha, she is revealed to be not Jo but an unknown woman who *looks like* her. I will come back to this scene, but it may be useful to note, anticipating what I will be discussing later on, that if Agatha's jealousy

de Lauretis

is consistently cast in heterosexual terms, as jealousy of men—whereas, to this viewer, the jeweller (played by Peggy Shaw) or Agatha's friend Julia (played by Elizabeth Cunningham) would seem much more likely causes for jealousy—it is not only because the film explicitly engages the standard codes of representation, which are of course straight, but also because it does not disavow the effective presence of the castration fantasy in jealousy itself, whatever the immediate cause of jealousy may be. (Speaking of her lover, Julia says: "With Kate, I know she's gay. She's been with women. I don't get jealous of men." Agatha replies: "So what? You get jealous of women.")

The origin of the castration fantasy is also inscribed in the film-within-the-film, in the scene where the young (pre-oedipal) Catalina and her girlfriend in the convent are threatened by a nun with God's punishment for an "evil" of which they have no knowledge. Enter the symbolic as deux ex machina: the prohibition at once producing fantasy and desire, the perversion is implanted in the subject, as Foucault might have said. Subsequently, and consistently with the film's overall treatment of fantasy, the castration fantasy is re-presented at the manifest level, framed in the terms of current lesbian practices and discourses around the vicissitudes of the sexual instincts, around sadomasochism, voyeurism, and exhibitionism: in the scene in the porno shop, where Agatha goes to confront the phallus in its humbler manifestation and commodity form, the dildo, the three fantasies come together and are in one deromanticized and denaturalized in the ironic figure of the "sex toys," the dildo and the rubber doll. The irony is underscored by the disgusted look of the sales*woman,* which remarks the male customer's insistence in wanting the window display doll, and by the unctuous, supercilious attitude of the sales*man* assisting Agatha in the selection of a "realistic" dildo. Gender asymmetry in male and female access to a sexuality defined by sexual commodities is made explicit in this exchange and is one of the points of the irony. However, if Agatha leaves the store without buying into the commodified heterosexual fantasy, nevertheless all of the primal fantasies rearticulated by the film in relation to a lesbian subject still necessarily include and have to come to terms with men. Which brings me to one of the problems of the film for many of its viewers, its inscription of and central concern with heterosexuality.[14] And would it were a problem only for the film.

The reception of *She Must Be Seeing Things* at the 1987 San Francisco Lesbian and Gay Film Festival and in Santa Cruz when I screened it for my Women and Cinema class was equally divided: some women loved it, others were profoundly upset by it. Lesbians especially were disturbed by the heterosexual fantasies, and many by the butch-femme role-playing: they either did not like that representation of a lesbian relationship, or if they did, they thought it shouldn't be made public on film but kept as the proverbial skeleton in the lesbian closet. It fared worse still in London: during a women-only screening, some women stormed the screen while others tried to rip the film from the

14
Other problems include the representation of gay men or gay sexuality, and especially the question of the relation of lesbian sexuality to race, which, though raised by the very casting of Sheila Dabney as Agatha, is not addressed as such by the film but instead is displaced by an emphasis on ethnic or cultural difference (Agatha is a middle-class Brazilian living in New York). Although the reasons for this displacement would be an interesting and important point of speculation in an interpretive account of the film, they are not directly relevant to the present argument.

15
See Victoria
Brownworth, "Dyke S/M
Wars Rage in London: Rac-
ism and Fascism Alleged,"
Coming Up! 10, no. 1 (Octo-
ber 1988), 14–15.

projector, claiming it was pornography, and s&m pornography at
that.[15] In an interview published in *Screen,* Sheila McLaughlin de-
fends her film by saying, among other things, the following:
Heterosexuality is the dominant code of the society that we live
in, and it defines and in a sense creates our own sexuality,
whether we choose to participate as literally heterosexuals or
not. I think it's somehow inescapable, that we're inextricably
bound up with that. We've gone through a long time of trying to
deny that, and yet it's important, if we ever want to get beyond
that stage, to find a "new language" or whatever you want to
call it, to work through that in some sort of discourse before we
can free ourselves from it, or figure out what our desire is
or is about. . . .

What I wanted to do in this film was to foreground the relationship between the two women and then have that act in
relation to male culture. I think it's positive because women
have been talking about difference, sexuality and desire for a
very short time, and I think that during the 60s and 70s we
came into danger of becoming our own police and being extremely moralistic and judgmental about what one can and can't
do as a "feminist." With this film, I wanted to open up the no-

16
Alison Butler,
" 'She Must Be Seeing
Things': An Interview with
Sheila McLaughlin," *Screen*
28, no. 4 (Autumn 1987),
20–21.

tions and possibilities of what women can do, to try to confront
and be iconoclastic towards what have become lesbian and feminist taboos. And hopefully by confronting them, to begin to
break down the power that they have, to digest them somehow.[16]
Indeed, heterosexuality is a ubiquitous institution in our culture,
pervasively embedded in practices of daily life as well as in the
media, language, art, science, literature, and the very structures

17
Monique Wittig,
"The Straight Mind," *Feminist Issues* 1, no. 1 (Summer
1980), 103–11. See also
Teresa de Lauretis, "The
Female Body and Hetero-
sexual Presumption," *Semi-
otica* 67, no. 3–4 (1987),
259–79; and Claire
Pajaczkowska, "The Het-
erosexual Presumption: A
Contribution to the Debate
on Pornography," *Screen* 22,
no. 1 (1981), 79–94.

of thought and knowledge that inform what Wittig has called
"The Straight Mind" (with pointed reference to Lévi-Strauss's
The Savage Mind), arguing that the social contract and symbolic
exchange that establish culture and society itself are *founded* on
the presupposition, or as I prefer to say, the presumption of
heterosexuality.[17] "When thought by the straight mind, homo-

sexuality is nothing but heterosexuality," writes Wittig (108), supporting McLaughlin's view that heterosexuality inevitably informs our conception of sexuality. And yet, why is it that the sex scenes with men in this film don't really work?

Whether they are bland or violent, the sex scenes with men in the film are not erotic but, rather, demonstrative and mechanical—not just the fantasies, daydreams, or hallucinations shot from the subjective point of view of Agatha, but also the scene with the "real" man who asks Jo to spend the night with him. I cannot imagine anyone being turned on by any of those scenes, in themselves. On the other hand, what I find erotic and emotionally engaging is Agatha's jealousy and her desire, figured in her look and position as outsider, as voyeur (and re-presented *en abîme* in the film-within-the-film, in Catalina watching, looking on, behind the curtain), and figured as well in the male suit she puts on to signify her desire in socially visible form, effectively to come out publicly and *visibly to herself* (as suggested by the scene in front of the mirror), to give herself courage. Or,

conversely, the desire figured in Jo's position as exhibitionist, the role she plays for Agatha in the boa striptease scene, clearly marked as a seduction fantasy, and a fully cinematic fantasy, with hints of Marlene Dietrich, Rita Hayworth, and Marilyn Monroe rolled into one, and Amina's aria from Bellini's *La sonnambula* on the soundtrack. In other words, it is *the active, conscious, and even flaunted assumption* of those positions as expressions of desire, signifiers of seduction, and the performance and reversal of sexual roles as a means of taking up and signaling, as modes of representing, the position of desiring subject, that are exciting for me, spectator—looking on the fantasy scenario that is the film—and certainly much more exciting, and much less banal, than the positions or the roles themselves.

The fact that they are roles, standard positions, as it were, in which desire is represented and defined, indeed prescribed, in a culture predicated on hetero-sexual difference, is foregrounded by the amateur quality of the performance, its being acted, marked as a performance (the scenes of Agatha's cross-dressing and Jo's femme masquerade open with each coming out from behind a curtain in their respective apartments), and distanced by irony (the hole in the stocking) or by lack of fit (Agatha in a man's suit). So that we see the face behind the mask, the mask doesn't quite fit, and the masquerade is never quite successful; or rather, it is successful *as a masquerade*—not an embodiment. For Agatha is clearly not a man (even as she "preferred identifying" with her father to falling in love with him), and Jo is not the female star in her full-drag impersonation of femininity but is in fact the filmmaker, the director, whose desire for Agatha is inscribed and figured, not to say sublimated, in her work. Which, when you think about it, is a very "masculine" position, as is her near-total absorption in her work. Unlike the previous inscriptions of original fantasies, the seduction fantasy is not reframed in the film-within-the-film, not narratively mediated by the characters serving as the relay of the spectator's look, as point of identification and spectatorial desire. It is constructed as a cinematic spectacle whose obvious iconographic references to movie stars and popular Hollywood scenarios of seduction frame the fantasy in an ironic, camp self-reflexivity. Here, then, the mediation, the reframing, is provided by the very codes and tropes of Hollywood cinema and camp aesthetic, by the figures of masquerade and cross-dressing with their long-term presence in the history of Western cinema and cultural representations, as well as their specific contemporary articulations.

The notions of masquerade, transvestism, and cross-dressing have been recurrent figures of feminist discourse in the 1980s, and in the theorization of female spectatorship in particular.[18] In her essay "Towards a Butch-Femme Aesthetic," Sue-Ellen Case takes up the issue of masquerade in the context of performance theory and a lesbian camp aesthetic. Discussing the Split

18
For example, Laura Mulvey, "Afterthoughts on 'Visual Pleasure and Narrative Cinema' inspired by King Vidor's *Duel in the Sun* (1946)," in *Visual and Other Pleasures* (Bloomington: Indiana University Press, 1989), 29–38; Mary Ann Doane, "Film and the Masquerade: Theorising the Female Spectator," *Screen* 23, no. 3–4 (September–October 1982), 74–87; Elaine Showalter, "Critical Cross-Dressing: Male Feminists and the Woman of the Year," *Raritan*, 3, no. 2 (1983), 130–49; Sandra Gilbert, "Costumes of the Mind: Transvestism as Metaphor in Modernist Literature," *Critical Inquiry* 7, no. 2 (Winter 1980), 391–417; and Jane Gaines, "The Queen Christina Tie-Ups," *Quarterly Review of Film and Video* 11, no. 1 (1989), 35–60.

Britches' production of *Beauty and the Beast,* where Peggy Shaw as the butch, "who represents by her clothing the desire for other women, becomes the beast—the marked taboo against lesbianism dressed up in the clothes of that desire," and Lois Weaver as the femme plays Beauty, "the desired one and the one who aims her desirability at the butch," Case writes:

This symbolism becomes explicit when Shaw and Weaver interrupt the Beauty/Beast narrative to deliver a duologue about the history of their own personal butch-femme roles. Weaver uses the trope of having wished she was Katherine [*sic*] Hepburn and casting another woman as Spencer Tracy, while Shaw relates that she thought she was James Dean. The identification with movie idols is part of the camp assimilation of dominant culture. It serves multiple purposes. One, they do not identify these butch-femme roles with "real" people, or literal images of gender, but with fictionalized ones, thus underscoring the masquerade. Two, the history of their desire, or their search for a sexual partner becomes a series of masks, or identities that stand for

19
Herbert Blau, "Disseminating Sodom," *Salmagundi*, no. 58–59 (1983), 233–34, cited by Case, 61. On the function of camp as a means to propose "female homosexuality as an aesthetic and not only a sexual choice," see Sabine Hake's interesting reading of Ulrike Ottinger's film, "'Gold, Love, Adventure': The Postmodern Piracy of *Madame X*," *Discourse* 11, no. 1 (Fall–Winter 1988–89), 97. Hake, however, unlike Case, seems unconcerned with distancing the postmodern taste for camp from the material and social realities of homosexuality, or with making any distinction between lesbian, gay, and "homosexual" consciousness, sensibility, or sexualities: "the retro mode characteristic of camp presupposes an alienated consciousness and an aesthetic appreciation that are essential both to the homosexual and the postmodern sensibility. Camp functions as an aesthetic position on sexual difference by exposing all categories of meaning production to a play with the pervasive/perverse levels of many sexualities." How important it is to distinguish between a lesbian and a gay camp aesthetic, a distinction that devolves from the sexual and gender asymmetry between "homosexual" subjectivities as they are constituted both discursively and materially at this moment in history in North America, is evident if one reads Case's essay with Leo Bersani's "Is the Rectum a Grave?" (*October* 43, [Winter 1987], now in *AIDS: Cultural Analysis/Cultural Activism*, ed. Douglas Crimp, [Cambridge, Mass.:

sexual attraction in the culture, thus distancing them from the "play" of seduction as it is outlined by social mores. Three, the association with movies makes narrative fiction part of the strategy as well as characters. [67–68]

The purpose of Case's essay is to articulate a feminist subject-position "outside the ideology of sexual difference and thus the social institution of heterosexuality" (56), and this, for her, can only be the position of "the butch-femme subject" (63). Her thesis requires, on the one hand, bringing "the lesbian subject out of the closet of feminist history" (57), which she does by retracing the steps of the interaction between feminism and lesbianism in North America to the early 1970s and the project of the Daughters of Bilitis, whose outcome was the alliance between lesbians and heterosexual feminists, an alliance that resulted in the elision of the material reality of the cross-dressing or passing woman and the appropriation of her strategies, safely metaphorized into discursive tropes, by a heterosexual feminist discourse primarily concerned with femininity and the female subject/body in relation to "sexual difference," and hence to masculinity and to men.

On the other hand, Case's own project requires recuperating the discourse of camp, the style and *mise en scène* of butch-femme roles—roles that "are played in signs themselves and not in ontologies" (70). But, in turn, the recuperation of camp to the side of a lesbian aesthetic and a lesbian (feminist) politics requires a distinction, a distancing of the latter from the discourse of a generalized "postmodernism." For, as Case remarks, "camp style, gay-identified dressing, and the articulation of the social realities of homosexuality have also become part of the straight, postmodern canon." And she cites Herbert Blau's homophobic authority ("becoming-homosexual is part of the paraphilia of the postmodern") in order to launch her critique of contemporary theory's appropriation of gay and especially lesbian discourses, an appropriation that again goes hand in hand

MIT Press, 1988], 197–222).
Bersani sees homosexual
camp not as irony or erotic
turn-on but as parody,
"largely a parody of wo-
men," and parody, he
states, "is an erotic turn-off,
and all gay men know this.
. . . The gay male parody of
a certain femininity [is
also] a way of giving vent to
the hostility toward women
that probably afflicts every
male": it "speaks the truth
of that femininity as mind-
less, asexual, and hyster-
ically bitchy, thereby
provoking, it would seem to
me, a violently antimimetic
reaction in any female
spectator" (208). I owe this
observation to my friends of
the Lesbian and Gay Fac-
ulty Research Group at the
University of California,
Santa Cruz.

20
Joan Riviere,
"Womanliness as a Mas-
querade," *The International
Journal of Psychoanalysis,*
vol. 10 (1929), reprinted in
Formations of Fantasy, 35–
44. On Joan Riviere and the
fortunes of masquerade as
the figure of femininity in
Lacanian psychoanalytic
theory and in cinema, see
Stephen Heath, "Joan Ri-
viere and the Masquerade,"
also in *Formations of Fantasy,* 45–61.

21
Doane, "Film and
the Masquerade," 80. The
internal reference is to
Mulvey, *Visual and Other
Pleasures,* 29–38.

with the elision of their social and material realities.[19] And hence her recapitulation of the vicissitudes of the figure of masquerade, first put forth by the Freudian analyst Joan Riviere in her analysis of a heterosexual woman patient.[20] After a brief and, itself, campy synopsis of Riviere's paper, Case concludes:

Thus began the theory that all womanliness is a masquerade worn by women to disguise the fact that they have taken their father's penis in their intellectual stride, so to speak. Rather than remaining the well-adjusted castrated woman, these intellectuals have taken the penis for their own and protect it with the mask of the castrated, or womanhood." [64]

Then she goes on to take issue with Mary Ann Doane's concept of masquerade as the term of a possible subject-position for female spectators. In order to make the argument fully intelligible, I will briefly summarize Doane's thesis, which is as follows: psychoanalytic and film theory, as well as dominant cinema, negate the female gaze, or rather inscribe it as overidentified with the image, and hence unseeing, empty of desire (she acutely points to the figure of the woman with glasses, a recurrent motif of classical Hollywood cinema, counterposed to the figure of the man with binoculars).

The pervasiveness, in theories of the feminine, of descriptions of such a claustrophobic closeness [to the image], a deficiency in relation to structures of seeing and the visible [result in] a tendency to view the female spectator as the site of an oscillation between a feminine position and a masculine position, invoking the metaphor of the transvestite. Given the structures of cinematic narrative, the woman who identifies with a female character must adopt a passive or masochistic position, while identification with the active hero necessarily entails an acceptance of what Laura Mulvey refers to as a certain "masculinisation" of spectatorship.[21]

But transvestism (by which both Doane and Mulvey mean a metaphoric, subjective transfer of female to male point of view) may be recuperated into the accepted notion of women's greater sexual mobility or bisexuality, on which both Freud and Hélène Cixous, for example, agree. On the contrary, masquerade as the hyperbolic, excessive demonstration of femininity as a cultural construct would not be recuperable, according to Doane, within the terms of current definitions of woman—her being body, as Cixous declared, or her being object and sign of cultural exchange, as Lévi-Strauss did, and so on—because masquerade "constitutes an acknowledgement that it is femininity itself which is constructed as mask" and because "in flaunting femininity [the masquerading woman] holds it at a distance" (81), the distance which Doane rightly deems "necessary for an adequate reading of the image" (87). Doane's effort, in other words, is to find a position in heterosexuality from which the woman (spectator) can see and signify her desire in her distance from the image. The question remains, however, whether this distance can in fact be assumed by the straight female spectator in relation to the image of woman on the screen: how would a spectator "flaunt" her femininity in the dark of the movie theater? Again, a question of vision and visibility—how does she look, how do I look? Finally, then, whether or not she can assume that distance without sliding into the "transvestite" position (that is the male point of view) is the theoretical problem Doane's essay poses but fails to elaborate.

Case criticizes Doane on two counts. First, that the masquerade of femininity as a position of spectatorship, whereby the (heterosexual) female viewer can "appropriate the gaze for [her] own pleasure," is still a passive, conventionally feminine position; and here Case's own frame of reference, which is *theatrical* representation and performance and the specific subject effects and positions in spectatorship produced in theatrical (as contrasted with filmic) representation, is most likely responsible for her erroneous assumption that film spectatorship is a *passive* or *object*like mode of subjectivity, as opposed to the *active* mode of stage performance, the femme who "performs her masquerade as the *subject* of representation" (66; emphasis added). As I have suggested earlier about cinema as fantasmatic production, in connection with Laplanche and Pontalis's paper on the originary role of fantasy in subjectivity and sexual identity, film spectatorship can be just as active and constitutive for the subject as a more public or *visible* "activity" (once again, the question of visibility, what *can be seen?*). In fact, Doane herself makes clear that what she is trying to articulate, against dominant views of the female spectator/subject as incapable of vision, is a position of (heterosexual) female spectatorship not only active, but distanced from the specular effects of the image, and so capable of acting as the subject of signification and desire. Unfortunately, as she herself admits, her effort is not successful.[22] On the second count of her critique, however, Case is not mistaken. The femme, she argues, "delivers a performance of the feminine masquerade rather than, as Doane suggests, continuing in Riviere's reactive formation of masquerading compensatorily before the male-gaze-inscribed-dominant-cinema-screen" (66). Between the femme, who foregrounds her masquerade of femininity by playing to a butch, and the butch, who foregrounds her own masquerade of the phallus to the femme, "the fictions of penis and castration become ironized and 'camped up'. . . . In other words, these penis-related posturings were always acknowledged [in lesbian bar culture] as roles, not biological birthrights" (64–65).

The problem with trying to claim masquerade as a "non-recuperable" position of agency for the female subject is precisely its compensatory nature of reaction-formation, that is to say, of defense mechanism against the male's requirement that women acquiesce and accept what he defines as femininity and lay no claim to masculine prerogative; as such, it is not only inscribed within a male-defined and male-dominant heterosexual order, but more inexorably, in the current struggle for women's

22
In the same issue of the journal where Case's essay appears, perhaps coincidentally, Doane's own afterthoughts on her 1982 article are published as well. Here the point is made even more explicit: "'Film and the Masquerade,'" she writes, is an "attempt (which fails in many respects) to tear the concept of masquerade out of its conventional context. Generally, masquerade is employed not to illuminate the agency usually associated with spectatorship, but to designate a mode of being for the other—hence, the sheer objectification or reification of representation" (Doane, "Masquerade Reconsidered: Further Thoughts on the Female Spectator," *Discourse* 11, no. 1 [Fall–Winter 1988–89], 42).

23

As Irigaray puts it in *Ce Sexe qui n'en est pas un*, "the masquerade . . . is what women do . . . in order to participate in man's desire, but at the cost of giving up theirs"; or as another woman laments, "When women give up the masquerade, what do they find in bed? Women analysts, how do they cause erections?" (cited in Heath, "Joan Riviere and the Masquerade," 54–55).

24

Laura Mulvey, *Visual and Other Pleasures*, 33.

25

Patricia White, "Madame X of the China Seas," *Screen* 28, no. 4 (Autumn 1987), 94, citing Doane, "Film and the Masquerade," 81.

"equal access" to pleasure in heterosexuality, the masquerade of femininity is bound to reproduce that order by addressing itself—its work, its effects, its plea—to heterosexual men.[23] This "daughter's seduction," in contemporary Western culture, is certainly recuperable and in fact recuperated even within the academic institution. What is not, on the other hand, is the female—butch, femme, bad girl, or good girl—who does not address her masquerade to men. That this possibility has not been seen or even contemplated in feminist theorizations of masquerade is the point made by Case and elaborated in another context by Patricia White.

In the course of a reading of Ulrike Ottinger's *Madame X,* White also discusses Doane's notions of masquerade and transvestism, retracing the latter to Mulvey, who put it thus: "as desire is given cultural materiality in a text, for women (from childhood onwards) trans-sex identification is a *habit* that very easily becomes *second nature*. However, this Nature does not sit easily and shifts restlessly in its borrowed transvestite clothes."[24] But "why must *transvestite* clothes be 'borrowed'?" asks White, pointing out the absurdity of the statement that for the transvestite "clothes make the man."[25] She thus makes explicit the assumptions of these feminist theorists that women are uncomfortable in masculine clothes due to their real sex (the first nature) and/or female desire, and that women can and do cross-dress, metaphorically and otherwise, *with impunity* by virtue of their alleged "sexual mobility." Such assumptions are all the more insidious in the frame of reference and visibility of contemporary theory alluded to by Case, in which lesbians and gay men who cross-dress and/or masquerade *must be seen* as simply and safely acting out "the paraphilia of the postmodern," like everyone else.

To return to McLaughlin's film, then, and in the terms I have been developing earlier, the butch-femme role-playing is exciting not because it represents heterosexual desire, but

because it doesn't; that is to say, in mimicking it, it shows the
uncanny distance, like an effect of ghosting, between desire
(heterosexually represented as it is) and the representation; and
because the representation doesn't fit the actors who perform
it, it only points to their investment in a fantasy—a fantasy that
can never fully represent them or their desire, for the latter
remains in excess of its setting, the fantasy that grounds it and
that continues to ground it even as it is deconstructed and de-
stabilized by the mise en scène of lesbian camp. It is in that
space between the fantasy scenario and the self-critical, ironic
lesbian gaze—a space the film constructs evidently and
purposefully—that I am addressed as spectator and that a
subject-position is figured out and made available in terms of a
sexual difference that is not a difference between woman and
man, between female and male sexuality, but a difference between heterosexual and lesbian sexuality. So I do not identify
with either woman or role, for the film works as a fantasy for

me as well, offering not the object but the setting of my desire. What I do identify with is the space of excess and contradiction that the role, the lack of fit, the disjuncture, the *difference* between characters and roles make apparent in each of them, the space in which that difference configures a lesbian subject-position, that is, the space of a desire that is at once for the same and for the other, but in a woman, and therefore quite distinct from the heterosexual notion of bisexuality as desire for both men and women, where the self is woman and the other is man, or vice versa.

The distinction I'm trying to make between, on the one hand, the representation of desire heterosexually conceived, even as it is attributed to a woman for another, and, on the other hand, the effort to represent a homosexual-lesbian desire is a subtle and difficult one. The reception of McLaughlin's film is evidence of that difficulty, which is not only due to the diverse meanings that have accrued to those two words *lesbian* and *desire,* but even more derives from the complexity of representation itself, the weight of its culturally established codes and expressive forms, and the overdetermination of its effects, the ways it engages the viewer's subjective processes, both conscious and unconscious. So let me backtrack a moment from this film to the historical and cultural ground from which it so singularly emerges. In all the culturally dominant forms of representation that surround us, from television to museum art, from the most banal love story to the most sublime one can think of, desire is predicated on sexual difference as gender difference, the difference of woman from man or femininity from masculinity, with all that those terms entail—and not as a difference between heterosexual and homosexual, or straight and gay sexuality. This is the sense in which I read McLaughlin's statement that heterosexuality "defines and in a sense creates our sexuality." She means, of course, the *institution* of heterosexuality, and not heterosexual behavior, the event of sexual intercourse between a woman and a man, which may or may not occur. But even for those whose sexual behavior or whose desire has never been heterodirected, even for them heterosexuality is "inescapable," though not determining. For, if sexuality is represented as gendered, as the direct result of the existence of two sexes in nature—on which basis culture has constructed gender and onto which in turn civilization has attached meanings, affects, and values, such as love, social relations, and the continuation of the human species—then it follows that sexuality is finally inescapable for every single human being, as is gender; no one can be without them, because they are part and parcel of being human. Thus sexuality is not only *defined* but actually *enforced* as heterosexuality, even in its homosexual form.

Moreover, as feminist theory has argued for two decades now, sexuality in the dominant forms of Western culture is defined from the frame of reference of "man," the white man, who has enforced his claim to be the subject of knowing, and woman—all women—his object: object of both his knowledge and his desire. Heterosexuality, therefore, is doubly enforced on women, as it were: enforced as hetero-sexuality, in the sense that women can and must feel sexually in relation to men, and enforced as hetero-sexuality in the sense that sexual desire belongs to the other, originates in him. In this standard frame, amazingly simplistic and yet authoritative, and reaffirmed again and again, not least by a woman theorist often invoked by feminists, Julia Kristeva, whatever women may feel toward other women cannot be sexual desire, unless it be a usurpation or a perverted, unnatural imitation of man's desire. Here is Kristeva: Lesbian loves comprise the delightful arena of a neutralized, filtered libido, devoid of the erotic cutting edge of masculine sexuality. Light touches, caresses, barely distinct images fading one into the other, growing dim or veiled without bright flashes into the mellowness of a dissolution, a liquefaction, a merger. . . . Relaxation of consciousness, daydream, language that is neither dialectical nor rhetorical, but peace or eclipse: nirvana, intoxication, and silence. When such a paradise is not a sidelight of phallic eroticism, its parenthesis and its rest, when it aspires to set itself up as absolute of a mutual relationship, the nonrelationship that it is bursts into view. Two paths are then open . . .[26]

26
Julia Kristeva, "Manic Eros, Sublime Eros: On Male Sexuality," in *Tales of Love*, trans. Leon S. Roudiez (New York: Columbia University Press, 1987), 81. See also, in the same volume, her "Stabat Mater," and my critique of it in "The Female Body and Heterosexual Presumption," cited above, note 17.

Lesbian sexuality, in other words, is a nonrelationship, or a *nonsexual* relationship: unless it is an adjunct, a sideline, an added attraction to the cutting edge of masculine sexuality (which is what this chapter of *Histoires d'amour* is specifically about), sex between women is a bland pre-oedipal soup. From it only two paths are open: return to the eroto-logic of the master-slave relationship, or death—loss of identity, psychosis, suicide ("identité perdue, dissolution léthale de la psychose, angoisse des frontières perdues, appel suicidaire du fond").

This, then, is what makes the Barbara Stanwyck character the villain in *Walk on the Wild Side,* and what Vera in Sergio Toledo's film of the same name has so well internalized that she is convinced she is a man because she desires a woman: one may not be born a woman or a man, but one can only desire as a man. And this is, of course, the classic representation of the mannish lesbian since Stephen Gordon in Radclyffe Hall's *The Well of Loneliness,* a novel continuously and widely read since its obscenity trial in 1928 and the focus of debate among lesbian feminists even recently. In fact, McLaughlin's film refers to that representation explicitly in the interchange between Agatha and Jo on the bed, after the striptease scene, where Jo taunts Agatha about phallic desire. Agatha admits to feeling it "maybe-sometimes" but also adds with clear conviction, "But I don't want to be a man." Shortly after, the scene in the porno shop further explores and ironizes this contradictory relation of Agatha's "masculine" identification to the representation of phallic desire signified by the gingerly held, ironically "realistic" dildo.

By calling up this iconographic and cultural history, in conjunction with current lesbian practices of both reappropriation and deconstruction of what is and is not our history, the film asks what in feminist film culture is clearly a rhetorical question: what are the things Agatha imagines seeing and those Jo "sees" in her film, if not those very images, "a terror and a dream" (as Adrienne Rich so sharply put it), that our cultural imaginary and the whole history of cinema have constructed as the visible, what can be seen, *and eroticized?* Namely, the female body displayed as spectacle for the male gaze "to take it in," to enter or possess it, or as fetish object of his secret identification; the woman as mystery to be pursued, investigated, found guilty or redeemed by man. Above all, what can be seen and eroticized— though it is not actually imaged or represented on the screen, but only figured, implied, in the look—is the gaze itself, the phallic power of the gaze invested in the male look as figure and signifier of desire.[27] Feminist film criticism and theory have documented this history of representation extensively. Now, the originality of McLaughlin's film, in my opinion, consists precisely in its foregrounding of that frame of reference, making *it* visible, and at the same time shifting it, moving it aside, as it were, enough to let us see through the gap, the contradiction; enough to create a space for questioning not only what *they* see but also what *we* see in the film; enough to let us see ourselves seeing, and with what eyes.[28] The importance and the novelty of the film's question—what are the "things" she must be seeing?— consist in that, insofar as the film addresses the spectator in a lesbian subject-position, the question is addressed to lesbians. Thus it is no longer a rhetorical question in the sense that the answer is already known or can be taken for granted, but is reactivated as a rhetorical question in the sense that it can turn around, suspend, subvert the expected answer.

This is not the case in films or other visual practices that simply set out to represent "lesbians" but without shifting or reworking the standard frame of reference, the conventions of

27

For an extensive reexamination of the concept of the gaze in relation to cinematic voyeurism, narcissism, and male subjectivity, see Kaja Silverman, "Fassbinder and Lacan: A Reconsideration of Gaze, Look and Image," *Camera Obscura*, no. 19 (January 1989), 54–84. Her thesis, that "Fassbinder's films work to ruin or deface" the phallus as "the image of the penis" (78) and consequently mark the look and the male body as the very site of castration, proposes Fassbinder as the subject of a radical cinematic practice. Whether or how this may relate to his homosexuality, Silverman does not suggest, but her argument is potentially rich nonetheless for a consideration of gay male spectatorship.

28

My argument here runs somewhat parallel to Marilyn Frye's essay "To Be and Be Seen," in *The Politics of Reality: Essays in Feminist Theory* (Trumansburg, N.Y.: The Crossing Press, 1983), 152–74. But I am less certain than she is that the simple visibility of lesbians is a sufficient condition for the representation or the formation of lesbian subjectivity. My argument for McLaughlin's film as a text that foregrounds the complexity and difficulty of lesbian visibility is also, in this sense, in dialogue with Frye.

seeing and the established modes and complex effects of representation, which are so closely anchored, if not altogether contained, by a frame of visibility that is still, alas, heterosexual. I am not convinced, for instance, by Jill Dolan's assertion that the reappropriation of pornographic imagery by lesbian magazines such as *On Our Backs* offers "liberative fantasies" and "representations of one kind of sexuality based in lesbian desire."[29] I'm not at all convinced by this argument, made in an otherwise convincing and important article, because its very premise, its basis, lesbian desire, is merely assumed to be, and taken for granted as, a property or a quality of individuals predefined as lesbians; whereas it is precisely that "lesbian desire" that constitutes the kind of subjectivity and sexuality we experience as lesbian and want to claim as lesbians; and which therefore we need to theorize, articulate, and find ways of representing, not only in its difference from heterosexual norms, its ab-normality, but also and more importantly in its own constitutive processes, its specific modalities and conditions of existence. The simple casting of two women in a standard pornographic scenario or in the standard frame of the hetero romance, repackaged as a commodity purportedly produced for lesbians, does not seem to me sufficient to disrupt, subvert, or resist the straight representational and social norms by which "homosexuality is nothing but heterosexuality" nor *a fortiori* sufficient to shed light on the specific difference that constitutes a lesbian subjectivity.

In Donna Deitch's *Desert Hearts* (1985), for instance, heterosexuality as sexual behavior remains off-screen and is diegetically cast off in a quick Reno divorce, but heterosexuality as institution is still actively present in the spectatorial expectations set up by the genre—the Western romance, with its seamless narrative space, its conventional casting and characterization—and by commercial distribution techniques, which make this love story between women in every other respect the same as any other.[30] No problem. If I single out

29
Jill Dolan, "The Dynamics of Desire: Sexuality and Gender in Pornography and Performance," *Theatre Journal* 39, no. 2 (May 1987), 171.

30
Consider, for example, the woman (who remains nameless in the film) whom Vivian sees in Kay's bed when she first goes to Kay's house, and who then reappears briefly, in the car scene, to be treated by Kay as the "slut" versus the love interest (here Vivian) of the classical Western: her narrative characterization as the stock character "whore" is completed by her makeup, looks, pose, speech, and so forth. *Desert Hearts* does not distance this image and role or reframe them in a lesbian camp tradition or in the lesbian history of the forties and fifties, as it might have done, but only invokes a general fifties mood typical of many films of the eighties. It remains squarely within Hollywood conventions, including the casting of two self- and media-identified heterosexual actresses. On the inscription of films about lesbians within iconographic and generic conventions, see Mandy Merck, "'Lianna' and the Lesbians of Art Cinema," in *Films for Women*, ed. Charlotte Brunsdon (London: British Film Institute, 1986), 166–75.

Desert Hearts for its failure to engage with the problem of representation—which is never just a problem of the film, but of the whole cinematic apparatus as a social technology and of the much larger field of audiovisual representation beyond that—it is because its project (though necessarily an independent, self-financed film) makes no attempt to pass itself off for anything but a mass-audience, commercially viable entertainment product, and nonetheless declares itself a lesbian's film. As such, therefore, it bears a social responsibility, a burden of accountability, perhaps greater than those of other, outright obnoxious commercial products (for example, *Black Widow,* *Personal Best* [1982] to say nothing of Lina Wertmuller's despicable *Sotto sotto* [1984]), which unabashedly exploited the currently fashionable discourse on lesbianism to the end of an effective delegitimation of the lesbian—and perhaps even the feminist—politics of sexual difference. Deitch's film is also less noxious, in my eyes, than other independent films apparently benign, "sensitive," or pro-lesbian, such as John Sayles's *Lianna* (1983) or Patricia Rozema's *I've Heard the Mermaids Singing* (1987), which more subtly appropriate the issue of lesbian difference for art-entertainment purposes and resolve it much too simply, and all too safely, in a banal notion of sexual preference.[31] There, as well, representation seems to pose no problem.

31
I have written of this at greater length in "Guerrilla in the Midst: Women's Cinema in the '80s," *Screen* 31, no. 1 (Spring 1990), 6–25.

And yet, problems there are aplenty. Not only problems manifested by the massive reaction to homosexuality and gay politics surfacing in the frightful misrepresentations and repressive strategies of the Right in the context of the AIDS crisis, but also problems in the representation of lesbianism within feminist theory itself. To many feminist critics and theorists, lesbian subjectivity is a subset, a variation, or a component of female subjectivity; few would agree with Wittig that "lesbians are not women." A case in point, and one that exhibits an interesting new trend in heterosexual feminist theorizing, is Eve Sedgwick's work on the representation of homosexual desire, which concerns itself exclusively with men because, in her words,

the *relatively continuous* relation of female homosocial and homosexual bonds [as opposed to] the *radically discontinuous* relation of male homosocial and homosexual bonds . . . links lesbianism with the other forms of women's attention to women: the bond of mother and daughter, for instance, the bond of sister and sister, women's friendship, "networking," and the active struggles of feminism.[32]

32
Eve Kosofsky Sedgwick, *Between Men: English Literature and Male Homosocial Desire* (New York: Columbia University Press, 1985), 2; emphasis added.

As you must have noticed, the word *desire* is conspicuously absent from this itemized list of what Sedgwick can only bring herself to call "women's attention to women." Yet, in the same page, she repeatedly stresses why she uses the word *desire* rather than *love* in the subtitle and throughout her book *Between Men: English Literature and Male Homosocial Desire*: she uses *desire* rather than *love* precisely in order "to mark the erotic emphasis." We cannot but conclude that, if desire—with the erotic emphasis—exists between women, it is of no great consequence; it is no source of conflict or contradiction, no bond as strong as that of mother and daughter, as significant as friendship, or as important as women's political struggles. This, she adds, "seems at this moment to make an obvious kind of sense." And it certainly must make sense to those feminists whose heterosexual commitment to men is apparently so impervious to theorization that more and more they turn to theorizing either men's stakes in feminism or male subjectivity itself, both gay and straight. But what is more disturbing, and more to my immediate point here, is the sweeping of lesbian sexuality and desire under the rug of sisterhood, female friendship, and the now popular theme of "the mother-daughter bond." In all three parts of the rug, what is in question is not desire, but identification.

By way of demonstration, I now turn to one of the few essays in film theory that attempt to engage the question of desire between women, which trips precisely on that rug, on the confusion of desire with identification. I hope that the importance of McLaughlin's film project, its recasting the question of lesbian desire so that it cannot be confused with simple narcissistic identification, will come into sharper focus, and that so will the consequence of my theoretical distinction between a representation of lesbianism that is heterosexually conceived and one that is not. Jackie Stacey's article "Desperately Seeking Difference" offers a reading of two films, the classic 1950 *All About Eve* (directed by Joseph Mankiewicz and starring Bette Davis and Anne Baxter) and the 1985 independent film *Desperately Seeking Susan* (directed by Susan Seidelman and starring Madonna and Rosanna Arquette). Stacey claims that, while these are not " 'lesbian films' " (her quotation marks), they offer particular pleasures to women spectators, pleasures connected with "women's active desire and the sexual aims of women in the audience in relationship to the female protagonist on the screen."[33]

33
Jackie Stacey, "Desperately Seeking Difference," *Screen* 28, no. 1 (Winter 1987), p. 49.

Moreover, she introduces her article thus: "While [the issue of the female spectator's pleasure] has hardly been addressed [in feminist film theory], the specifically homosexual pleasures of female spectatorship have been ignored completely. This article will attempt to suggest some of the theoretical reasons for this neglect" (48).

Unfortunately, after such a promising beginning, the readings of the films prove what any spectator can easily conclude, that in both cases one woman—the younger or more "childlike" of each pair—wishes to be *like,* to become or literally to impersonate the other, either in order to take her place in the world, to become a famous star like her, and to replace her as the object of desire of both her husband and the audience (*All About Eve*), or in order to acquire her image as a woman liberated, free, and "saturated with sexuality" (as Stacey says of the

Susan, played by Madonna, in *Desperately Seeking Susan*). In short, both are terminal cases of identification, the first with an oedipal mother/rival image, the second with a feminine ego ideal. In psychoanalytic terms, this "childlike" wish is a kind of identification that is at once ego-directed, narcissistic, and *desexualized,* devoid of sexual aim. It is, if we attend to Freud, either "a direct and immediate identification [with a parental figure, the ego-ideal] and takes place earlier than any object-cathexis" (*SE,* XIX, 31), or an object-identification, "an object-cathexis [that has been given up, introjected, and] has been replaced by an identification" (*SE,* XIX, 28). In the latter case, Freud specifies, "the transformation of object-libido into narcissistic libido which thus takes place obviously implies an abandonment of sexual aims, a desexualization—a kind of sublimation, therefore" (*SE,* XIX, 30). The distinction between object-libido and narcissistic or ego-libido is crucial here, for one is sexual and has to do with desire, wanting to have (the object), the other is desexualized and has to do with narcissistic identification, wanting to be or to be like or seeing oneself as (the object).

The issue, however, is complicated by the fact that narcissism operates in several ways in psychic life: Freud speaks of a primary narcissism, original in all humans ("an allocation of the libido such as deserved to be described as narcissism might be present far more extensively, and . . . might claim a place in the regular course of human sexual development" [*SE,* XIV, 73]), and a secondary narcissism, acquired during development ("the narcissism which arises through the drawing in of object-cathexes" [*SE,* XIV, 75]). The latter is what constitutes the narcissistic or ego-libido and, if not predominant over object-cathexes, determines a narcissistic object-choice—as, Freud suggests, in "perverts and homosexuals" (*SE,* XIV, 88). If, however, it is predominant—as in "narcissistic women," whose need does not "lie in the direction of loving, but of being loved" and who love only themselves "with an intensity comparable to that of the man's love for them"—then the narcissistic or ego-libido stands in the way of a "complete object-love" or "is unfavourable to the development of a true *object-love*" (*SE*, XIV, 88–89).[34] The introduction of the term *object-love* (*Objektliebe*), which appears in this section of the essay interchangeably with *object-choice* (*Objektwahl*), makes it possible for Freud to salvage the woman from total self-absorption in her own narcissism by allowing that she may develop an object-love (he could hardly call it object-choice!) for her child, as an externalized part of her self or a retrieval of her own long-abandoned "boyish nature" (*SE*, XIV, 90). But Freud is typically ambiguous in the theory of narcissism. Particularly with regard to (heterosexual) women, he does not say when or how the narcissistic object-choice of "the purest and truest" female type (*SE*, XIV, 88) trespasses into the "self-sufficiency" of secondary narcissism with its inaptitude for object-love. Thus one is left to wonder: if the narcissistic choice of object is made with ego-directed and hence passive aims (the need for "being loved" rather than "loving"), does it still count as object-choice or object-libido, or is it rather ego-libido? The addition of the term *object-love* only muddles the matter further.

Perhaps, then, one may follow the royal road mapped out by Freud himself and look for an answer in one's personal and experiential history: it seems to me fairly incontrovertible, since I have known them both, that the ego-libido or narcissistic disposition is not to be confused with the object-choice component of *sexual* desire toward an other that characterizes adult, post-oedipal, lesbian homosexuality, whether that object-choice be of the anaclitic type or of the narcissistic type, which latter, says Freud (with his characteristic incapacity to envision lesbians), is most evident in homosexual men, though by no means exclusive to them.

Indeed, both film narratives bear out my point, and Stacey herself confirms it: "Roberta's desire to become more like her

34
I have slightly altered the *SE* translation of this phrase, substituting the italicized word *object-love* for its "object-choice," because the German reads: "der Gestaltung einer ordentlichen . . . Objektliebe ungünstig ist" (Sigmund Freud, "Zur Einführung des Narzissmus," in *Studienausgabe*, vol. 3 [Frankfurt am Main: Fischer Verlag, 1982], 55).

ideal—a more pleasingly coordinated, complete and attractive feminine image—is offered narrative fulfilment" (61); and as for *All About Eve,* Stacey concludes her analysis with these words: "The reflected image, infinitely multiplied in the triptych of the glass, creates a spectacle of stardom that is the film's final shot, suggesting a perpetual regeneration of intra-feminine fascinations through the pleasure of looking" (57). In sum, the "feminine desire" Stacey hopes to have unveiled theoretically, as Eve is transformed into Madonna in the 1980s, is still a form of identification with the image of woman, if a powerful and attractive womanhood, a feminine role model or ego ideal, and a quintessentially heterosexual one; it is not desire between women but indeed "intra-feminine," self-directed, narcissistic "fascinations." And so if the article does suggest some of the reasons why "the specifically homosexual pleasures of female spectatorship have been ignored," it does so quite unintentionally and precisely by its own equivocation of the very terms of its argument, not only the term *desire* but also the term *homosexual,* which, very much as Sedgwick sees it, when it comes to women, really means homosocial, that is, woman-identified female bonding.[35]

In plainer words, for Stacey as for Sedgwick, desire between women is not sexual. This is what I mean by a representation of lesbianism that is heterosexually conceived—and in fact heterosexist. Far from conceiving another kind of sexuality for women and between women, a lesbian sexuality as the material, physical ground of lesbian desire, both Stacey and Sedgwick imply, as Kristeva states outright, that sex, "real sex," only happens with men: between women and straight men or between gay men. When you think about it, this is another way of putting the old question "what do lesbians do in bed?" now in the language of feminist and film theory.

Going back to She Must Be Seeing Things, then, let me re-emphasize the significance of its taking the question of lesbian desire seriously and trying to work through the difficulty of

35
In this sense, I would also have to disagree with Kaja Silverman's argument for the "convergence of object-choice and identification" in female subjectivity, in *The Acoustic Mirror: The Female Voice in Psychoanalysis and Cinema* (Bloomington: Indiana University Press, 1988), 153. Although I'm totally in favor of her revaluation of the negative Oedipus complex and the "intersection of desire for and identification with the mother" that it may produce in "the early history of the female subject" (154), I would insist that failing to distinguish object-choice, of whatever type, from narcissistic-maternal identification can only lead to what Silverman calls a "*choric* fantasy," using—not by coincidence—Kristeva's term: a vision of female-bonding, homosocial collectivity under the sign of "a primary and passionate desire for the mother" (139). This is all well and good as a feminist utopia, but what about lesbians? More often than not, adult lesbians don't sleep with their mothers, and to reduce lesbian subjectivity to the negative Oedipus complex would, of course, be crude. Though I cannot do justice here to the complexity of Silverman's formulation, her reading of the "*choric* fantasy" in films such as Robert Altman's *Three Women* and Laura Mulvey and Peter Wollen's *Riddles of the Sphinx* speaks to the heterosexual nature of this feminist fantasy.

representing it against this barrage of representations, discourses, and theories that negate it, from Freud to Hollywood to contemporary feminism and film theory. In contrast to the romance or fairy-tale formulas adopted by films such as *Lianna, Desert Hearts,* or *I've Heard the Mermaids Singing,* McLaughlin's film locates itself historically and politically in the contemporary North American lesbian community, with its conflicting discourses, posing the question of desire within the context of actual practices of both lesbianism and cinema. It both addresses and questions spectatorial desire by disallowing a univocal spectatorial identification with any one character or role or object-choice and by foregrounding instead the relations of desire to fantasy, and desire's mobility within the fantasy scenario. Further, as Martha Gever has observed, the film reclaims the cinematic function of voyeurism, rearticulating it in lesbian terms and so indeed allowing an account of the "specifically homosexual pleasures of female spectatorship" and why they have been ignored, mistaken, or misplaced in feminist film theory.[36]

36
Martha Gever, "Girl Crazy: Lesbian Narratives in *She Must Be Seeing Things* and *Damned If You Don't,*" *The Independent* 11, no. 6 (July 1988), 14–18.

In conclusion, I want to return to a short scene in the film that condenses many of the issues I have been discussing, the scene where Agatha, from her office window, sees Jo kissing a man in the street below. What marks Agatha's "seeing" as a hallucination is the profilmic substitution of another woman for Lois Weaver, whom the viewer recognizes as Jo. The other woman, unknown to perhaps most spectators but not to all, is played by Sheila McLaughlin herself, who thus makes a very interesting cameo appearance, inscribing herself in a particular role in the film written and directed by her. This directorial choice supports my reading that Agatha is not the only desiring subject of the film—the subject of the Catalina fantasy, the voyeur, the "she" who must be seeing things, the cross-dressing woman, the visible representation of lesbian desire. McLaughlin's appearance in the place of Jo/Lois Weaver, that is to say, in the place of the object of Agatha's desire, is a performative personal statement, a femme's masquerade as the desired one "who aims her desirability at the butch," as Case would put it. But by the very fact that McLaughlin is the filmmaker, and that she is also, therefore, in the place of Jo, the diegetic filmmaker, whose film gives visual, symbolic form to her desire for Agatha in Catalina, McLaughlin's appearance in this scene sustains my reading that she, too, is the desiring subject in the Catalina fantasy, the voyeur and exhibitionist, the "she" who must be seeing things, and the desiring subject of her film as a whole. The scene represents, finally, the lesbian subject as a double one, as Case suggests, and renders performative my earlier statement that it takes two women, not one, to make a lesbian. But it also suggests that other visible representations of lesbian subjectivity and desire are already there for all to see, if only we know how to look.

Discussion

Nancy Graham

Can you say something about the critique of *She Must Be Seeing Things* in regard to its treatment of racial difference.

Teresa de Lauretis

In discussions in which I've participated, a common objection seems to be that the film poses the question of racial difference, but then avoids it by collapsing it into questions of cultural or ethnic difference. This observation strikes me as correct, but I don't think the film allows one to deal with it beyond locating it as a problem. That is why my work focuses on the question of fantasy—an issue that I do think is seriously considered within the film itself.

Mandy Merck

I wonder if you would mind returning for a moment to Riviere's essay on masquerade. My recollection of this essay is that it is a case history of a very successful professional woman, which is remarkable given that it dates from the 1920s . . .

de Lauretis	. . . and the case history of a heterosexual woman . . .
Merck	. . . yes. Her profession isn't stated, but what she's very good at

is going to conferences and giving impressive speeches, after
which she inevitably feels guilty and deals with that feeling in
a very self-demeaning and hyperfeminized way, that is, by ap-
proaching her male colleagues as a sort of flirtatious cuddle-
bunny. Riviere diagnoses this as a masquerade of femininity and
goes on to say that there is no authentic femininity for any
woman, that *all* femininity is a masquerade.

With that in mind, I wonder if we could turn to the regime of visibility that we've seen at this conference—with the
exception, perhaps, of the Arzner photos. Mostly we have been
shown images of active gay male sex or of its art historical an-
odyne, the male nude. I find this interesting in relation to the
difficulties and asymmetries of picturing women's pleasure in
terms of their bodies or organs. For when we did see women's
bodies close enough to see a significant organ, in the lesbian safe
sex tape—if you regard the clitoris or vagina as analogous to
the penis, and that's an interesting question—it was immediately covered up by what have been described as the signifiers
of safe sex. That is, the central signifier in the lesbian sex sequences might be a rubber glove, a dental dam, or a dildo,
whereas clearly the central signifier in the gay male tapes was
the cock itself.

Now, Lacan argued that that which is not visible cannot be
made into a symbol—a dubious proposition if we think of the
number of unseen cavities that organize our symbolic system,
notably black holes . . . I wonder, therefore, whether what we're
looking for, to paraphrase Richard Fung, is not our penis but
what in other and more prehistoric times might have been
called our phallus—notwithstanding the masculine connotations
of that term.

Your question began with the notion of masquerade, which
raises issues regarding its relation to femininity, on one hand,

and to feminist film theory, on the other. Then you moved to another, not unrelated but more problematic question—the representability of female sexuality, of which bodily organs might be the female equivalent of the penis as visible signifier of desire in visual representation (for example, in porno film).

According to Lacan, the relation between masquerade and penis resides in the phallus, since with the masquerade the (straight) woman turns herself into the phallus and therefore becomes desirable to men. But whereas the penis and the masquerade are eminently visible, the phallus is not. In other words, the visibility of the masquerade is precisely what veils and signifies the phallus, what signifies man's desire for the veiled phallus. So, according to Lacan, both the masquerade of femininity and the penis signify the phallus, or male desire; female desire does not exist in a form analogous to male desire, but in a form complementary to and dependent on it: the woman desires to be desired, and therefore she turns herself into the phallus. For Lacan, that is the only kind of desire there is. Of course, this doesn't account for lesbian desire (and I don't know whether or not it accounts for gay male desire). So, yes, in a way I am looking for something that is not a penis but that can function as the signifier of another kind of desire, that is to say, lesbian desire. And I would be willing to call it phallus if the masculine and paternal inferences built into the term could be discarded. At this moment, it seems unlikely that they can, but perhaps it's worth trying, and perhaps I will try. But I certainly do not think the solution lies in finding an organ in the female body equivalent to the penis. And I do not think a lesbian pornography organized in the same way as gay male pornography can tell us very much about our sexuality or our desire.

Which brings me to your other point, about the amazingly different ways we—lesbians and gay men, filmmakers and critics—have been dealing with sexuality in both visual and discursive representation in this conference. These differences, which I have long felt existed, from things I read and from films and other kinds of images that circulate in lesbian and gay subcultures, have become quite apparent, even glaring during the past two days. In a sense, it is not surprising that these differences between lesbians and gay men exist when you think of how differently women and men deal with sexuality in practice because of all sorts of factors—from anatomy and physiology to socialization, from gender constraints to sex-specific discourses and representations available in most cultures, up to the well-known historical disparity in the social perception and handling of male and female homosexuality. To begin to discuss these differences would require another conference altogether. It would be a most appropriate and, I think, radical topic for a gay and lesbian conference, but perhaps a very uncomfortable one.

For now, going back to your question, I would agree with you that, in this conference, gay men's discourse on sexuality and the visual representation of gay male sexuality in the safe sex tapes were organized around the cock, whereas the lesbian discourse on lesbian sexuality and desire, in Judith's and my talks, was concerned with fantasy and the scenarios, reframings, and variously mediated forms in which lesbian erotic fantasy is staged. For example, the safe sex porno tape with two women (I would not call it *lesbian* pornography) proved to me that dildos and rubber gloves do not work the way the penis does in gay male porno, or perhaps in straight porno as well. Insofar as they appear to imitate the established codes of visual pornography, dildos and rubber gloves appear to be indeed inferior substitutes for the erect penis; but, on the other hand, they may work precisely insofar as they can be seen as forms of masquerade, aspects of performance, fantasy objects of desire, more like a fetish than a penis, as I was arguing for the masquerades in Sheila's film. For me personally, the safe sex tape of the two women did not work at all; it was more boring than exciting because it was too much like standard pornography. And I will add that the only male porno tape that worked for me, among the ones we saw here, was the one that foregrounded the interracial fantasy scenario.

Ada Griffin   I apologize for raising the issue of fair representation in the context of your talk, because I really would like to register a criticism of the conference as a whole. But your response to the earlier question about racial difference did provoke me to make these comments now. To begin with, to speak in terms of representation and then fail to represent black lesbians as presenters at this conference seems problematic. Maybe it's just because I'm black, but I am astonished that race does not have to be a priority for women, especially for lesbians, because it always is for me. And when people casually make references to black holes or imply that things aren't significant enough in a film to be considered, it really puts me in a position of hostility, not to mention boredom.

de Lauretis   I think you're quite right in general, but my response had to do with the fact that this film does not, for me, lend itself to an understanding or examination of racial difference in a lesbian relationship. Other people have made the same criticism you just made of my talk and of the film. After hearing them, I thought a lot about the inscription of race in the relationship between Agatha and Jo, but I concluded that the film intentionally focuses on other aspects of their relationship. And though it makes clear that the role of Agatha is marked by her *cultural* difference as a Brazilian, a black Latina, it doesn't even attempt to address the *racial* difference between the women. So it's not that race is not a crucial issue in lesbian and feminist relationships, politics, and theory. It certainly is. But it is not represented as an issue in this film. Perhaps I could have talked about other lesbian texts that do not elide race, like Audre Lorde's *Zami: A New Spelling of My Name* [Trumansburg, N.Y., The Crossing Press, 1982], which is a book that centers precisely on the constitution of the subject as a black lesbian. I have written about *Zami*, about

Cherríe Moraga's play *Giving Up the Ghost* [Los Angeles: West End Press, 1986], about other works by lesbians of color, and about the issue of race in feminist theory and in lesbian representation. But not in film. Part of the problem is that I have not seen a film made by or about lesbians of color, although there are now many that deal with race in various other relationships between women. I fully agree with you that this conference lacks representation of lesbian filmmakers and critics of color; I've often wondered why, when lesbians of color have produced so many outstanding works of literature, theater, criticism, and theory, they have not worked very much with film or video. This is a very interesting question, especially given the fact that gay men of color, by contrast, seem to work more in film and video than in fiction, criticism, or theory.

Marusia Bociurkiw   It seems that in this conference people of color have had the burden of responsibility to talk about race. This leads me to the realization that there are ways in which lesbian work always gets laden with huge agendas because there's relatively little of it out there to discuss. This burden seems especially heavy for those women who attempt to work in the area of lesbian sexuality in representation, where the usual responses run the gamut from "Couldn't you have done more?" to "Shouldn't you have shown less?" Whenever there's such a dearth of imagery, there will always be these unmanageable kinds of criticisms.

That said, I still think it's unfortunate that you didn't address questions of race in your paper—especially since you talked about the position of Agatha as outsider. One can imagine asking if this is meant to be Agatha's literal acting out of her position as a person of color, or a comment on it.

Awkward or not, I think it is crucial for us to raise certain issues in our work. It would be interesting to hear what the filmmaker has to say on this subject. I don't think we should apologize for raising it here, where it is clearly an issue.

de Lauretis   You've said something that I'd like to repeat, which is that lesbian work, and feminist work as well, always gets overlaid with "the agenda of everything." I agree, precisely because of the multiplicity of aspects involved in the formation of subjectivity and the political claims rightly advanced by different social subjects, that "everything" has to be considered. But I also think that everything cannot be done at the same time and fitted into a single, comprehensive theory. If you are going to articulate these large questions as being structurally related, they have to first be analyzed conceptually one at a time. From teaching women's studies I am quite familiar with the pressure of dealing with all things together—with the mantra, as Kobena Mercer called it, of race, class, gender, and sexuality. And I agree with him when he says that at this point in history it's disingenuous simply to recite or pay lip service to this mantra. The question of racial difference is a huge and very profound one. It should be addressed very seriously, as the central focus of one's work over time and not superficially, as one would end up doing if one chose a film that is working very seriously on another question, even though related. Kobena's and Richard Fung's talks focused on visual texts that foregrounded the question of race and allowed them to address it in its complexity and contradictions.

I want to be clear, I'm not saying that I don't want to think about racial difference in the representation of lesbianism in film; what I'm suggesting is that the work I've done on the role of lesbian fantasy in Sheila's film could be very useful to others in thinking about how fantasy may work or may be used in film to address racially as well as sexually different spectators.

Richard Fung   I think that part of the problem is that the film itself is guilty of evoking the mantra. On the one hand, by casting the role of Agatha as a person of color, a whole cultural baggage is invoked; on the other hand, one feels that people of color are simply inserted to legitimate the liberal credentials of the film or of the white characters in it.

de Lauretis   That's a very legitimate criticism. If I understand you correctly,

you're saying that the film tries to be politically correct and to legitimate itself by casting a black Latina in a role that doesn't really deal with her as a black lesbian, that is to say, a person whose multiple and complex identity is necessarily shaped by the oppressive presence of racism, as well as of heterosexism, in the society in which she lives. I don't know if that is what the filmmaker intended, but I agree that it can be seen that way: she is a lesbian, but not a lesbian of color. So I agree with you that that is a part of the problem. But another part is that I didn't point it out as a problem, and thus in a sense I compounded or added to the nonrepresentation of lesbians of color both in the film and in the conference.

Isaac Julien   Regarding the way Agatha has been represented in this film, I think I have to agree with your conclusions, but with reservations, because for me there was a another sort of masquerade occurring. In terms of racial difference, Agatha was masquerading as Eurasia, becoming a mythologized, fetishized black subject within the narrative. This might be one way to rethink an analysis of masquerade in relation to fantasy and to broach issues of race at the same time.

That said, and though I had trouble with the degree of slippage and mythologizing in the construction of Agatha's role, I found your observations about the filmic strategies for imaging fantasy to be very useful and on target. Your elaboration of Jo's, the filmmaker's, use of the film-within-the-film and Agatha's relation to that differently experienced though shared signifier was very convincing. Which reminds me of just how much I admire this film.

de Lauretis

I've heard something similar to what you said in the first part of your comment from women who felt that Agatha's character was not strong enough, too apologetic, not butch enough, and not black enough, that is, not really a black woman. That strikes me as a very just criticism of the film, as I said, although the stereotype implied in the association of strong, butch, and black, frankly, is rather disturbing. So I like the way you put it, "masquerading as Eurasia," much better. And I'm very glad that your comment zeroed in on what I was trying to analyze in my paper, the original use of fantasy and of the film-within-the-film as strategies of lesbian representation and address. That was really what my paper was about. In fact, it seems to me that the way this discussion has been going until now—and in part it's my own fault—has had the unfortunate effect of avoiding those issues that I did raise in my paper, that is, the difficulties and problems in representing lesbian sexuality as distinct from both heterosexual female sexuality and gay male sexuality— difficulties and problems that clearly exist for white lesbians as well as lesbians of color. So that it seems as if the specificity of lesbian sexuality must remain unspoken or unspeakable even in the context of a gay and lesbian conference. This is very disturbing.

Jeff Nunokawa

I would like to turn for a moment to your critique of Eve Sedgwick, by way of suggesting an analogy to your responses to

	the challenge of why you did not consider the question of race in the film. A response that Sedgwick might make to your critique of her work . . .
de Lauretis	You're going to speak for her?
Nunokawa	I'm just imagining . . . You insist that your reticence about the issue is simply symptomatic of the text's silence; you don't talk about such things because the film doesn't. Now, Sedgwick's position, as I understand it, is that the continuity between (and concomitant invisibility of) lesbian desire and, say, the mother-daughter dyad contrasts with the radical discontinuity between male homosexual desire and male bonding. This is not meant as a description of lesbian versus male homosexual desires, but rather of the way it looks through the cultural lens Sedgwick is using. You see, she also maintains that she is simply describing a cultural situation as it exists.
de Lauretis	I don't see that the comparison holds. First, I didn't say, "It's not in the film, therefore, I cannot talk about it." I said it is in the film but not in such a way that allows me to rethink and say something interesting about the relations of race, sexuality, and desire. Second, I think that Sedgwick is not concerned at all with lesbians or lesbian desire. She is concerned with the nature of bonds between men, which is what occupies her book. In and of itself, this would be fine. However, in her book, she speaks as a feminist, and that means that her elision of desire and sex in relationships between women is presented as the feminist position. Now, I am a feminist, too, and so are other lesbians whom Sedgwick's argument would erase from existence. For when she says, as she does, that for women there is no distinction between homosexuality and female bonding or homosociality, she implies that sex and desire don't really matter or present problems among women, are not really important or central to their relationships, and consequently, there is no sexual difference between lesbians and heterosexual women. This amounts to denying lesbianism altogether. This may be a wishful position

held by some, mostly straight feminists, but it is certainly not the position of most lesbian feminists, and therefore it is not the feminist position, as Sedgwick's straight readers and many gay men seem only too eager to believe.

Nunokawa   The question was simply whether Sedgwick herself was ignoring lesbianism or describing a culture that symptomatically ignores it.

de Lauretis   Sedgwick buttresses her argument by citing feminists and lesbians, citing a few specific feminist texts. What I'm saying is that there are many other feminist and lesbian texts equally available that tell a very different story, and they must be reckoned with. In other words, Sedgwick is not describing "the social" (in the sense of the patriarchal status quo), she's discussing feminism, she's taking a very partial position within feminism and passing it off as the feminist position on lesbianism. This is the conceit operating in her book and one that I find to be deeply offensive to lesbians. She dismisses the history, the theory, and the reality of lesbianism just as much as "the social" does. On the other hand, I'm not saying that racism doesn't exist or that racial difference is unimportant in lesbian relationships because we're all sisters anyway, and I'm not speaking for all lesbians, white or of color. It's true that I did not consider the issue of racial difference in the film, but I did not try to say or even suggest that it didn't matter.

Ruby Rich   While the question of race has been discussed in relation to *She Must Be Seeing Things,* I was led to think back to the Mapplethorpe images Kobena showed us, and I began wondering about the explosiveness of the subject of race and homosexuality. In Linda Nochlin's essay on orientalism in nineteenth-century French painting ["The Imaginary Orient," in Linda Nochlin, *The Politics of Vision: Essays on Nineteenth-Century Art and Society* (New York: Harper and Row, 1989), 33–59], she discussed the popular trope of picturing a black woman and a white woman together as a signifier of lesbianism. I think that racial difference operates for lesbians in the same way as, let's say, butch-femme, or s&m roles do, that is, as a form of differentiation between two people of the same gender. And I suspect that it isn't merely coincidental that this figures as an issue not only in *She Must Be Seeing Things,* but also in Mapplethorpe's work and in Isaac Julien's *Looking For Langston.* I don't have anything more to say about it right now, other than to make this observation, since I believe that with issues of power and representation, nothing can be taken for granted.

Tom Waugh   Lizzie Borden is, of course, another filmmaker whose work takes up this problematic. However, I would like you to address the question of popular or mainstream sensibilities. There has been some discussion of the vernacular at this conference, and you position *She Must Be Seeing Things* both in relation to popular films like Patricia Rozema's *I've Heard the Mermaids Singing* and Donna Deitch's *Desert Hearts,* and in relation to the avant-garde strategies of Yvonne Rainer. Yet you seem to dismiss those popular films in which lesbian directors, working in conventional formats, succeeded in reaching a very responsive audience. This might even be seen as the way in which McLaughlin's film fails: she borrowed from the popular narrative format, yet couldn't elicit the same kind of popular response. What do you think is the responsibility of the lesbian or gay critic regarding these various levels of cultural hierarchy?

de Lauretis   I'm sorry if my brief remarks about *Mermaids* and *Desert Hearts* came through as a dismissal. On the contrary, I was proposing a critique of them. Both films have been very successful; for that very reason they cannot be dismissed and in fact might be taken as exemplary of current trends in popular cinema. Very briefly, my criticism of those films, as well as Hollywood products like *Black Widow,* is that their representation and popularization of lesbianism directly or indirectly delegitimate lesbian and feminist politics. By the way, I must correct one point: *Mermaids* was not made by a lesbian. This might seem like a minor point to insist upon, but, as Kobena said earlier, a film's reception is largely contingent on the discourses that circulate around it and what the filmmaker describes as her project. Everything that Rozema had to say about her film, as well as the film itself, makes it very clear that lesbianism was purely a ploy, an attention getter, something by which "to blow Polly's mind," not to mention the viewer's. Those were her words, in a published interview she gave to Chris Bearchell for the Canadian gay and lesbian magazine *Epicene* (Bearchell herself commented that this was no "dyke tale"). I was criticizing Rozema's film precisely for its failure to take "responsibility," for attempting to reach a wider audience by exploiting the currently fashionable topic of lesbianism and trivializing a long and continuing history of homophobia and lesbian oppression.

To come back to your question, I certainly believe there is a need for diverse cinematic practices and media interventions on all levels, from popular to avant-garde, and I think the lesbian or gay critic has a responsibility toward all of them. But, to me, critical responsibility does not mean "accommodating" or applauding and celebrating an independent film simply because it manages to reach popular audiences regardless of how it does so. In a way, the larger the audience, the greater the responsibility of the filmmaker. In the sixties and seventies we used to say that a filmmaker "sold out" to Hollywood. Nowadays it seems more likely that one buys into a superficial notion of pluralism where the various "others" are shown to be just like everybody else (to wit, Steven Spielberg's *The Color Purple* [1985]). I've written more on this in an article entitled "Guerrilla in the Midst" [*Screen* 31, no. 1 (Spring 1990), 6–25]. There I criticize *Desert Hearts* and *Mermaids* in different ways and for different reasons, because in my opinion they're trying to do, and succeed in doing, very different things.

Concluding Discussion

Terri Cafaro

I want to comment on something that has been a fairly persistent theme in this conference—namely a challenge to lesbian butch-femme role-playing. Ruby Rich mentioned, very rightly I think, how the confluence of issues of gender, sexuality, and race complicates attempts to theorize lesbian sexuality, or lesbian spectatorship. Teresa's paper offered a new theory of female same-sex object-choice in relation to inherited definitions of heterosexual power relations—a theory that tells us much about butch-femme roles. But I feel that the very great challenges of Teresa's work were displaced by the equally urgent issue of race, deferring once again the question of the psychic structures of butch-femme role-playing.

Tom Kalin

I think the necessary process of acknowledging all the different aspects of our identities is something that, for the most part, hasn't been allowed. In the AIDS struggle, for example, perhaps again because of the sense of urgency, identity has been described through some single factor, seen as determining. However, I think that Kobena Mercer's discussion of ambivalence opens up possibilities for revising positions and embracing things that previously might have been considered irrelevant—for example, the significance of biographical information in relation to one's political practice.

Stuart Marshall's talk suggested something similar with regard to the use of the pink triangle by the AIDS activist movement. His attempt to disentangle the complex levels of reference in that symbol are very useful for thinking about ambivalence in the different allegiances and alliances within the movement. So the "slippage" between meanings is more relevant than ever before.

Ruby Rich

I'm sorry that Cindy Patton isn't here today [Patton had to leave the "How Do I Look?" conference to attend the Second International Conference on AIDS Education and Information sponsored by the World Health Organization and held in Cameroon], because the reference to ambivalence reminded me of a comment she made in her question-and-answer session, a comment that I thought was one of the most astounding statements of the conference, precisely because it was left unexamined. I'm referring to her admission that, when she showed the video porn segments after her talk at Duke University, she stopped the tape before coming to the lesbian one. For me, her ambivalence as a lesbian speaker provides a starting point for a whole other discussion, one about the real differences between the lesbian and gay male presentations and representations we've seen at this conference. Of course, this has everything to do with the element of danger in the representation of lesbian sexuality, the fact that there isn't any safe public space for these images. Knowledge of this inequity profoundly influences the kinds of images that can be created—or even imagined.

Kalin   More than a few gay men also experienced discomfort in watching pornographic videotapes in a room full of people. White hairless bodies do not necessarily constitute every person's object of desire. A range of responses, or ambivalences, to the dominant discourse of gay male erotica or pornography needs to be acknowledged, so that there's not a kind of monolithic figuring of desire.

Marusia Bociurkiw   I would also like to comment on Cindy's assumption that the lesbians in the room would be uncomfortable with seeing lesbian porn. Actually, my discomfort was in not being able to see more of it. The lesbian audiences I've encountered persistently express the desire to see more and more work like that. And it seems to me that the time for talking about our fear of representations of lesbian sexuality, or the damage done to lesbians because of them, has passed. We need to be talking about how to get more lesbian work produced and about the differences in the conditions of production for lesbian and gay male work. I think that for various reasons—some good, some bad—those differences have been obscured. Perhaps this is because feminism has reoriented the question to one of spectatorship, so we no longer consider earlier feminist discussions about inequality or lack of access to resources.

Liz Kotz   I also want to add to Ruby's comment. It's been very noticeable at this conference that all the men's presentations had some sort of autobiographical element in them, whereas none of the women's presentations did. This seemed like a rather funny reversal of the stereotype of women's work in the seventies. In fact, the accusations about women's autobiography grew so persistent that it seems to have come to a point where we feel we have to be hyper-distant.

I was frustrated with both Judith Mayne's and Teresa de Lauretis's contestations of the predominantly heterosexual and heterosexist academic feminist film discourse, because those of us in the film and video communities either never took it seriously in the first place or have long since abandoned it. So these papers had a somewhat dated and less relevant feel to me than, say, Richard Fung's or Kobena Mercer's, which dealt with what are for me more contemporary issues. And I agree with Marusia's comment that the time when we needed to contest either straight feminist dogma or the notion that lesbian representation can be reappropriated for heterosexual viewers has passed for the lesbian film community.

Judith Mayne   I feel I have to answer that. I work in academia and obviously can't pretend to be something I'm not, but I can't believe that lesbian film history is irrelevant to people who work within gay and lesbian media.

Kotz   I don't think the history is irrelevant at all. Rather, it's the contestation of feminist film theory that is irrelevant.

Mayne   But how can you do any kind of history that doesn't deal with the way in which these issues have been constructed? It's no longer possible to do a simple-minded documentary history. I realize these splits are very real, between activist and academic communities, between people who are film and video producers and people who work in the university, but I also think that these divisions need to be contested. And I still maintain that lesbian film history cannot be divorced from the concerns of media activists.

Bociurkiw I think that one really admirable thing about this conference is that it included—at great expense to itself, no doubt—producers from different places to participate in these conversations, and I appreciate that. But it has also made me realize that I sometimes feel like an invisible worker, producing the work that gets theorized. But I do use that theory; it really is important to my work. I found Judith's talk very interesting and helpful, but I still find the separation between theory and practice vexing.

As a producer I am affected by theory in a very practical sense. For example, discussions focusing on issues of presence and absence—I'm thinking of Teresa's talk—or on problematic aspects of lesbian representation have been important for my work. At the same time, I sometimes find these discussions debilitating. When I speak about my work, or about lesbian representation, I try to do so from a position of presence rather than absence. That might sound simple, but I actually find it a very complicated thing to do. I'm present, I'm producing work, and there are other people producing work as well. To begin a discussion about representation from the position of presence as a producer is a difficult but necessary task.

Mayne I think Teresa would agree that we're speaking from a position of presence also, and it's not as though the kind of work that we do is totally valued by feminist film theorists or people in the academy, either. There is a misconception that, because we are academics by profession, we comfortably speak academic discourse. In fact, it's a division that we inhabit sometimes very uncomfortably.

Teresa de Lauretis Not only do we speak from a position of presence ourselves as critics, but we're also speaking about films. For example, I'm speaking about several films, all of which are "present." So I don't understand what you're saying about absence.

It's one thing to criticize codes of representation and another to say that lesbians don't exist or that women don't exist. We're not saying that; we're trying to construct a representation that is not simply one using the dominant codes. Though we might be speaking from within the lessons of theory, I think we are trying to develop, whether as women critics or film- and videomakers, representations that are simultaneously deconstructions of dominant codes. But this can only be done through codes of representation; otherwise it would be an entirely solipsistic endeavor. In other words, what we produce has to be legible. What we are trying to explore in our work are ways in which certain presences, certain lesbian presences, are—precisely—*legible,* in spite of theories that say they're not.

Stuart Marshall   I am just a little concerned, because I feel a rift opening between people who are committed to theoretical practice and those committed to film or video practice. I think it's really important to recognize that, at a very fundamental level, we are talking about two discrete areas of practice, each with its own problems, its own institutional struggles, its own history. What has been so powerful about the independent film movement, from the 1970s on, is that it offered the opportunity for these practices to come together. I'm sure the situation in the U.S. is the same as in Britain, where you actually have film theorists making films—I'm thinking of Laura Mulvey, for instance—and you also find film practitioners producing theory. I think this has been an extremely healthy thing.

Bociurkiw   You make a very good point that touches on what I said earlier, namely, that on both sides of this "rift" we're producing theory, albeit in different ways. And this is a similarity that is really important to recognize. We each enable the other's work.

Marshall   The artist-theorist relationship is problematic—and properly so. I think there should be a constant yet supportive friction be-

	tween these two areas of practice. And it's up to us to find ways to make these two areas of practice intersect productively.
Kalin	I agree. The model is usually one of discontinuity between theory and practice. But theory and practice actually inform each other to such a degree that any notion that theory comes after the fact, that practice is what theory is constructed on, is absurd. I know that this imaginary divide simply does not function in my own film and video practice. There's a constant informing back and forth—complete with contradictions—between what might be discretely labeled as a theoretical text, on the one hand, and a visual product on the other.
José Arroyo	I'd like to comment on what Judith said about not taking for granted the difficulties in contesting hegemonic theories from within the academy. I want to remind people that these difficulties exist not just within theoretical work and/or filmmaking, but also within other areas of criticism such as reviews or simply networks of information. People working to contest the difficulties in different spaces should work together and reinforce each other, thus contributing to the opening of spaces. Ruby reminded us how the closing off of spaces for lesbians affects even the imaginary. So I think we can't take any of these areas of practice for granted. Whether the battles are fought five years later or five years earlier, the fact that they are being conducted on different fronts is very important, because they are all for a common good.
Rich	In response to what you just said, it occurred to me that one of the advantages that men working on gay male representation have is precisely invisibility and the lack of theory. And one of the disadvantages that lesbians have is the necessity to work out of an enveloping blanket of feminist theory. I just hope that Teresa's and Judith's work will be expanded upon, because there's been such a problem of erasure of lesbian film theory in general.

Douglas Crimp	There's only one place that gay men can go for film theory. We obviously can't produce it sui generis. We have to deal with feminist film theory, too.
Mandy Merck	But I worry about that, because I'm not sure that's what's happening. I didn't see a lot of evidence of men borrowing from feminist film theory here. I see a certain evidence of the iconography of male homosexuality attempting to add in female homosexuality. I think that was the real question about Cindy's presentation, and the issue of safe sex representation in general, indicated by her difficulty with showing the lesbian video at Duke. Because AIDS and safe sex are such emergency issues, there was a strange way that the template became the male body and a very particular rhetoric of male sexuality that does not seem to me an adequate one. It was a sort of thermodynamic, "he's gotta have it" model of male sexuality, a model of men needing to get off, but, for safety's sake, without a liquid exchange.

That doesn't at all coincide with my discussions with gay male friends, where a lack of desire is often something they complain about. They're not getting it, but they're not necessarily wanting to get it. This shift in desire cannot be represented by an industry that has to sell its wares on the thermodynamic model. And if this isn't an adequate model for men, I assure you it's not adequate for women. We want to join the struggle against AIDS, but we can't simply be added in as analogues to that particular penile economy.

Crimp	I don't think that's exactly where women have come into the struggle against AIDS. In fact, at least in this country, women have been engaged in the AIDS struggle from the beginning, primarily around broad issues of health care. Gay men have learned a great deal from the feminist health care movement, to mention just one example. But I was actually referring to feminist theoretical models. As you know, feminist theory has been very useful to people such as Simon Watney in theorizing representations of AIDS.

Martha Gever

I want to go back to Douglas's earlier comment and amend it. I think that feminist theory has at times proved difficult for lesbians and gay men, but it has also given us many tools with which to work on problems of representation. But there are other theoretical traditions we borrow from and refer to that have taught us crucial lessons. I am thinking specifically of work on issues of race and representation. And although, as Kobena pointed out, theories on different aspects of identity should never be conflated, I think they provide us with very important models. Of course, feminism has explored identity as well, but other models exist, and their contributions must be acknowledged.

Isaac Julien

Listening to Judith's and Teresa's papers, it was almost scary to see the extent to which feminist film theory is heterosexist and homophobic, to see the lengths to which one has to go in disentangling that theory in order to get to a point where one can begin to talk about lesbian desire. I, for one, never undervalue that as a practice. This kind of work indirectly influences the film practices that I try to engage with. Theories of masquerade, for example, have been incredibly important to me as a filmmaker. Maybe this is not directly reflected in my work, but it is certainly a foundation for my thinking.

Of course, one takes risks in raising these issues. It is interesting to me that they are discussed here, because they're not really coming up in debates about black cinema, or "third cinema." They're coming up in debates about gay and lesbian culture, precisely because this is where all kinds of differences intersect. Historically, gay and lesbian culture has always had to confront this hybridity, and with the AIDS crisis we're facing all of these differences again in new and difficult ways.

Selected Bibliography

Alcock, Beverly, and Jocelyn Robson, "Cagney and Lacey Revisited," *Feminist Review*, no. 35 (Summer 1990), 42–52.

Als, Hilton, "Negro Faggotry," *Black Film Review* 5, no. 3 (Summer 1989), 18–19.

Arbuthnot, Lucie, and Gail Seneca, "Pre-Text and Text in 'Gentlemen Prefer Blondes,'" *Film Reader*, no. 5 (Winter 1981), 13–23.

Arroyo, José, "Look Back and Talk Black: The Films of Isaac Julien in Postmodern Britain," *Jump Cut*, no. 36 (forthcoming 1991).

———, "Pedro Almodovar: Law and Desire," *Descant* 20, no. 1–2 (Spring–Summer 1989), 53–70.

Becker, Edith, et al., "Special Section: Lesbians and Film," *Jump Cut*, no. 24–25 (March 1981), 17–51. Includes Bonnie Zimmerman, "Lesbian Vampires"; Claudette Charboneau and Lucy Winer, "Lesbians in 'Nice' Films"; Jacquelyn Zita, "Counter-Currencies of a Lesbian Iconography"; Andrea Weiss, "Lesbian Cinema and Romantic Love"; Michelle Citron, "Comic Critique"; Judy Whitaker, "Hollywood Transformed"; Julia Lesage, "Subversive Fantasy"; B. Ruby Rich, "From Repressive Tolerance to Erotic Liberation."

Bociurkiw, Marusia, "Territories of the Forbidden: Lesbian Culture, Sex and Censorship," *Fuse*, March–April 1988, 27–32.

Boffin, Tessa, and Sunil Gupta, eds., *Ecstatic Antibodies: Resisting the AIDS Mythology*, London, Rivers Oram Press, 1989.

Bordowitz, Gregg, "Picture a Coalition," in *AIDS: Cultural Analysis/Cultural Activism*, ed. Douglas Crimp, Cambridge, Mass., MIT Press, 1988, 183–96.

Bordowitz, Gregg, and Jean Carlomusto, "Do It! Safer Sex Pornography for Girls and Boys Comes of Age," *Outweek*, August 28, 1989, 38–41.

Bronski, Michael, *Culture Clash: The Making of a Gay Sensibility*, Boston, South End Press, 1984.

Butler, Alison, "'She Must Be Seeing Things': An Interview with Sheila McLaughlin," *Screen* 28, no. 4 (Autumn 1987), 20–29.

Case, Sue-Ellen, "Towards a Butch-Femme Aesthetic," *Discourse* 11, no. 1 (Fall–Winter 1988–89), 55–73.

Castiglia, Christopher, "Rebel without a Closet: Homosexuality and Hollywood," *Critical Texts* 5, no. 1 (1988), 31–35.

Chris, Cynthia, "Policing Desire," *Afterimage* 17, no. 5 (December 1989), 19–20.

Citron, Michelle, "Films of Jan Oxenberg: Comic Critique," in *Films for Women*, ed. Charlotte Brunsdon, London, British Film Institute, 1986, 72–78.

Crimp, Douglas, "Fassbinder, Franz, Fox, Elvira, Erwin, Armin, and All the Others," *October,* no. 21 (Summer 1982), 63–81.

———, "Portraits of People with AIDS," in *Cultural Studies Now and in the Future,* ed. Lawrence Grossberg, Cary Nelson, and Paula Treichler, New York and London, Routledge, forthcoming 1991.

Danzig, Alexis, "Acting Up: Independent Video and the AIDS Crisis," *Afterimage* 16, no. 10 (May 1989), 5–7.

de Lauretis, Teresa, "Guerrilla in the Midst: Women's Cinema in the '80s," *Screen* 31, no. 1 (Spring 1990), 6–25.

———, "Sexual Indifference and Lesbian Representation," *Theatre Journal* 40, no. 2 (May 1988), 155–77.

———, *Technologies of Gender: Essays on Theory, Film, and Fiction,* Bloomington, Indiana University Press, 1987.

Diamond, Sara, "As a Wife Has a Cow: The Work of Cornelia Wyngaarden," *Video Guide* 8, no. 2 (1986), 4.

———, "Of Cabbages and Kinks," *Parallelogram* 8, no. 5 (Summer 1983), 12–18.

———, "Pornography: Image and Reality," in *Women Against Censorship,* ed. Varda Burstyn, Toronto, Douglas MacIntyre, 1985, 40–57.

———, ed., "The Sex Issue," *Video Guide* 8, no. 4 (December 1986).

DiCaprio, Lisa, "Lianna: Liberal Lesbianism," *Jump Cut,* no. 29 (February 1984), 45–47.

Dyer, Richard, "Coming to Terms," *Jump Cut,* no. 30 (March 1985), 27–29.

———, *Heavenly Bodies: Film Stars and Society,* New York, St. Martin's Press, 1986.

———, *Now You See It: Studies on Lesbian and Gay Film,* New York and London, Routledge, 1990.

———, "Pasolini and Homosexuality," in *Pier Paolo Pasolini,* ed. Paul Willemen, London, British Film Institute, 1977, 56–63.

———, "Seen to Be Believed: Some Problems in the Representation of Gay People as Typical," *Studies in Visual Communication* 9, no. 2 (Spring 1983), 2–19.

———, "Victim: Hermeneutic Project," *Film Form,* no. 1 (1977), 3–22.

———, ed., *Gays and Film,* London, British Film Institute, 1977; New York, Zoetrope, 1984. Includes Caroline Sheldon, "Lesbians and Film: Some Thoughts"; Richard Dyer, "Stereotyping"; Jack Babuscio, "Camp and the Gay Sensibility"; Andy Medhurst, "Notes on Recent Gay Film Criticism."

Ellsworth, Elizabeth, "Illicit Pleasures: Feminist Spectators and *Personal Best,*" *Wide Angle* 8, no. 2 (1986), 45–56.

Fani-Kayode, Rotimi, "Traces of Ecstasy," *Ten.8,* no. 28 (Summer 1988), 36–43.

Finch, Mark, "Business as Usual: Substitution and Sex in *Prick Up Your Ears* and other Recent Gay-Themed Movies," in *Coming on Strong: Gay Politics and Culture*, ed. Simon Shepherd and Mick Wallis, London, Unwin Hyman, 1989, 76–89.

————, "Mauritz Stiller's *The Wings* and Early Scandinavian Gay Cinema," *European Gay Review*, no. 2 (1987), 26–31.

————, "Sex and Address in 'Dynasty,'" *Screen* 27, no. 6 (November–December 1986), 24–42.

Finch, Mark, and Richard Kwietniowski, "Melodrama and 'Maurice': Homo Is Where the Het Is," *Screen* 29, no. 3 (Summer 1988), 72–80.

Frechette, David, "What's Wrong with This Picture," *Black Film Review* 5, no. 3 (Summer 1989), 22–23.

Gever, Martha, "Girl Crazy: Lesbian Narratives in *She Must Be Seeing Things* and *Damned If You Don't*," *The Independent* 11, no. 6 (July 1988), 14–18.

————, "The Names We Give Ourselves," in *Out There: Marginalization and Contemporary Cultures*, ed. Russell Ferguson, Martha Gever, Trinh T. Minh-ha, and Cornel West, New York, New Museum of Contemporary Art, and Cambridge, Mass., MIT Press, 1990, 191–202.

————, "Pictures of Sickness: Stuart Marshall's *Bright Eyes*, in *AIDS: Cultural Analysis/Cultural Activism*, ed. Douglas Crimp, Cambridge, Mass., MIT Press, 1988, 109–26.

————, "Where We Are Now," *Art in America* 75, no. 7 (July 1987), 43–49.

Gever, Martha, and Nathalie Magnan, "The Same Difference: On Lesbian Representation," *Exposure* 24, no. 2 (1986), 27–35.

Goldsby, Jackie, "What It Means to Be Colored Me," *Out/Look*, no. 9 (Summer 1990), 8–17.

Goldstein, Richard, "The Gay New Wave," *Village Voice*, 22 April 1986, 51–53.

Greyson, John, "Compromised Strategies: AIDS and Alternative Video Practices," in *Voices of Dissent*, ed. Mark O'Brian and Craig Little, Bloomington, Indiana University Press, 1990, 60–74.

————, "Homo Video," *Jump Cut*, no. 30 (March 1985), 36–38.

————, "Proofing," in *AIDS: The Artists' Response*, ed. Jan Zita Grover, Columbus, Hoyt L. Sherman Gallery, Ohio State University, 1989, 22–25.

————, "Two Men Embracing: Gay Video Images," *Video Guide* 8, no. 4 (December 1986), 10–11.

Gupta, Sunil, "Desire and Black Men," *Ten.8*, no. 22 (Summer 1986), 17–22.

Hake, Sabine, "'Gold, Love, Adventure': The Postmodern Piracy of *Madame X*," *Discourse* 11, no. 1 (1988–89), 88–110.

Hemphill, Essex, "Brother to Brother" (interview with Isaac Julien), *Black Film Review* 5, no. 3 (Summer 1989), 14–17.

Julien, Isaac, and Kobena Mercer, "True Confessions: A Discourse on Images of Black Male Sexuality," in *Male Order: Unwrapping Masculinity,* ed. Rowena Chapman and Jonathan Rutherford, London, Lawrence and Wishart, 1988, 131–41.

Julien, Isaac, and Pratibha Parmar, "In Conversation," in *Ecstatic Antibodies: Resisting the AIDS Mythology,* ed. Tessa Boffin and Sunil Gupta, London, Rivers Oram Press, 1990, 96–102.

Kelly, Keith, "The Sexual Politics of Rosa von Praunheim," *Millennium Film Journal,* no. 3 (1979), 115–18.

Kleinhans, Chuck, et al., "Special Section: Gays and Film," *Jump Cut,* no. 16 (1977), 13–28. Includes Tom Waugh, "Films by Gays for Gays"; Richard Dyer, "Homosexuality and Film Noir"; Bob Cant, "Fassbinder's *Fox*"; Andrew Britton, "Foxed"; Will Aitken, "Leaving the Dance"; Tom Waugh and Chuck Kleinhans, "Gays, Straights, Film, and the Left."

Koch, Stephen, *Stargazer: Andy Warhol's World and His Films,* New York, Praeger, 1973.

Kuhn, Annette, "Encounter between Two Cultures—Discussion with Ulricke Ottinger," *Screen* 28, no. 4 (Autumn 1987), 74–79.

Landers, Timothy, "Bodies and Antibodies: A Crisis in Representation," *The Independent* 11, no. 1 (January–February 1988), 18–24.

Lord, Catherine, "Plotting Queer Culture," *Artpaper* 9, no. 7 (March 1990), 16–17.

Marshall, Stuart, "Picturing Deviancy," in *Ecstatic Antibodies: Resisting the AIDS Mythology,* ed. Tessa Boffin and Sunil Gupta, London, Rivers Oram Press, 1990, 19–36.

———, "Taxi zum Klo," *Undercut,* no. 3–4 (March 1982), 1–3.

Matthews, Peter, "Garbo and Phallic Motherhood: A 'Homosexual' Visual Economy," *Screen* 29, no. 3 (Summer 1988), 14–39.

Mayne, Judith, "A Parallax View of Lesbian Authorship," in *Inside/Out: Lesbian Theories, Gay Theories,* ed. Diana Fuss, New York and London, Routledge, forthcoming 1991.

———, *The Woman at the Keyhole: Feminism and Women's Cinema,* Bloomington, Indiana University Press, 1990.

McDowell, Cyndra, and Lee Waldorf, "Close Up: A Conversation with Toronto Film-maker Midi Onodera," *The Body Politic,* March 1986, 34–35.

Mercer, Kobena, "Dark and Lovely: Notes on Black Gay Image-Making," *Ten.8,* forthcoming 1991.

———, "Imaging the Black Man's Sex," in *Photography/Politics: Two,* ed. Pat Holland, Jo Spence, and Simon Watney, London, Comedia/Methuen, 1987, 61–69.

———, "Reading Racial Fetishism: The Photographs of Robert Mapplethorpe," in *Fetishism: Gender, Commodity, Vision,* ed. Emily Apter and Bill Pietz, Ithaca, N.Y., Cornell University Press, forthcoming 1991.

Mercer, Kobena, Jacqueline Rose, Gayatri Spivak, and Angela McRobbie, "Sexual Identities: Questions of Difference," *Undercut*, no. 17 (Spring 1988), 19–30.

Merck, Mandy, "Desert Hearts," *The Independent* 10, no. 6 (July 1987), 15–17.

———, "Difference and Its Discontents," *Screen* 28, no. 1 (Winter 1987), 2–9.

———, " 'Lianna' and the Lesbians of Art Cinema," in *Films for Women*, ed. Charlotte Brunsdon, London, British Film Institute, 1986, 99–108.

Meyer, Richard, "Rock Hudson's Body," in *Inside/Out: Lesbian Theories, Gay Theories*, ed. Diana Fuss, New York and London, Routledge, forthcoming 1991.

Miller, D. A., "Anal Rope," in *Inside/Out: Lesbian Theories, Gay Theories*, ed. Diana Fuss, New York and London, Routledge, forthcoming 1991.

Moon, Michael, "Flaming Closets," *October*, no. 51 (Winter 1989), 19–54.

Navarro, Ray, and Catherine Saalfield, "Not Just Black and White: AIDS Media and People of Color," *The Independent* 12, no. 6 (July 1989), 18–23.

———, "Shocking Pink Praxis: Race and Gender on the ACT UP Frontlines," in *Inside/Out: Lesbian Theories, Gay Theories*, ed. Diana Fuss, New York and London, Routledge, forthcoming 1991.

Oswald, Laura, "The Perversion of the I/Eye in *Un Chant d'amour*," *Enclitic* 7, no. 2 (1983), 106–15.

Pally, Marcia, "Women in Love," *Film Comment*, April 1986, 35–39.

Parkerson, Michelle, "Beyond Chiffon: The Making of *Stormé*, in *Blasted Allegories: An Anthology of Writings by Contemporary Artists*, ed. Brian Wallis, New York, New Museum of Contemporary Art, and Cambridge, Mass., MIT Press, 1987, 375–79.

———, "Diva Under Glass," *Heresies*, no. 16 (1983), 11.

Parmar, Pratibha, "Black Feminism: The Politics of Representation," in *Identity: Community, Culture, Difference*, ed. Jonathan Rutherford, London, Lawrence and Wishart, 1990, 101–26.

Patton, Cindy, "The Cum Shot: Three Takes on Lesbian and Gay Sexuality," *Out/Look*, no. 3 (Fall 1988), 72–77.

———, "Hegemony and Orgasm, or The Instability of Heterosexual Pornography," *Screen* 30, no. 3 (Fall 1989), 72–77.

Pearce, Frank, "How to Be Immoral and Ill, Dangerous and Pathetic, All at the Same Time: Mass Media and Homosexuality," in *The Manufacture of News*, ed. Stanley Cohen and Jock Young, London, Constable, 1973, 284–301.

Rich, B. Ruby, "From Repressive Tolerance to Erotic Liberation: *Maedchen in Uniform*," in *Re-vision: Essays in Feminist Film Criticism*, ed. Mary Ann Doane, Patricia Mellencamp, and Linda Williams, Frederick, Md., The American Film Institute and University Publications of America, 1984, 100–130.

Riggs, Marlon, "Marlon Riggs Untied" (interview by Revon Kyle Banneker), *Out/Look*, no. 10 (Fall 1990), 15–18.

Russo, Vito, *The Celluloid Closet: Homosexuality in the Movies*, New York, Harper and Row, 1981, 1987.

————, "A State of Being," *Film Comment*, April 1986, 32–34.

Saalfield, Catherine, "Positive Propaganda: Jean Carlomusto and Gregg Bordowitz on AIDS Media," *The Independent* 13, no. 10 (December 1990), 19–21.

Shaw, Nancy, "On a Trumped-Up Charge: Two Video Films," *Vanguard* 18, no. 3 (Summer 1989), 20–25.

Silverman, Kaja, "Fassbinder and Lacan: A Reconsideration of Gaze, Look and Image," *Camera Obscura*, no. 19 (January 1989), 54–84.

Simmons, Ron, "Other Options," *Black Film Review* 5, no. 3 (Summer 1989), 20–22.

Smith, Jack, "The Perfect Filmic Appositeness of Maria Montez," *Film Culture*, no. 27 (1962–63), 28–32.

Smyth, Cherry, "The Pleasure Threshold: Looking at Lesbian Pornography on Film," *Feminist Review*, no. 34 (Spring 1990), 152–59.

Stacey, Jackie, "Desperately Seeking Difference," *Screen* 28, no. 1 (Winter 1987), 48–61.

Steakley, James, "Gay Film and Censorship: A 1919 Case Study," in *Homosexuality, Which Homosexuality?*, Amsterdam, Free University, 1987, vol. 2, 147–55.

Steven, Peter, "Gay and Lesbian Cinema," in *Jump Cut: Hollywood, Politics and Counter Cinema*, New York, Praeger, 1985, 278–323.

Straayer, Chris, "'Personal Best': Lesbian/Feminist Audience," *Jump Cut*, no. 29 (February 1984), 40–44.

Tartaglia, Jerry, "The Gay Sensibility in American Avant-Garde Film," *Millennium Film Journal*, no. 4–5 (1979), 53–58.

Tyler, Parker, *Screening the Sexes: Homosexuality in the Movies*, New York, Holt, Rinehart and Winston, 1972.

Watney, Simon, "Hollywood's Homosexual World," *Screen* 23, no. 3–4 (September–October 1982), 107–21.

————, *Policing Desire: Pornography, AIDS, and the Media*, Minneapolis, University of Minnesota Press, 1987.

Waugh, Thomas, "Hard to Imagine: Gay Erotic Cinema in the Postwar Era," *CineAction!*, no. 9 (Fall 1987), 65–72.

————, "A Heritage of Pornography: On the Gay Film Collection of the Kinsey Institute," *The Body Politic*, no. 90 (January 1983), 29–33.

————, "Lesbian and Gay Documentary: Minority Self-Imaging, Oppositional Film Practice, and the Question of Image Ethics," in *Image Ethics: The Moral Rights of Subjects in Photographs, Film, and Television*, ed. Larry Gross, John Stuart Katz, and Jay Ruby, New York, Oxford University Press, 1988, 248–72.

————, "Men's Pornography: Gay and Straight," *Jump Cut,* no. 30 (March 1985), 30–35.

————, "Murnau: The Films Behind the Man," *The Body Politic,* no. 51 (March–April 1979), 31–34.

Weiss, Andrea, "Lesbian as Outlaw: New Forms and Fantasies in Women's Independent Cinema," *Conditions* 11, no. 12 (1985), 117–31.

White, Patricia, "Female Spectator, Lesbian Spectre: The Haunting," in *Inside/Out: Lesbian Theories, Gay Theories,* ed. Diana Fuss, New York and London, Routledge, forthcoming 1991.

————, "Madame X of the China Seas," *Screen* 28, no. 4 (Autumn 1987), 80–95.

Williams, Linda, "'Personal Best': Women in Love," in *Films for Women,* ed. Charlotte Brunsdon, London, British Film Institute, 1986, 146–54.

Contributors

Teresa de Lauretis, Professor of the History of Consciousness at the University of California, Santa Cruz, is the author of *Alice Doesn't: Feminism, Semiotics, Cinema* (Indiana University Press, 1984) and *Technologies of Gender: Essays on Theory, Film, and Fiction* (Indiana University Press, 1987), as well as articles on lesbian representation and feminist theory. She is the editor of a special issue of *Differences* on "Queer Theory" and is working on *The Practice of Love,* a book on sexual structuring, fantasy, and lesbian subjectivity.

Richard Fung is a Toronto-based videomaker and community activist. His videotapes include *Orientations* (1984), *Chinese Characters* (1986), *The Way to My Father's Village* (1988) and *Safe Place,* coproduced with Peter Steven (1989). In 1990 he completed three videotapes: *My Mother's Place, Fighting Chance,* and *Steam Clean/Vapeurs sans peur* (for the Gay Men's Health Crisis Safer Sex Shorts series).

Stuart Marshall is a British film- and videomaker and co-chair of Positively Healthy, an organization of people with AIDS. His many video works include *A Question of Three Sets of Characteristics* (1980), *Bright Eyes* (1984), and *Pedagogue* (1988). His films *Desire* (1988) and *Comrades in Arms* (1990) were opening-night features at New York's New Festival in 1989 and 1990, respectively. He is currently at work on a film about AIDS and lesbian and gay activism for Britain's Channel Four television.

Judith Mayne is Professor of French and Women's Studies at Ohio State University. Her books include *Private Novels, Public Films* (University of Georgia Press, 1988), *Kino and the Woman Question: Feminism and the Soviet Silent Film* (Ohio State University Press, 1989) and *The Woman at the Keyhole: Feminism and*

Women's Cinema (Indiana University Press, 1990). She is currently working on a book about Dorothy Arzner.

Kobena Mercer is Assistant Professor of Art History at the University of California, Santa Cruz. Formerly Television and Video Officer of the British Film Institute, London, he has written extensively on race and sexuality in visual representation. He is the editor of *Black Film/British Cinema* (ICA Documents, 1988) and a special issue of *Screen* titled "The Last Special Issue on Race" (with Isaac Julien, 1988). He recently completed a doctoral thesis on Enoch Powell and the discourse of British racism.

Cindy Patton, activist and writer, is a consultant to the World Health Organization for its Global Program on AIDS. Her books include *Sex and Germs: The Politics of AIDS* (South End Press, 1985), *Making It: A Woman's Guide to Sex in the Age of AIDS,* with Janis Kelly (Firebrand Books, 1987), and *Inventing AIDS* (Routledge, 1990). She currently teaches in the Department of Women's and Gender Studies at Amherst College, Massachusetts.

Other titles of interest from Bay Press

Out of Site

A Social Criticism of Architecture

Edited by Diane Ghirardo

If You Lived Here

A Project by Martha Rosler

Edited by Brian Wallis

AIDS Demo Graphics

Douglas Crimp and Adam Rolston

Democracy

A Project by Group Material

Edited by Brian Wallis

The Critical Image

Essays on Contemporary
Photography

Edited by Carol Squiers

Remaking History

Edited by Barbara Kruger
and Phil Mariani

The Work of Andy Warhol

Edited by Gary Garrels

The Anti-Aesthetic

Essays on Postmodern Culture

Edited by Hal Foster

Recodings

Art, Spectacle, Cultural Politics

Hal Foster

**Discussions in
Contemporary Culture**

Edited by Hal Foster

**Suite vénitienne /
Please Follow Me**

Sophie Calle / Jean Baudrillard

Line Break

Poetry as Social Practice

James Scully

Vision and Visuality

Edited by Hal Foster

5.4.93   16.95   Hacker   53979